IMAGES
of America

SOUTH WINDSOR

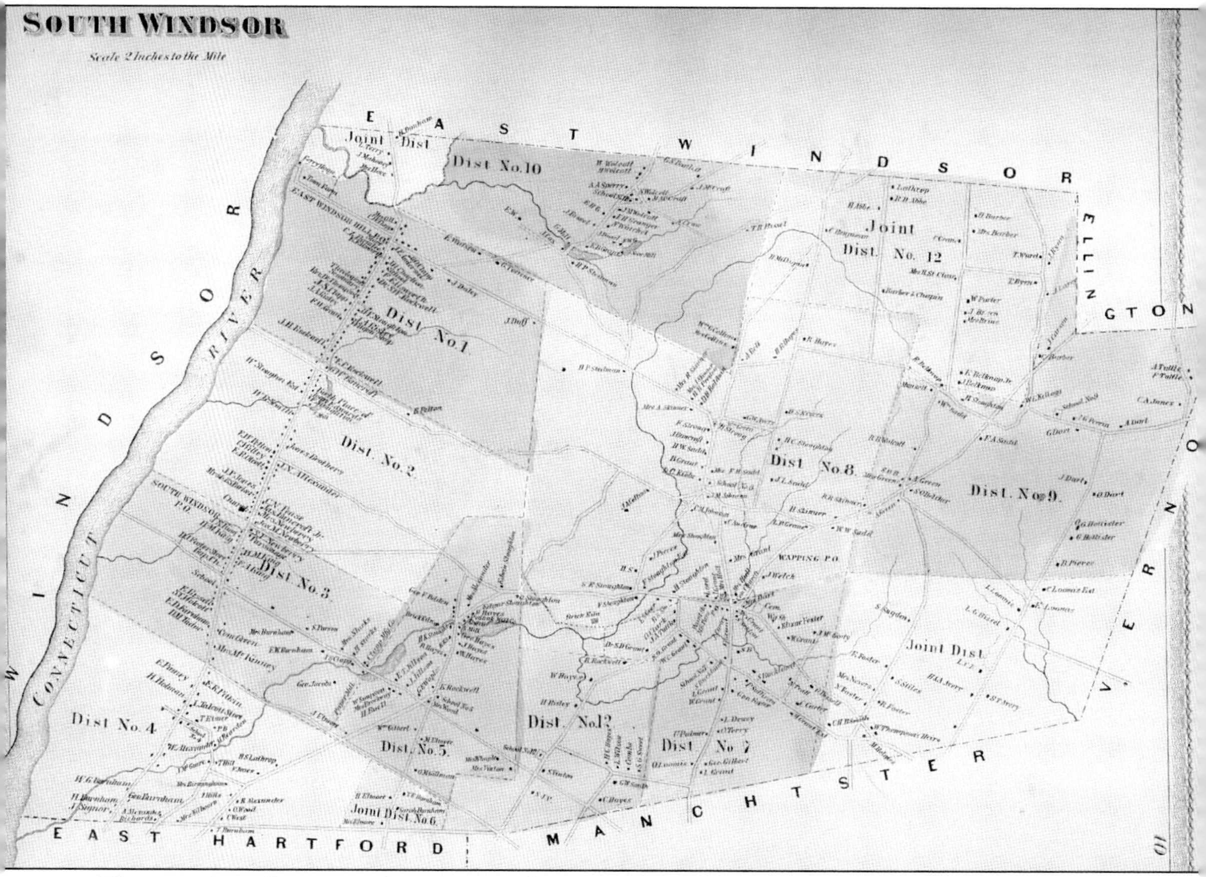

This map from the 1869 *Atlas of Hartford City and County*, published by Baker and Tilden, shows the town of South Windsor, incorporated in 1845. The map shows the school districts at the time, along with the names of businesses and landowners throughout the approximately 28.5-square-mile town. (Wood Memorial Library and Museum.)

ON THE COVER: Started by John Bissell in 1641, the Bissell Ferry operated on the Connecticut River until 1921 and connected the east and west sides of the river. Originally, John Bissell ferried livestock for farmers on the west bank to grazing land on the east bank, but eventually, human passengers traveling by foot, cart, buggy, and bicycle took the place of cows. (Hildred Raymond Collection, Wood Memorial Library and Museum.)

IMAGES *of America*

SOUTH WINDSOR

Claire Lobdell for
Wood Memorial Library & Museum

ARCADIA PUBLISHING

ISBN 978-1-4671-2523-9

Published by Arcadia Publishing
Charleston, South Carolina

Printed in the United States of America

Library of Congress Control Number: 2017932972

For all general information, please contact Arcadia Publishing:
Telephone 843-853-2070
Fax 843-853-0044
E-mail sales@arcadiapublishing.com
For customer service and orders:
Toll-Free 1-888-313-2665

Visit us on the Internet at www.arcadiapublishing.com

To the volunteers of the Friends of Wood Memorial Library and Museum, without whom none of this would have been possible.

Contents

Acknowledgments		6
Introduction		7
1.	River Town	9
2.	Main Street	25
3.	Sullivan Avenue and Wapping	59
4.	Business and Industry	85
5.	Farming	99
6.	Pleasant Valley, Long Hill, and the South Side of Town	115
Bibliography		126
About the Organization		127

ACKNOWLEDGMENTS

I am eternally indebted to the generations of South Windsorites who have valued their town's history and taken pains to ensure that its records would be preserved. Doris Burgdorf, Sally Edlund, Jean Klein, Mike Salvatore, and the South Windsor Historical Society have been enormously helpful and generous with their encyclopedic knowledge of the town and its residents. Thank you to Ginny and Tony Macro for reading over the manuscript of this book (and for everything else you do here!), and to Mike Salvatore for fact-checking and edits. The Wood Memorial Library and Museum board and staff, especially Jan Grace and Jess Vogelgesang, have been stellar supporters and colleagues. I am grateful to my editors at Arcadia Publishing, Erin Vosgien and Stacia Bannerman, for seeing the project to fruition. The Wood's legion of volunteers past and present also made this book possible, especially Fran Nadeau, the Oral History Committee, and all those who were integral in founding the Wood's archives in 1990. Thank you also to all the individuals, families, organizations, and businesses that answered my obscure questions and lent me photographs to use in the book, especially Charlotte Collins, Phil Crombie, Kelly Foster, Debbie Hay, Ernie Hintz, Frank Niederwerfer, Gary Pitcock, Priscilla Snow, and Edie Vibert-Johnson.

Throughout the book, you will see quotes from oral histories. These interviews were conducted by volunteers and staff members at the Wood. All of the interviews quoted in this book are available to researchers at the Wood archives. Many of the images come from the Wood Memorial Library and Museum (WMLM) and from the South Windsor Historical Society (SWHS).

My grandparents Joan Lobdell and Jerry Schillo instilled in me a love of history and storytelling, for which I will always be grateful. Finally, a million thank-yous to Mom, Dad, Joan, Jack, Simona, and Annelise for your love, support, and patience.

INTRODUCTION

In 1614, Adriaen Block, a Dutch explorer, set off from New Amsterdam to explore Long Island Sound and nearby waterways. He discovered the headwaters of the Connecticut River, which he sailed up as far as a fortified Native American village on its east shore at a place called Nowashe, between the Scantic and Podunk Rivers—South Windsor. In 1636, English settlers from Plymouth and Dorchester, Massachusetts, moved to a site along the Connecticut River at the behest of Wahginnacut, the sachem of the Connecticut River tribes, who hoped the colonists might provide protection from the Pequots and undercut the Pequot monopoly on trade goods. This settlement, purchased from Wahginnacut's tribe, was called Windsor and was the first colonial settlement in what is now Connecticut. At the time, Windsor encompassed both the east and west sides of the river, although colonists did not move to the east side of the river until 1641, when John Bissell established the Bissell Ferry. The ferry first ran between Windsor and what is now East Windsor, but was moved near the end of what is now Ferry Lane by the early 1650s.

The original land grants to settlers on the east side of the river were in narrow, three-mile-long strips that extended east from the river. The earliest houses and earliest church were built on East Windsor Hill, which forms a bluff east of the river above the usual flood plain. The street that ran in front of the houses, now called Main Street, followed the well-worn Podunk Path, which Native Americans had used for generations. Timothy Edwards, father of firebrand preacher Jonathan Edwards and great-grandfather to Aaron Burr, was the first pastor on the east side of the river, and his congregants worshiped in a rustic meeting house built around 1694.

Beyond the three-mile land grants, another area of settlement, Wapping, grew up less dependent on the river. Wapping residents established their own parish and meetinghouse, and the town developed a rather bifurcated existence, with Main Streeters and Wappingites keeping to their own churches, schools, and social organizations until well into the 20th century, when main roads were paved, cars became common, and South Windsor built Ellsworth Memorial High School, joining all the town's teenagers under one roof.

In 1786, East Windsor broke off from Windsor on the west side of the river and formed its own municipality. In 1845, after a petition to the state legislature by Harvey Elmore, South Windsor was incorporated as its own town. In 1895, trolley tracks were laid down Main Street, connecting the town with Hartford and allowing men and women to travel to the big city to the south for work, often in the insurance industry. Even so, South Windsor remained an overwhelmingly agricultural, rural town dotted with small mills and other small businesses until around World War II, when the population began rapidly expanding. During the 1950s and 1960s, thousands of new residents joined the town, moving to the area to work in the aerospace industry or taking advantage of the new Interstates 84 and 91 to commute to jobs in Hartford and Springfield.

Today, South Windsor is a bustling, populous, multi-ethnic community that in 2013 elected Connecticut's first Muslim mayor. Large industrial and commercial distribution centers have grown up around Sullivan Avenue and John Fitch Boulevard, and new housing developments snake through with streets named for the farm families that once owned the land. Even so, the town's history pokes through if you know where to look: here, a one-room school has been turned into a house; there, a gristmill has been turned into a popular restaurant; on that corner, a century-old tobacco shed still leans into the wind, its shutters open, broadleaf tobacco leaves drying from the rafters.

This book takes the reader on a photographic tour of South Windsor from the 1860s, which is the date of our oldest photographs of the town, to the late 1970s. It is largely a tour of the town's public face: until the 1940s or 1950s, it is rare to find images of people in South Windsor in their homes doing things like cooking, sewing, or even relaxing in a sitting room. Instead, we have photographs of people in their Sunday best, standing outside their homes or posing with their crops in the field. It is a picture of life in times gone by, but it is an incomplete picture. Also, there were some places and activities that this author was unable to find photographs of despite much searching. For example, numerous South Windsor residents tell stories of harvesting ice from mill ponds and farm ponds to fill ice houses and ice boxes, but no photographs could be found of ice harvests. Similarly, a sprawling slaughterhouse stood for decades by the railroad tracks, near what is now John Fitch Boulevard. Parents would tell their children stories of feral, carnivorous pigs that inhabited the woods nearby, probably in hopes of keeping youngsters from playing near the tracks. Again, no pictures remain of the slaughterhouse. In many places throughout the book, there are quotes from oral histories from the Wood Memorial Library and Museum collections. These interviews, many of which are available online, tell the stories of the people and places shown in the photographs as well as the intimate family life that evaded photography.

Our tour of South Windsor starts by the Connecticut River, with an exploration of early life around the river and its tributaries and transportation across the river. The first chapter also illustrates the effects that cycles of flooding have had on nearby residents.

Chapter two looks at Main Street: the houses, businesses, churches, schools, and other community buildings that shaped life on the street, as well as some of the street's notable residents.

The third chapter focuses on life along the old Wapping Road (now known as Sullivan Avenue) and the community of Wapping itself as it transitioned from playing second fiddle to Main Street in the 18th and early 19th centuries to the thriving center of civic life in the 20th century.

South Windsor's business and industry is spotlighted in the fourth chapter, with small mills and light industry giving way to high-tech manufacturing.

Chapter five explores the role of agriculture in the town's life. Tobacco, of course, takes a central role, but other crops and livestock farming are shown as well.

The final chapter looks at the south side of town: a section sometimes called a wilderness that nonetheless played a vital role in South Windsor's history.

One

River Town

The Connecticut River is the reason South Windsor exists. Since the end of the last ice age around 13,000 years ago, the river has periodically flooded, leaving behind nutrient-rich soils in the low-lying fields that flank the river. Patches of marshland at the riverside are thick with game, attracting hunters and birdwatchers alike. Archaeological artifacts found in South Windsor show that humans have lived on this land for at least 5,000 years, and artifacts elsewhere around the state show human habitation more than 10,000 years old. Farmers, as well as amateur and professional archaeologists, have found thousands of Native American stone tools, projectile points, beads, and burial grounds in fields along the Connecticut River.

In 1614, Dutch explorers visited a fortified Native American village at a place called Nowashe, between the Podunk and Scantic Rivers. The first colonial settlement in what is now South Windsor was the Bissell Ferry, which linked the west and east banks of the river. Settlement radiated out from that point, as well as along the Scantic and Podunk, the two main Connecticut River tributaries in town. From the late 17th century to the mid-19th century, the Connecticut River thrummed with traffic. In the days before motorized transportation, riverboats were one of the most efficient methods of moving people and goods from place to place. Farmers, craftsmen, and merchants in South Windsor shipped their wares downriver and out to the West Indies.

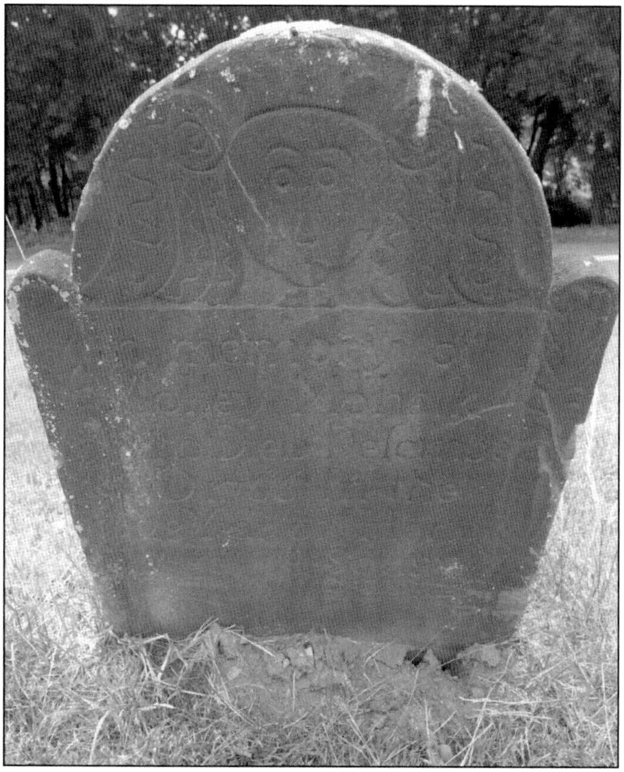

This gravestone is the oldest in Old Wapping Cemetery and is one of the only physical reminders here of native and colonial coexistence. Little is known about the woman, though her burial place and Christian first name suggest she was baptized. The stone reads, "In memory of Molley Mohalk who Dieb Desember AD 1766. In the 28 Year of Her Age. A squaw." (Photograph by Claire Lobdell, WMLM.)

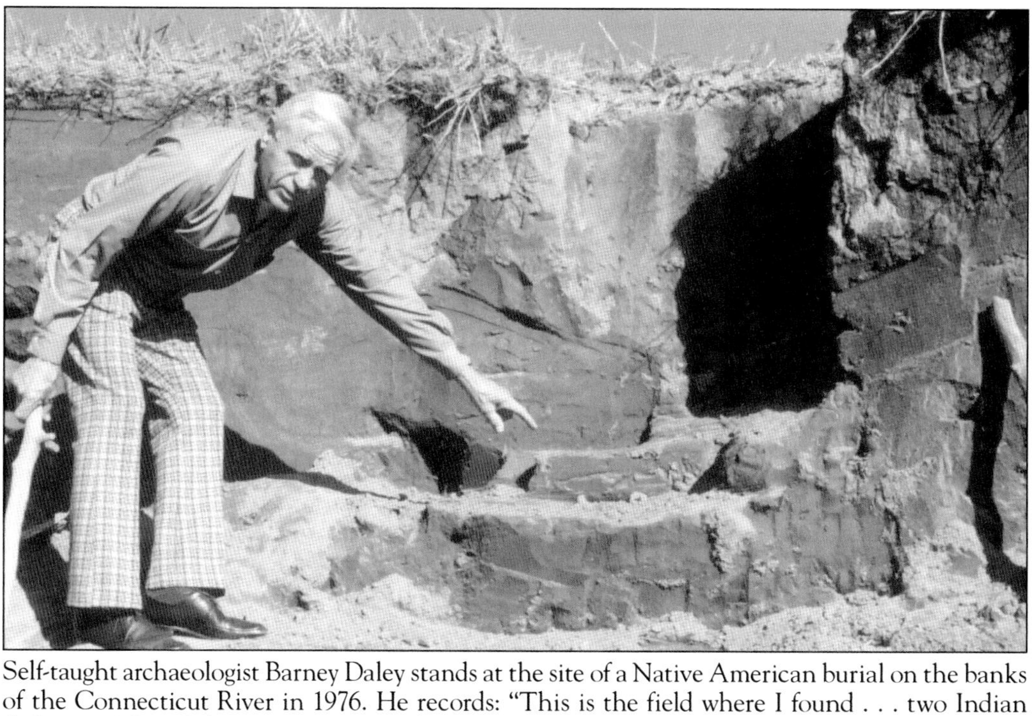

Self-taught archaeologist Barney Daley stands at the site of a Native American burial on the banks of the Connecticut River in 1976. He records: "This is the field where I found . . . two Indian skeletons. I found them on Easter Sunday and dubbed them the 'JC' site, since they came to life on Easter Sunday." (Barney Daley Collection, WMLM.)

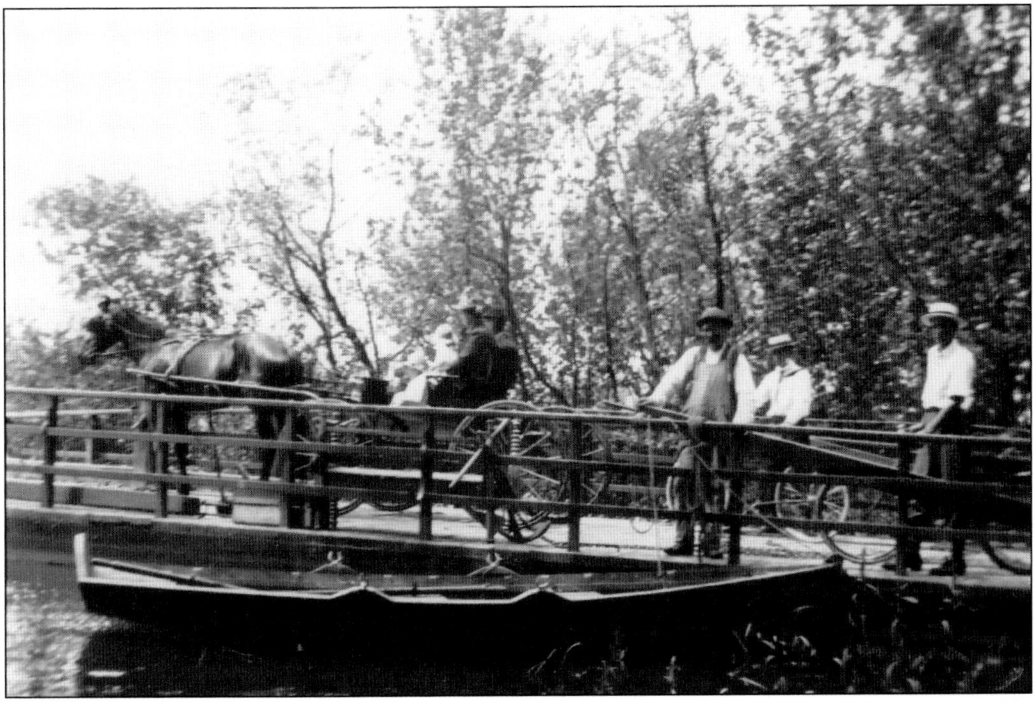

This photograph shows the Bissell Ferry, also pictured on the cover. Ruth Baker Risley recalls: "[A] cable lay on the river bottom until it was picked up in the pulleys of the ferry, and you pulled on the cable to propel yourself along. If the wind was blowing hard, it could give you a bad time." (Hildred Raymond Collection, WMLM.)

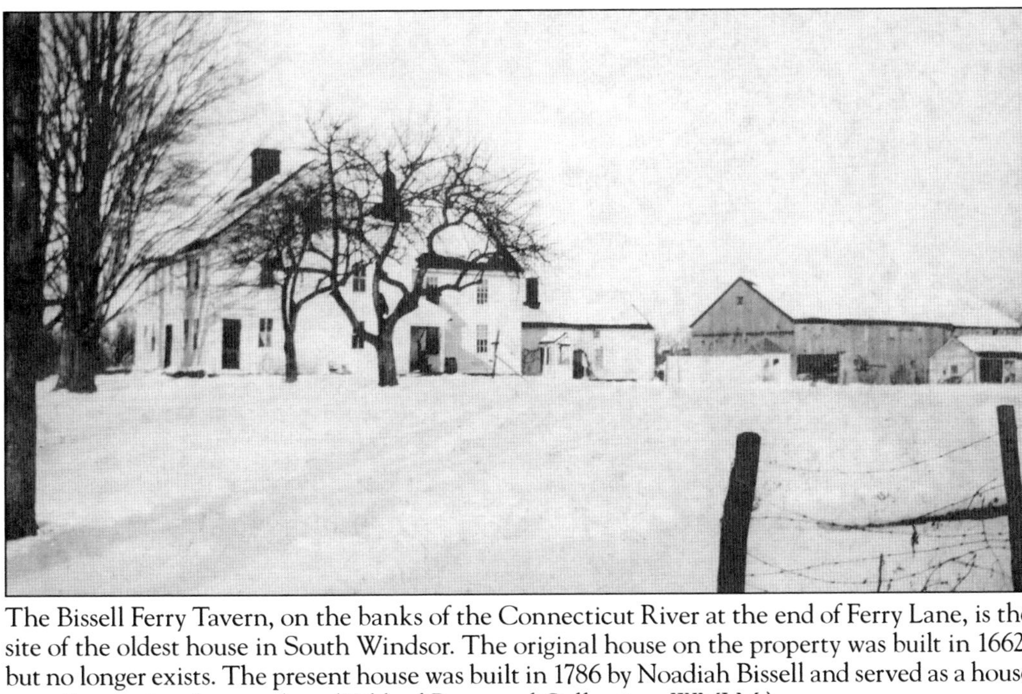

The Bissell Ferry Tavern, on the banks of the Connecticut River at the end of Ferry Lane, is the site of the oldest house in South Windsor. The original house on the property was built in 1662, but no longer exists. The present house was built in 1786 by Noadiah Bissell and served as a house as well as an inn for travelers. (Hildred Raymond Collection, WMLM.)

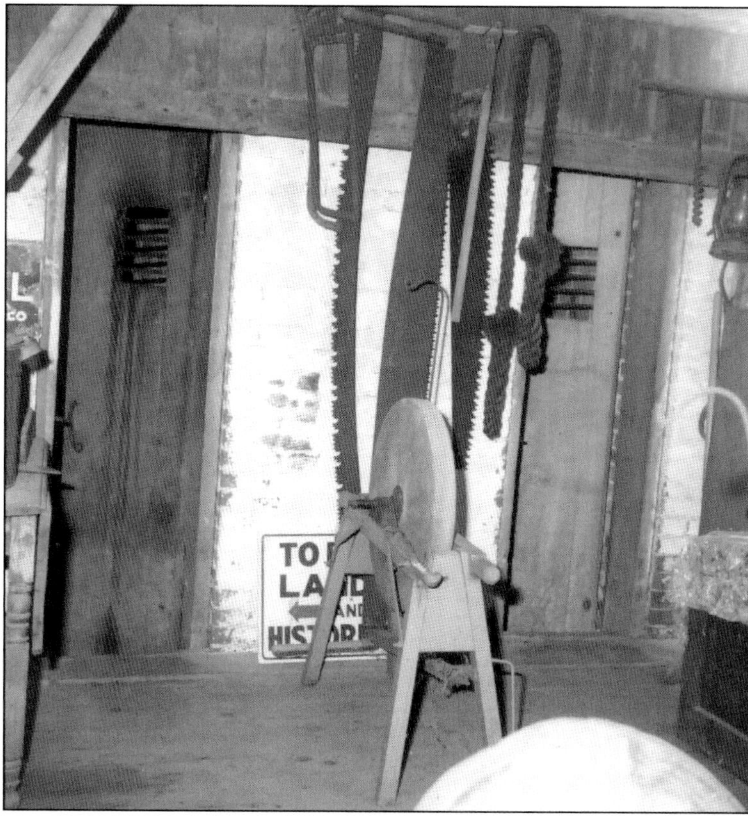

The Bissell Ferry Tavern also served as the town jail. According to Ruth Baker Risley, "there were two cells with their strong doors and iron bars across them that townspeople could be put into if they needed to be contained. Once in a great while we would have someone in there that had too much to drink." (Photograph by Dexter Burnham, South Windsor Chamber of Commerce.)

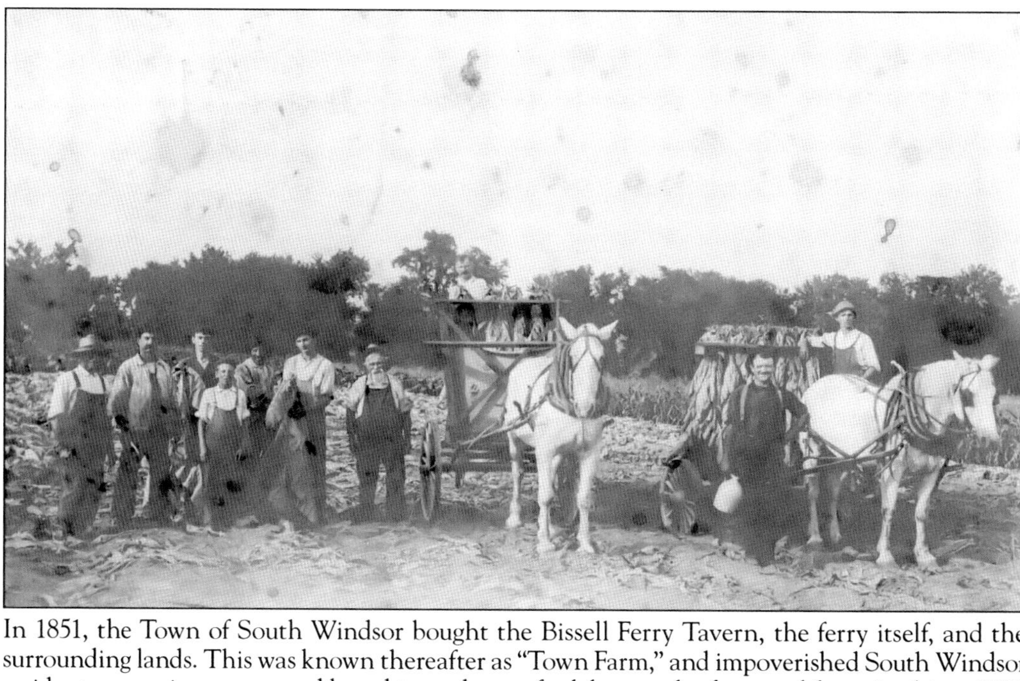

In 1851, the Town of South Windsor bought the Bissell Ferry Tavern, the ferry itself, and the surrounding lands. This was known thereafter as "Town Farm," and impoverished South Windsor residents were given room and board in exchange for labor on the farm and ferry. In this c. 1890 image, Town Farm laborers harvest the tobacco crop. (Hildred Raymond Collection, WMLM.)

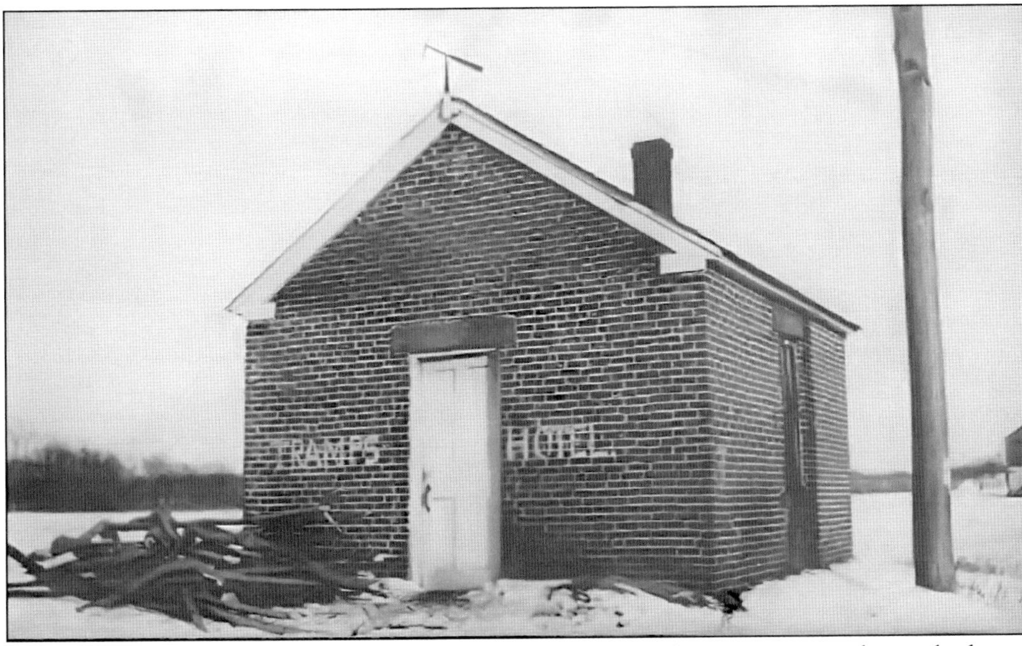

Tramps Hotel on the Town Farm provided temporary shelter for transients until it washed away in the Connecticut River flood of 1936. Ruth Baker Risley recalls: "there were bunks built into it, and there was a stove and either those who stayed there or some kind soul would provide enough wood for kindling so they could have warmth." (Hildred Raymond Collection, WMLM.)

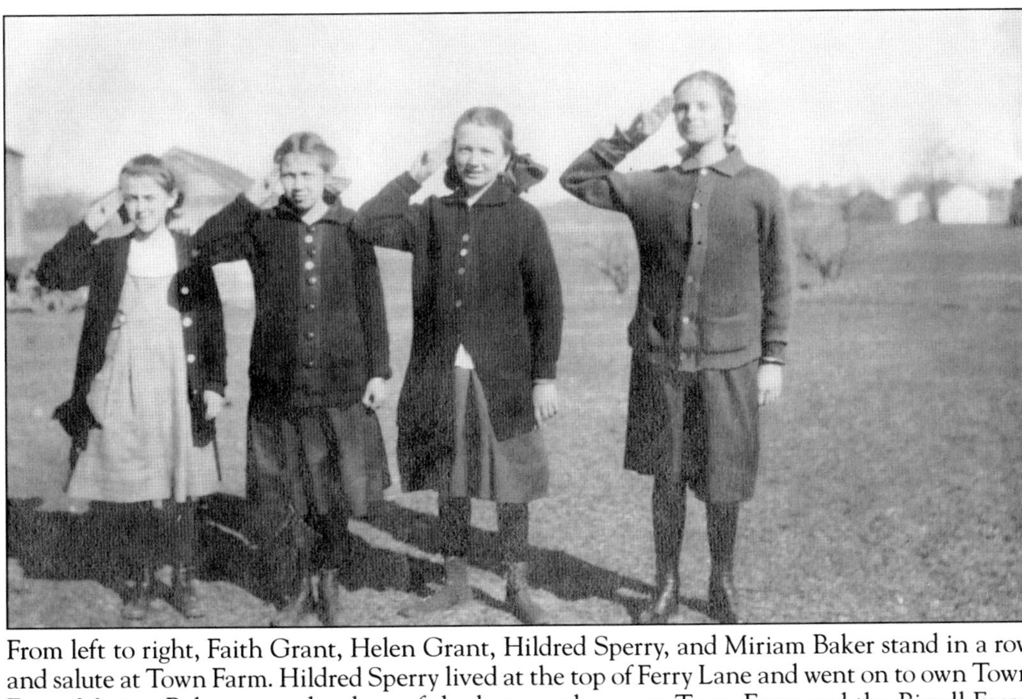

From left to right, Faith Grant, Helen Grant, Hildred Sperry, and Miriam Baker stand in a row and salute at Town Farm. Hildred Sperry lived at the top of Ferry Lane and went on to own Town Farm. Miriam Baker was a daughter of the last couple to run Town Farm and the Bissell Ferry. (Hildred Raymond Collection, WMLM.)

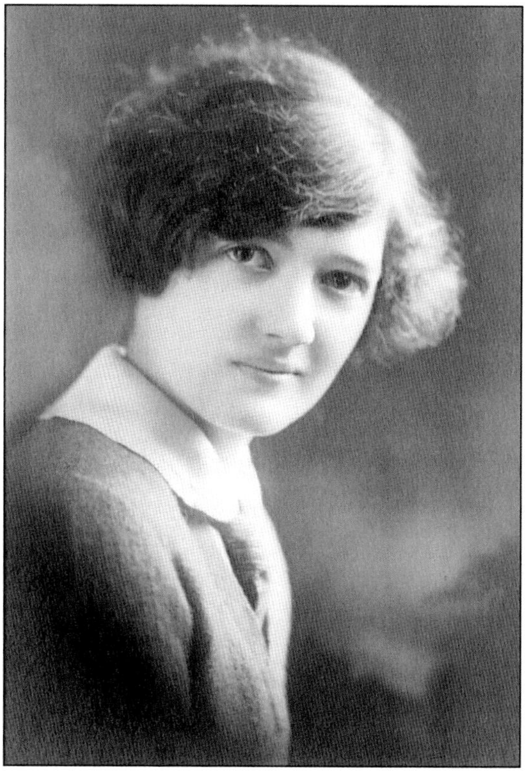

Catherine Hildred Sperry Raymond (1907–1992, left), better known as Hildred, was an ardent historic preservationist as well as one of the first aviatrixes in Connecticut. With her friend Helen Pelton (1903–1977, below), Hildred purchased Town Farm from South Windsor in order to preserve the historic house. They also organized to save Wood Memorial Library. Hildred's extensive collection of photographs of South Windsor was donated to Wood Library after her death. Doris Burgdorf recalls: "[Helen] and Hildred would do a lot of things together, and it was a concern of all of them. . . . Hildred did want to see [Wood] be a library again, and they were just racking their brain how it could happen, and Nancy Caffyn happened to be in town then and helped them because she was very good at organizing. . . . They established the Friends and got a lawyer to draw up their Friends corporation." (Both, Hildred Raymond Collection, WMLM.)

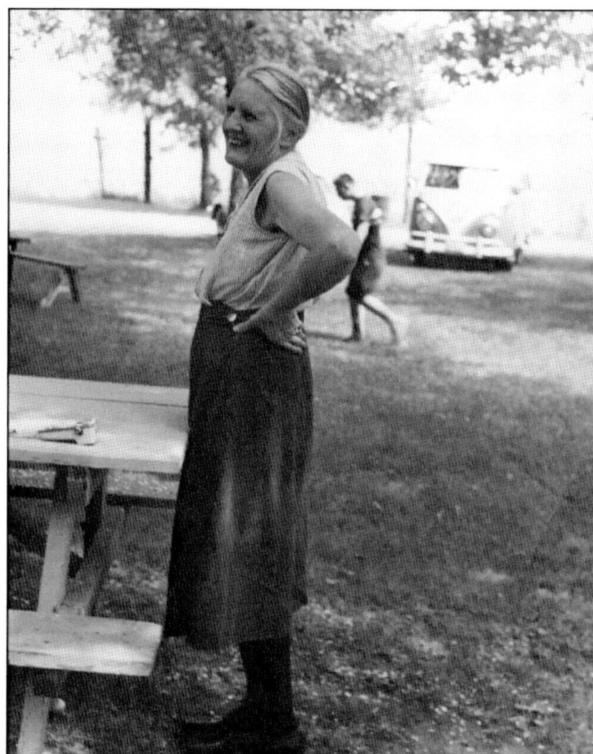

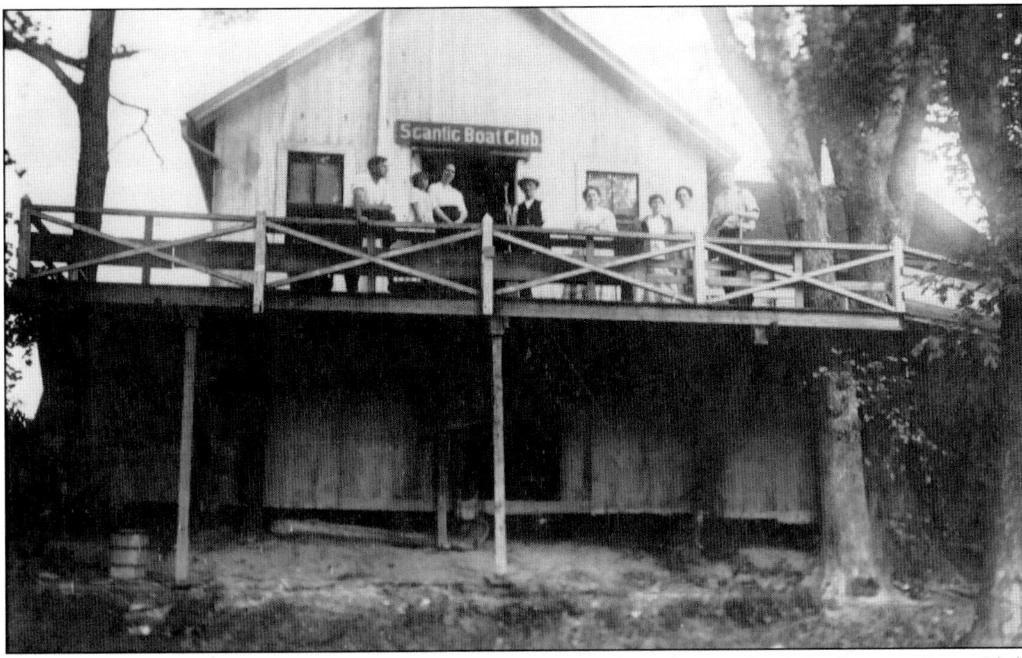

Members of the Tule, Porter, and Washburn families stand on the porch of the Scantic Boat Club, which was near the end of Ferry Road. Doris Burgdorf notes: "They had a commodore of their boat club, and they had jackets that looked like fireman's jackets. They were quite an official little boat club. . . . And they had canoes or rowboats." (Hildred Raymond Collection, WMLM.)

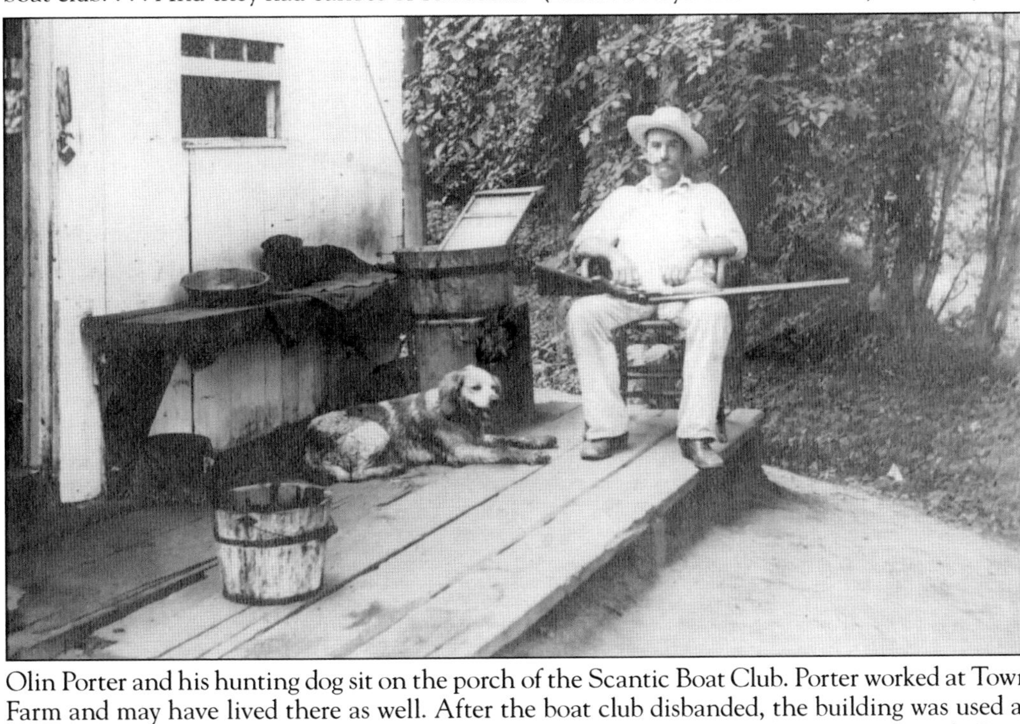

Olin Porter and his hunting dog sit on the porch of the Scantic Boat Club. Porter worked at Town Farm and may have lived there as well. After the boat club disbanded, the building was used as a house until it burned down in the mid-20th century while someone known as "Bicycle Pete" lived there. (Hildred Raymond Collection, WMLM.)

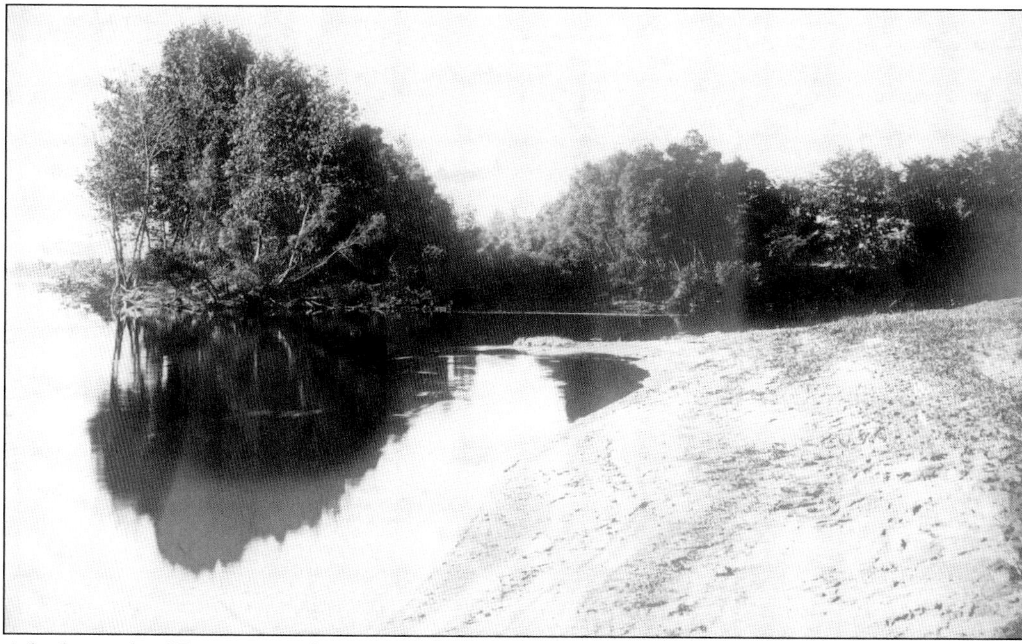

A little north of Ferry Lane, the Scantic River meets the Connecticut River at a spot that was the site of Ebenezer Grant's shipyard in the late 18th and early 19th centuries. Spelled "Scantuck" in early American documents, the Scantic River starts in Hampden, Massachusetts, and is slightly more than 40 miles long. (Hildred Raymond Collection, WMLM.)

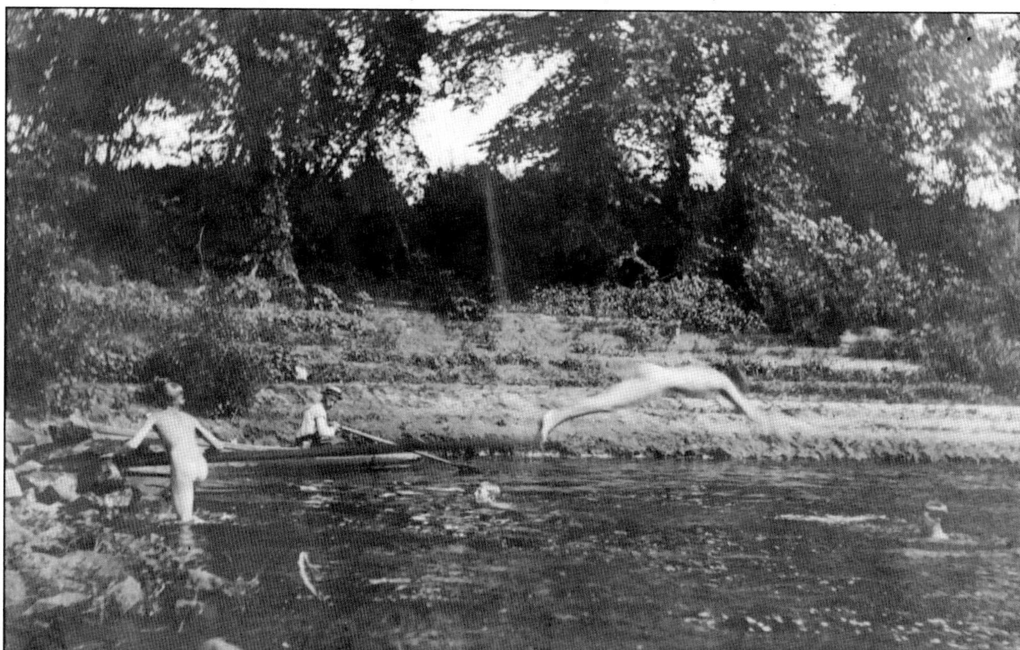

The current in the open channel of the Connecticut River is often too strong for swimming, but generations of South Windsor youth have swum in protected bends of the river as well as swimming holes in the Podunk and Scantic Rivers. Pictured around the turn of the 20th century, skinny dippers cool off in a cove between Vibert and Newberry Roads. (Roger Newberry Collection, WMLM.)

A granite marker in front of 454 King Street, near the East Hartford town line, marks the spot where John Fitch's (1743–1798) birthplace once stood. Perhaps inspired by the bustle of river traffic he saw on the Connecticut during his childhood, Fitch invented the steamboat in the 1780s. (Photograph by L. Ellsworth Stoughton, WMLM.)

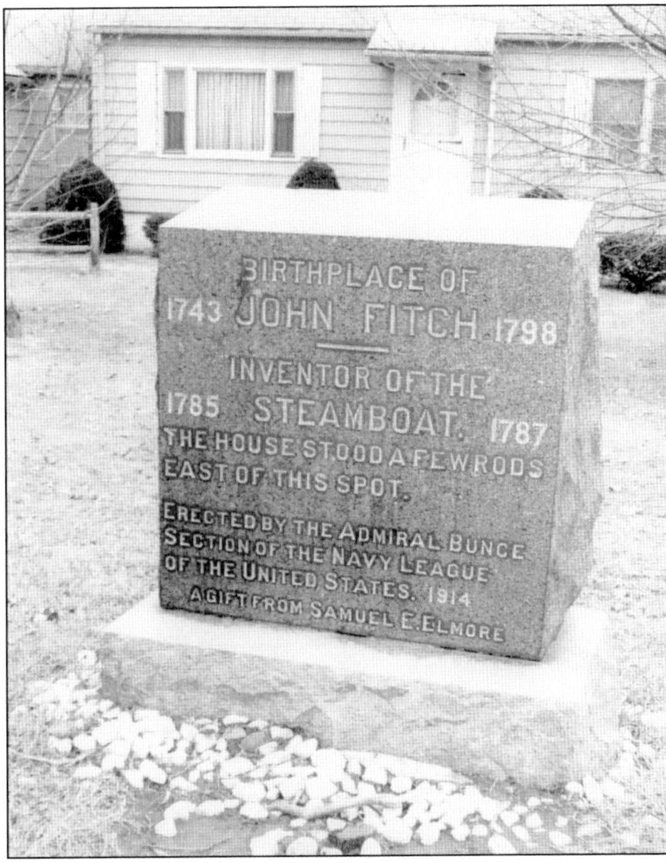

Children ride on and march alongside a parade float from the 1975 Wapping Fair Parade, memorializing native son John Fitch's steam-powered rowboat, the *Perseverance*. Fitch won praise for his invention, but not financial success. He died penniless in Bardstown, Kentucky, in 1798, and it was not until 1807 that Robert Fulton designed a commercially successful steamboat. (WMLM.)

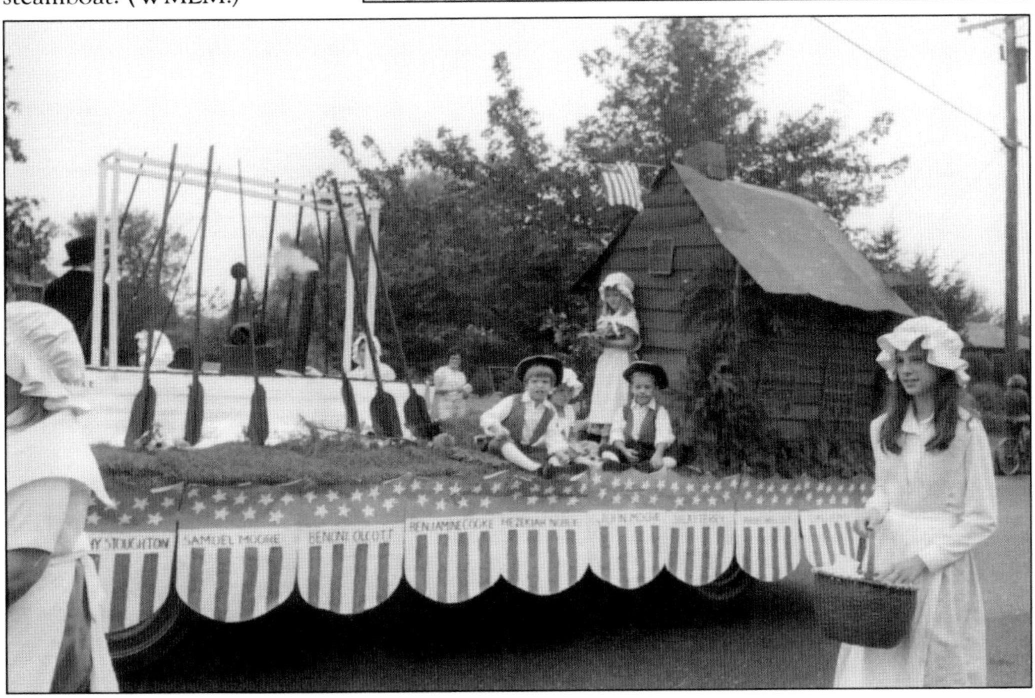

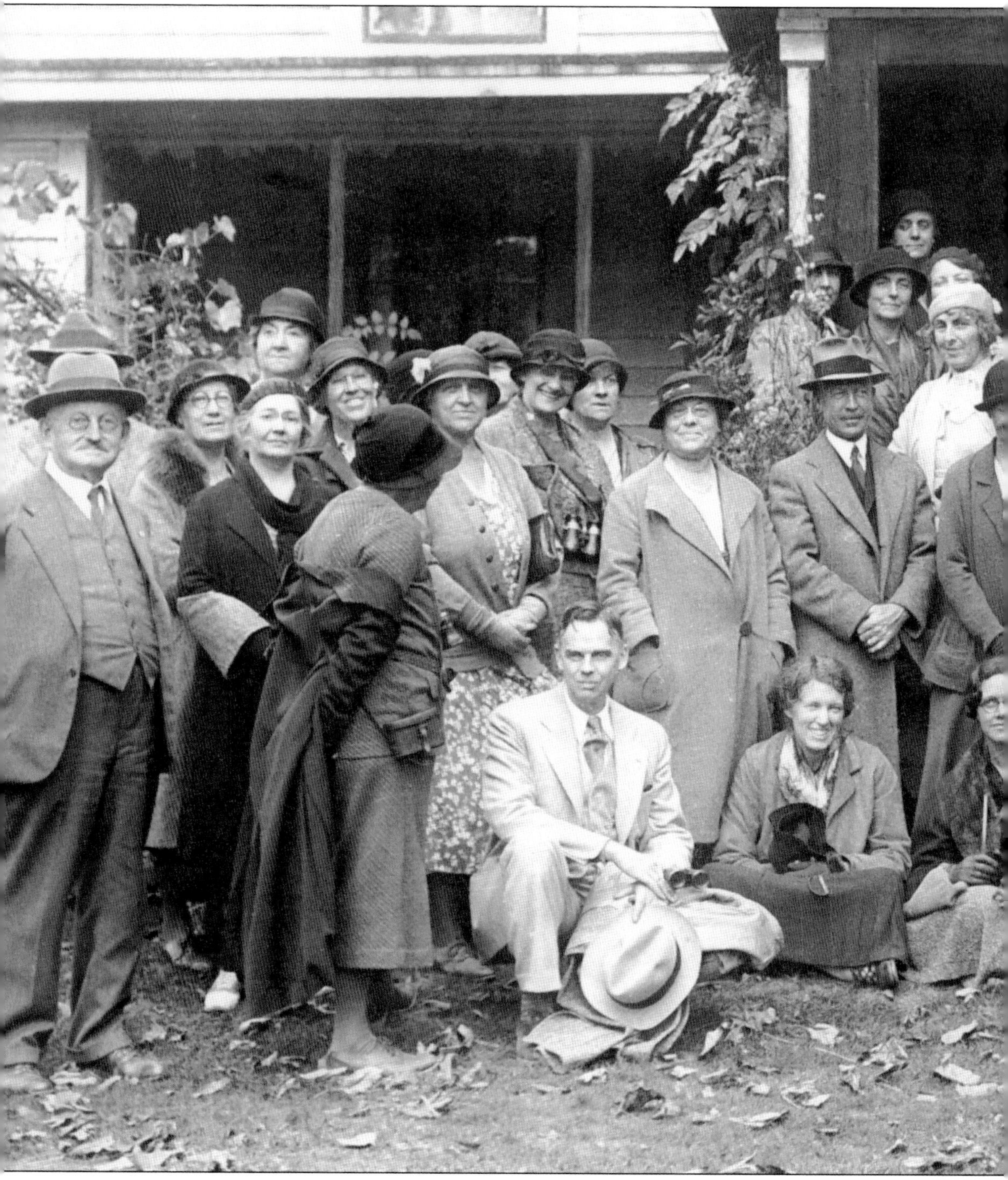

Members of the Hartford Bird Study Club stand in front of 809 Main Street. The club was founded in 1909 and later changed its name to the Hartford Audubon Society. South Windsor residents, including Charles Watson Vibert (standing near the center, with white hair and beard), were founding members, and the club often went on birdwatching excursions in the South Windsor Meadows. Charles Nielsen stated: "It was about the time that conservation was becoming a

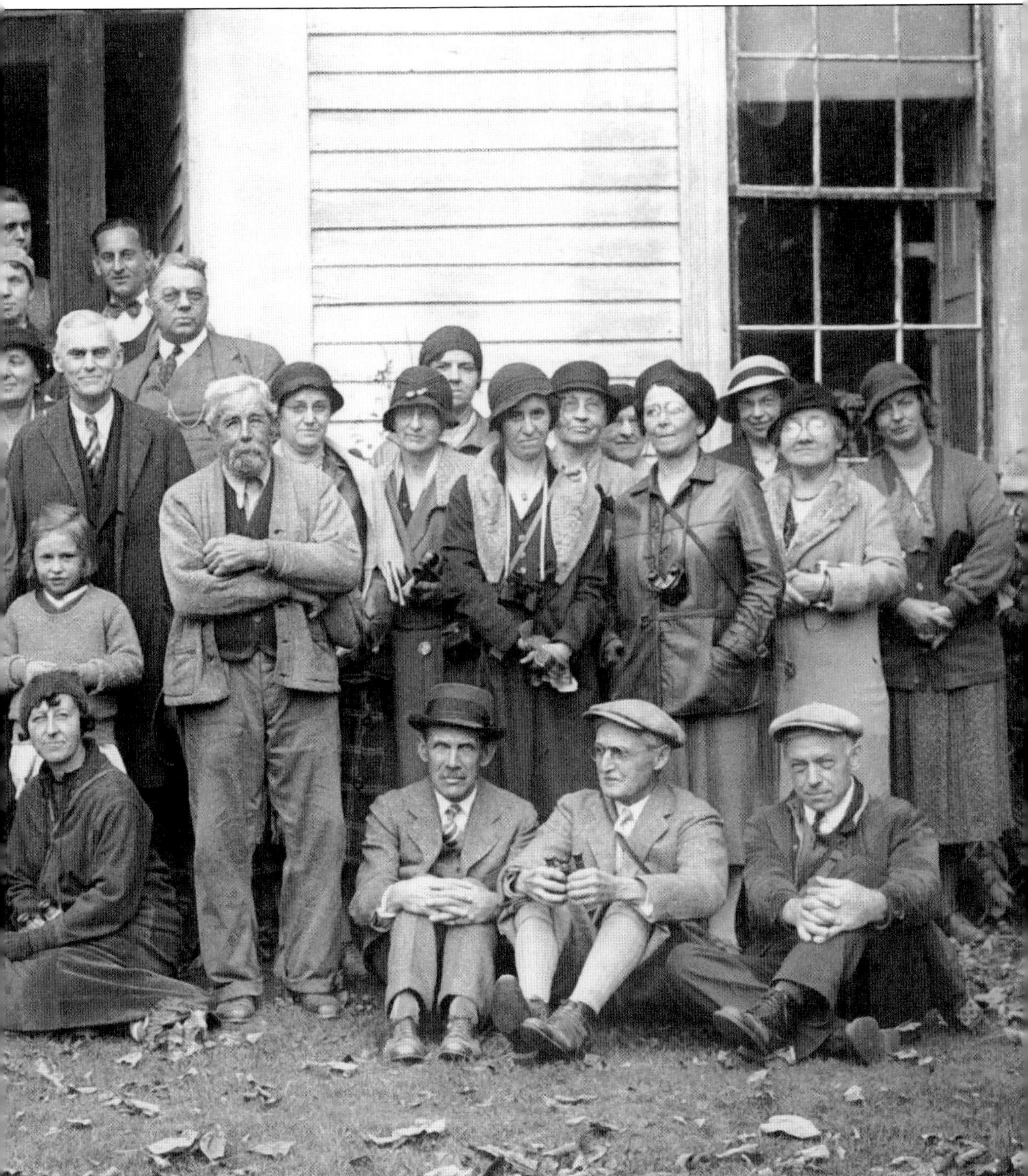

popular subject. . . . In the legislature he [Charles Watson Vibert] got introduced to that kind of philosophy, and he found he endorsed it. He came home, and he hung up his guns . . . and he bought a pair of binoculars." In the late 20th century, the society acquired a marshy 10-acre area next to the river and designated it the Station 43 Marsh Preserve, named for the number of the former trolley stop nearby. (Vibert family.)

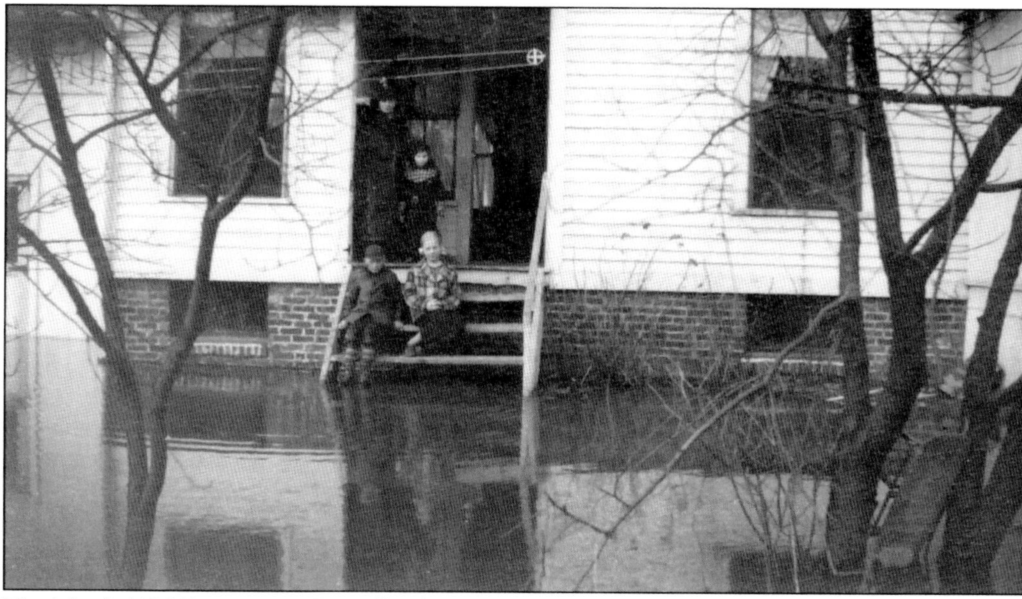

The March 1936 Connecticut River flood was a perfect combination of ice jams, snowpack melt, and heavy rains, which caused massive damage from New Hampshire to Connecticut. In Hartford, the peak of the flood was measured at 37.6 feet. In South Windsor, the flood waters inundated homes and businesses along the river and on Main Street. (Hildred Raymond Collection, WMLM.)

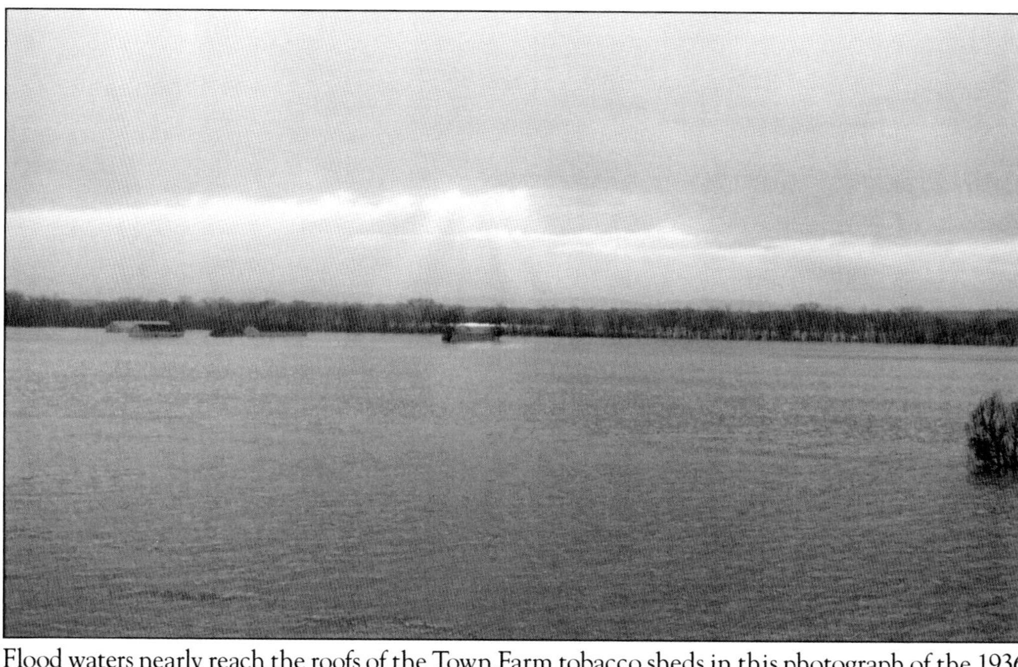

Flood waters nearly reach the roofs of the Town Farm tobacco sheds in this photograph of the 1936 flood. People in the Town Farm house had to be rescued by boat from a second-story window. The banks of the river at its normal height are beyond the row of trees in the background. (Hildred Raymond Collection, WMLM.)

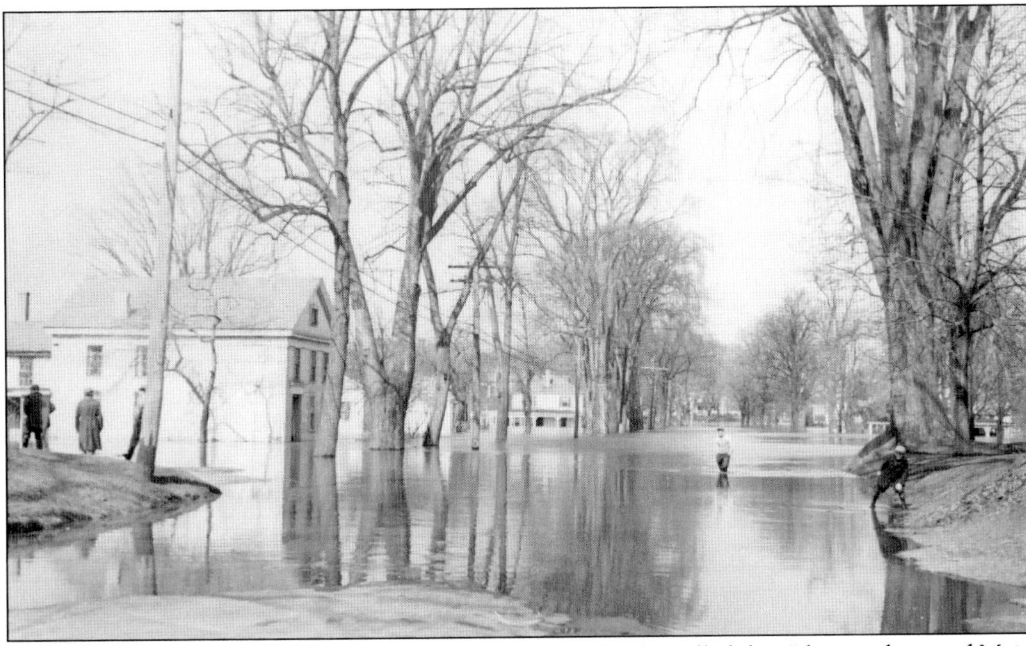

This image shows 1936 flooding on Main Street. Sally Edlund recalled that "the meadows and Main Street in South Windsor was so badly flooded that my dad drove me over one day and we stood in back of the Masonic Hall. . . . I still remember it—this huge brown ocean with little whitecaps . . . and as far as you could see, just brown muddy water." (Hildred Raymond Collection, WMLM.)

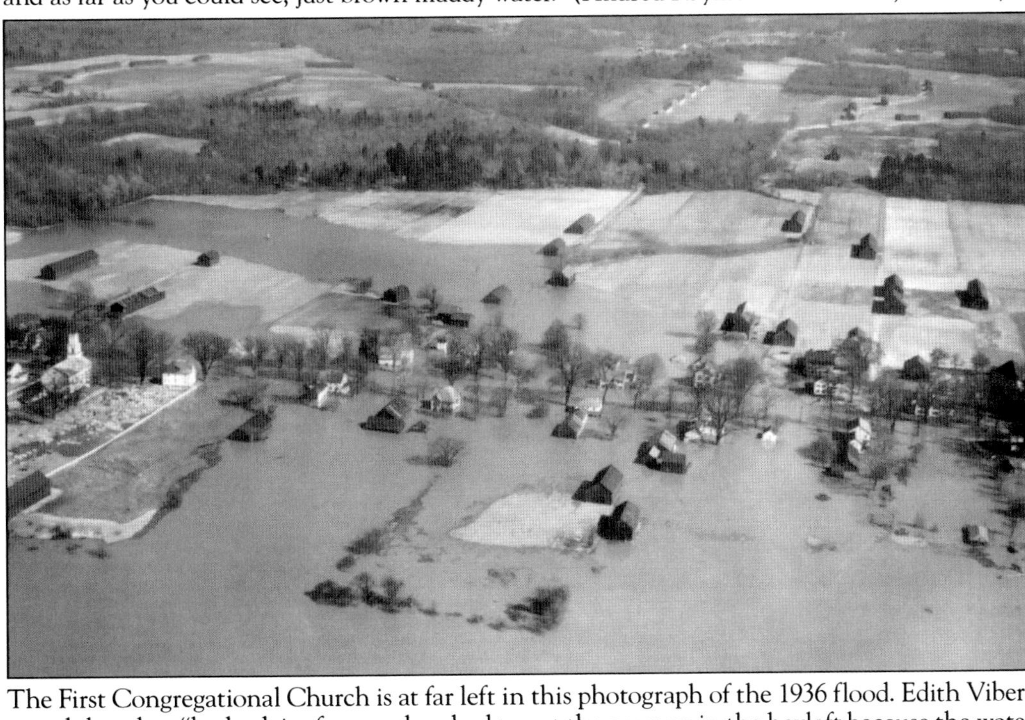

The First Congregational Church is at far left in this photograph of the 1936 flood. Edith Vibert stated that they "had a dairy farm and we had to put the cows up in the hayloft because the water started coming in the barn. We had, oh, I think it was maybe 25 cows all tied up in the hayloft on the second floor of the barn." (WMLM.)

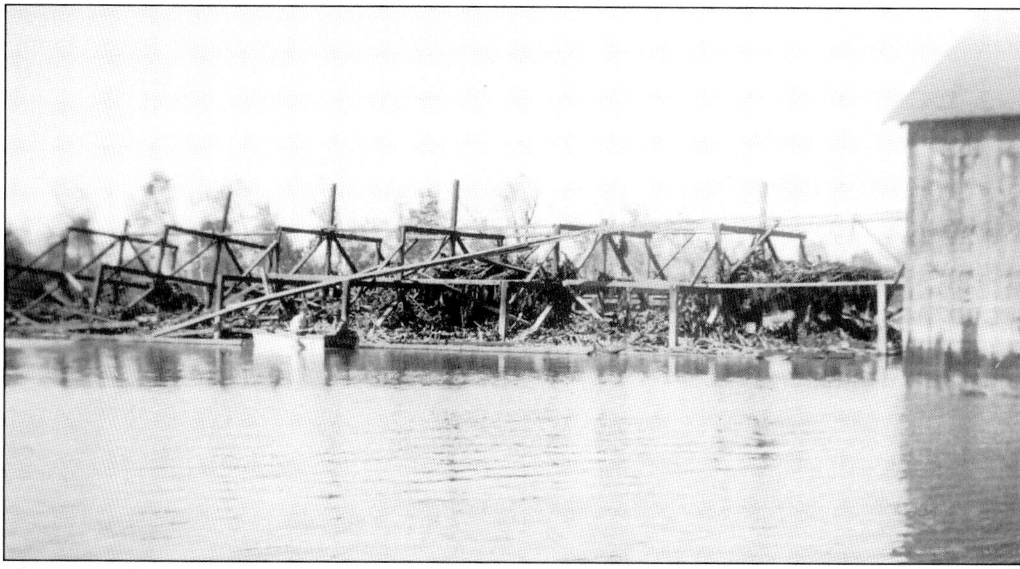

The September 1938 hurricane also caused widespread damage, including flooding and collapsed buildings. Sally Edlund said, "After the hurricane many sheds and barns blew down, and my Uncle Pete . . . brought loads and loads of lumber that had been used on tobacco sheds that blew down. . . . Since it was full of nails . . . we kids spent lots of time out there with a hammer, pounding out nails to re-use." (WMLM.)

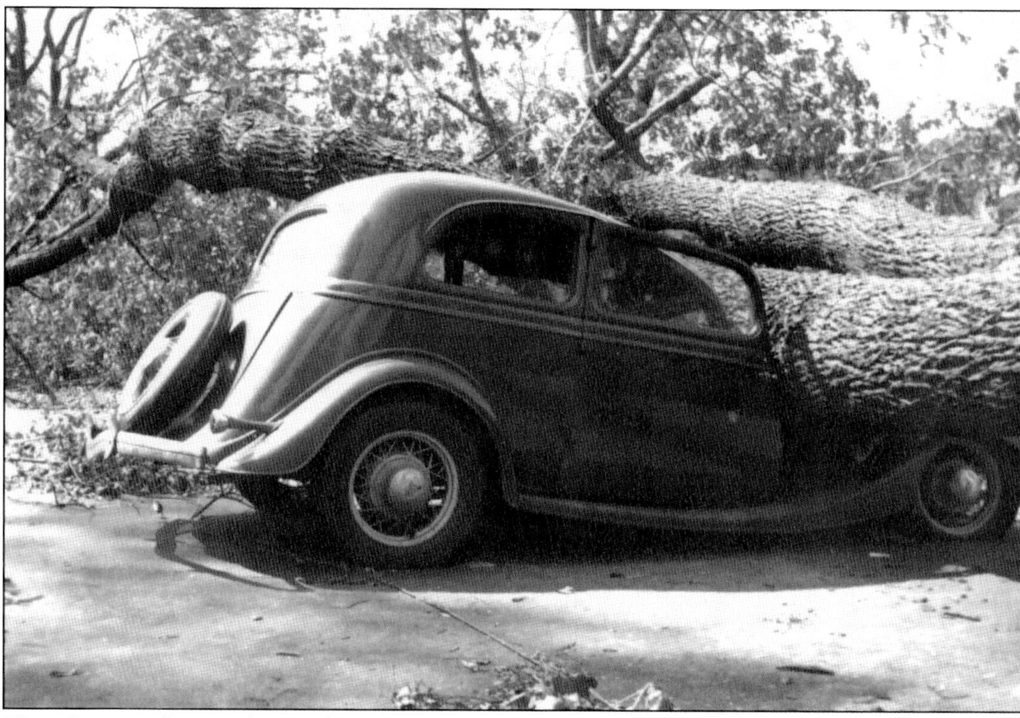

This photograph was taken at the intersection of Main Street and Sullivan Avenue. Butch Carney noted, "I could remember very vividly the hurricane of 1938 in this house how it shook. We hoped we'd escape with our lives. . . . We had a tobacco shed down in the field here and you could see it going rolling like a cardboard box." (Hildred Raymond Collection, WMLM.)

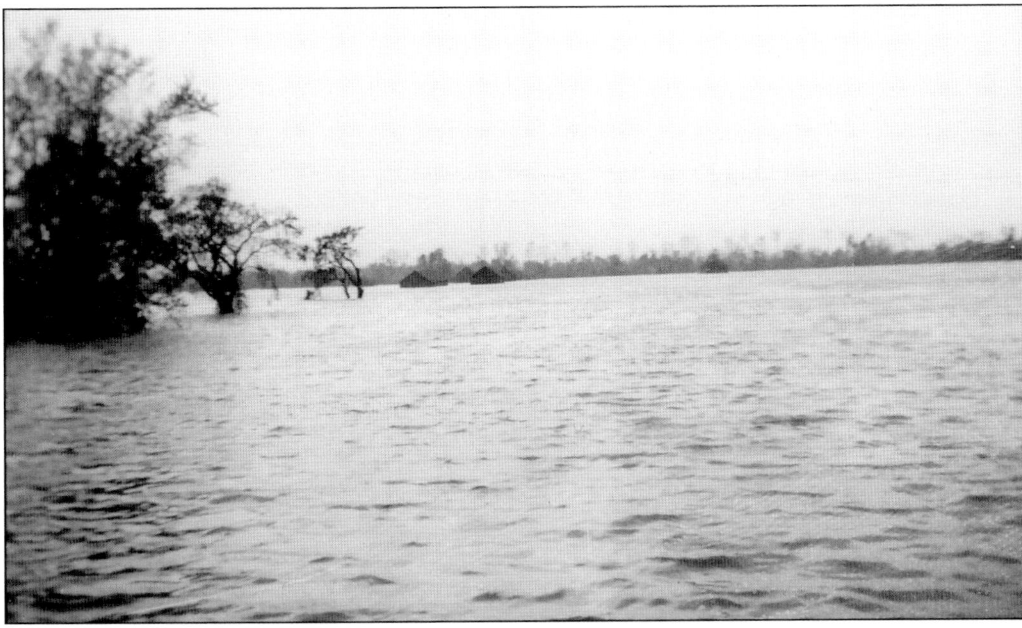

The hurricane caused flooding nearly as bad as the 1936 flood just two years before. Doris Burgdorf recalled: "That was quite an event because it took us by surprise. We had no knowledge of hurricanes before that . . . the road washed out. You couldn't get anywhere." This image shows partially submerged barns in the South Windsor Meadows after the hurricane. (Helen Carpy Photographs Collection, WMLM.)

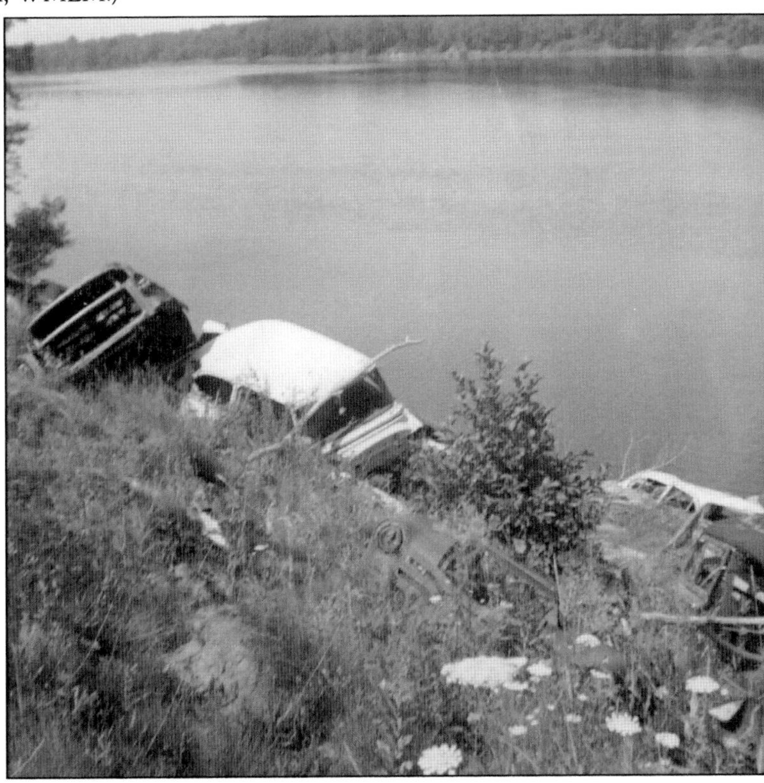

Both the 1936 flood and 1938 hurricane carved wide swaths out of the Connecticut River bank. Afterwards, locals jury-rigged some inelegant solutions to prevent further erosion. This photograph, taken during the 1940s, shows car frames and other heavy detritus piled on the riverbank to control erosion. (Barney Daley Collection, WMLM.)

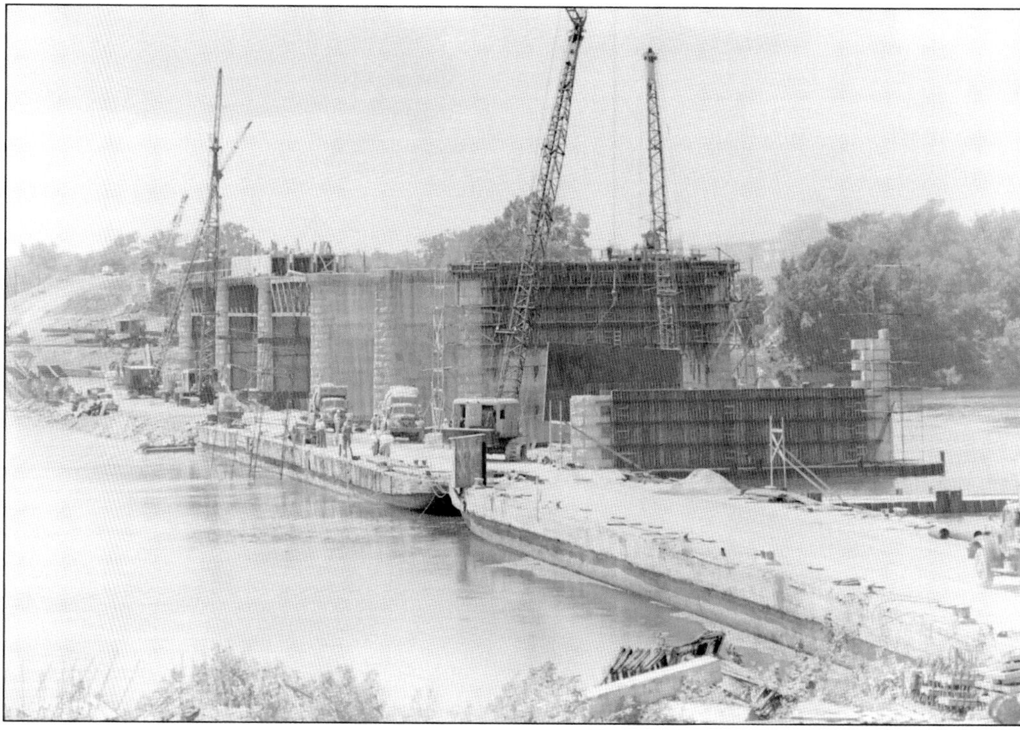

The Bissell Bridge is shown under construction, above, and after it opened in 1957, below. Originally a toll bridge, the structure was overhauled in 1994 when it began carrying Route 291 linking I-91 and I-84. Richard Nicholson remembered: "I grew up as a child in the 1950s when that bridge was being constructed. It was an enormous construction project, because it went through a very, very lengthy corridor of the South Windsor meadow, which is essentially a flood plain. . . . There was a huge, huge construction involved in moving that earth, and for a kid growing up . . . nothing could be more fascinating to watch than construction [taking] place and all of these huge payloaders . . . to move the dirt and pack it down and everything." (Both photographs by Ellsworth Fairbanks, Barney Daley Collection, WMLM.)

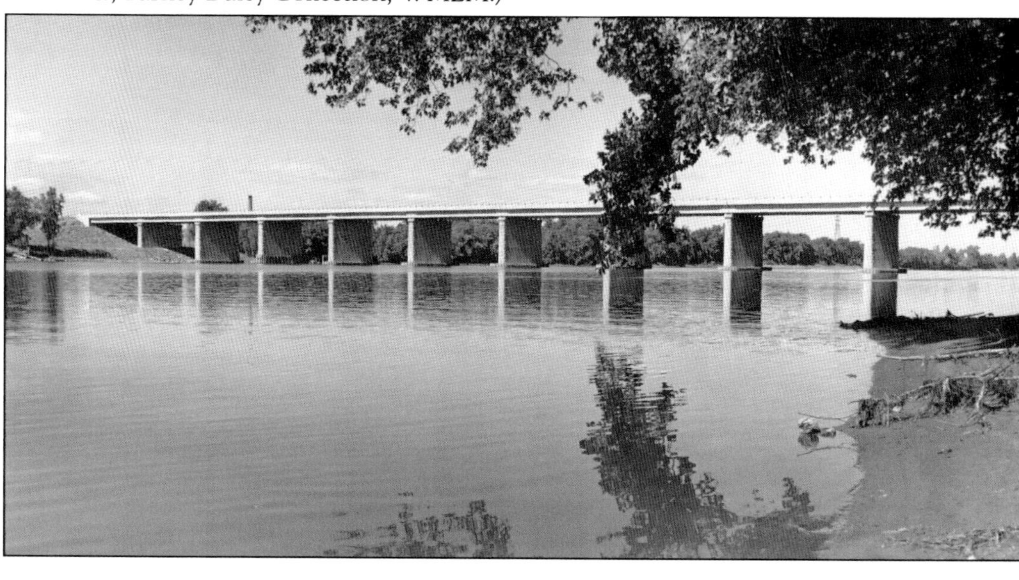

Two

Main Street

The original 1640 land grants on the east side of the Connecticut River to settlers from Dorchester, Massachusetts, were in narrow strips that extended three miles east from the river. Because the land directly adjacent to the river lies in a floodplain, early South Windsor settlers built their homes along Main Street, which was laid out in 1672 parallel to the river. This location was no accident: the street runs along what had been a well-worn Native American thoroughfare known as the Podunk Path. The northernmost end of the street, from the Scantic River to approximately one mile south, just beyond the God's Acre burying ground, is known as East Windsor Hill. Main Street of the 17th and 18th centuries was a much busier place than it is today. Many of the homes along Main Street also had workshops and stores attached to them. Families were much larger, and many households had servants, farmhands, and apprentices living with them in addition to relatives. In April 1771, more than two decades before he would become the second president of the United States, John Adams traveled down Main Street and wrote in his diary: "I have spent this morning in riding thro paradise. My eyes never beheld so fine a country."

In the early 20th century, a trolley line ran from Springfield, Massachusetts, down Main Street, to Hartford, transporting students to school and people to jobs in the city in the days before it was common for every family to own automobiles. In the 1940s, the construction of Route 5 cut Main Street off from much of the rest of South Windsor, but many of South Windsor's young people still went to school on Main Street until the 1960s, when the post–World War II baby boom, along with the influx of families moving into new subdivisions throughout the town, necessitated newer, larger schools. Main Street today is much quieter than it once was, but tractors still traverse the street in the summer on their way from one field to another, and many 18th- and 19th-century houses remain, giving a glimpse of earlier times.

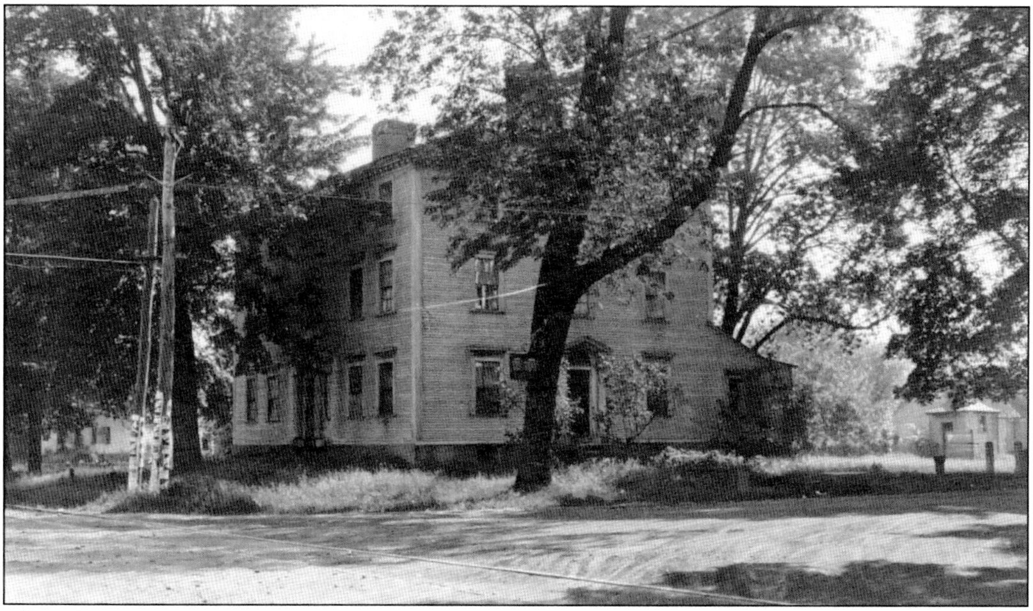

The John Watson house, at 1876 Main Street, was built in 1789. Seen here in 1922, this three-story house on the corner of Main Street and Sullivan Avenue is one of the largest on the street. Trolley tracks can be seen running in front of the house. The ornate four-holed outhouse (far right), which was built at the same time as the main house, still stands. (WMLM.)

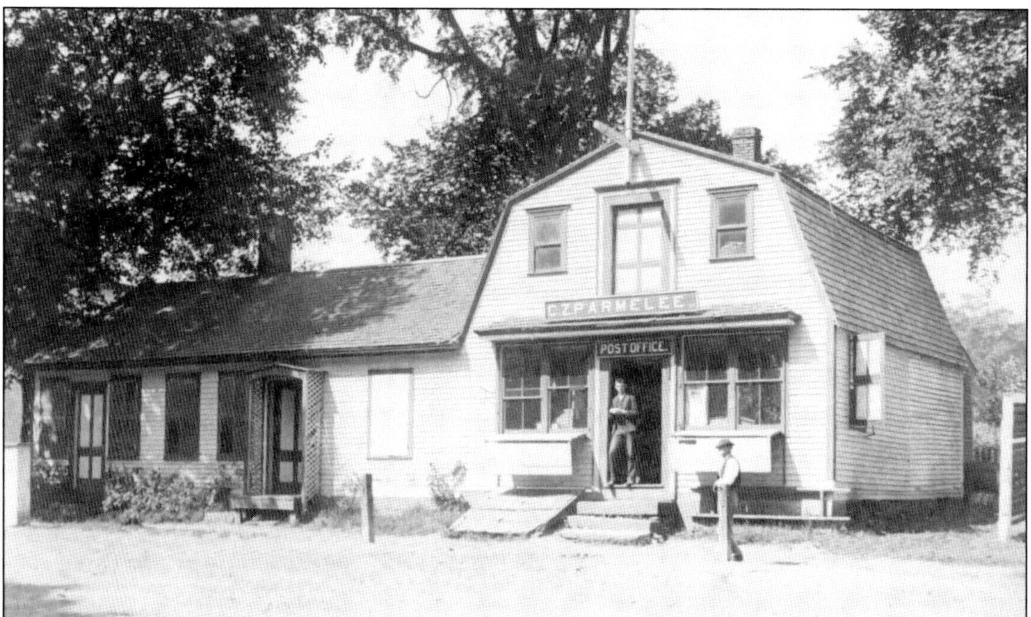

Harry Bancroft stands in the doorway of the C.Z. Parmelee Store around 1890. This building is also known as the East Windsor Hill Post Office and is one of the oldest continuously operating post offices in the country. The left section was built in 1757, while the two-story section at right was built 10 to 15 years later. Over the centuries, the building has been a saddle shop, gold- and silversmith, publishing house, post office, and general store. (Hildred Raymond Collection, WMLM.)

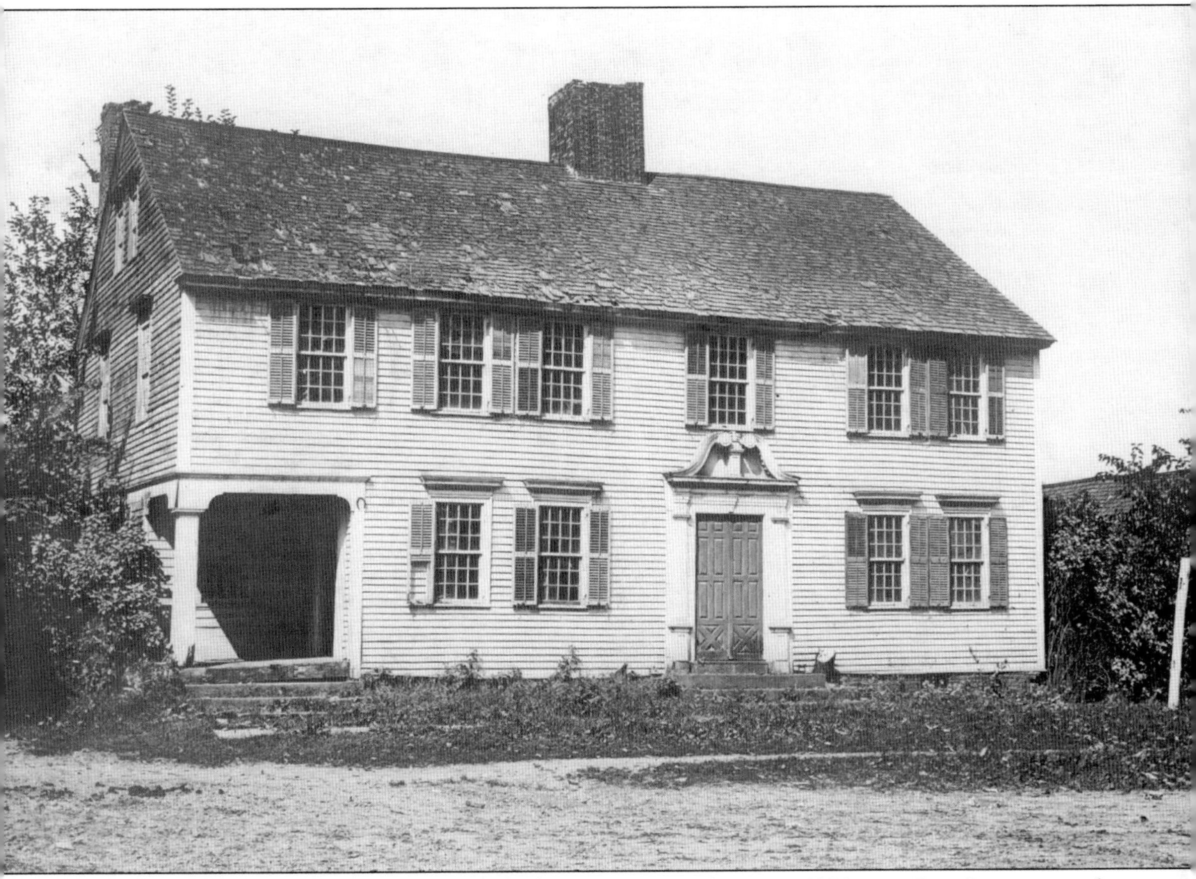

The Bissell Tavern, shown here shortly before it was torn down in 1901, stood at the corner of Ferry Lane and Main Street. Not to be confused with the Bissell Ferry Tavern at the bottom of Ferry Lane, this Bissell Tavern was built in 1760 and featured a ballroom with a fiddler's gallery. John Adams stayed at the tavern in 1771. He wrote in his diary, "Rode along the great river to Windsor, and put up at Bissell's, that is, in East Windsor; for the town of Windsor, it seems, lies on the west side of the river. . . . I want to hear the news and politics of the day. But here I am at Bissell's, in Windsor, hearing my landlord read a chapter in the kitchen, and go to prayers with his family in the genuine tone of a puritan." (Hildred Raymond Collection, WMLM.)

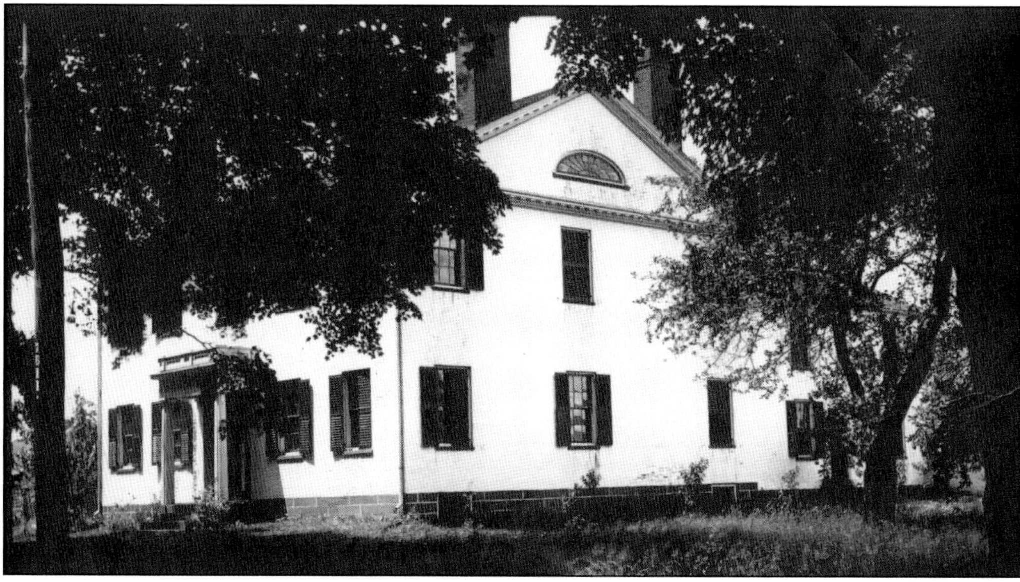

In 1812, Aaron Bissell Jr., proprietor of the tavern shown on the previous page, built the imposing brick house at 1909 Main Street as a wedding present for his daughter and son-in-law. Bissell liked the house so much that the following year he had a nearly identical house built for himself next door at 1891 Main Street (pictured). (Hildred Raymond Collection, WMLM.)

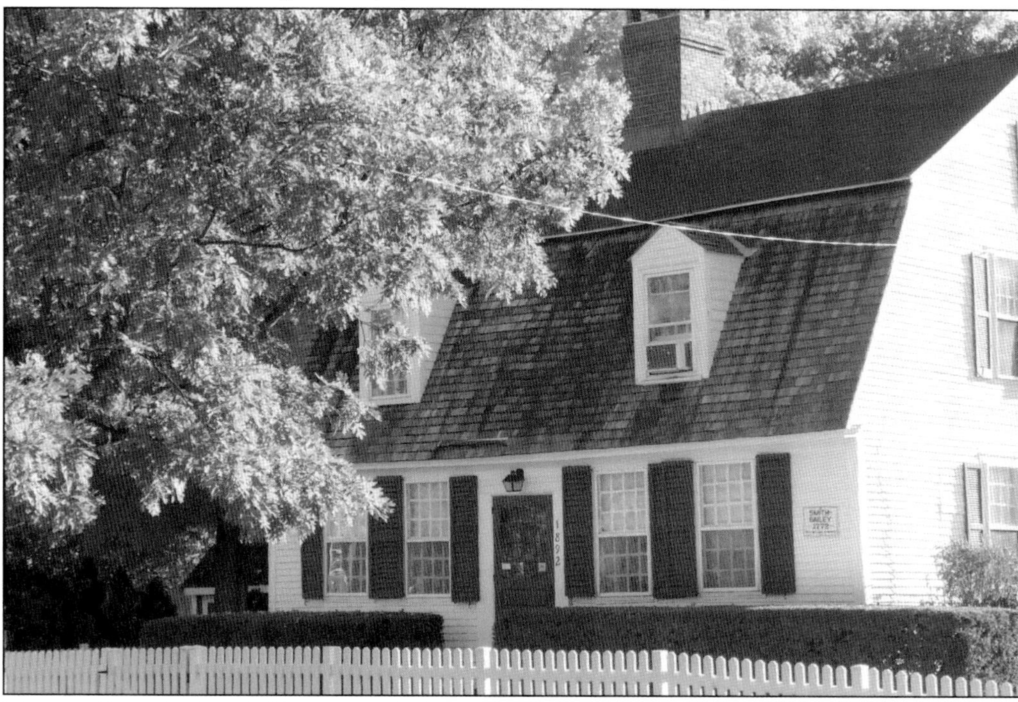

The small gambrel-roofed house at 1892 Main Street was built in 1772 by silver- and goldsmith Smith Bailey, who sold his wares in the shop pictured on page 26. In 1786, tall case (grandfather) clockmaker Daniel Burnap bought the house and had his shop and foundry in the back. Burnap trained a number of apprentices in his shop, among them Eli Terry, the clockmaker whose family Terryville, Connecticut, was named for. (Photograph by Claire Lobdell.)

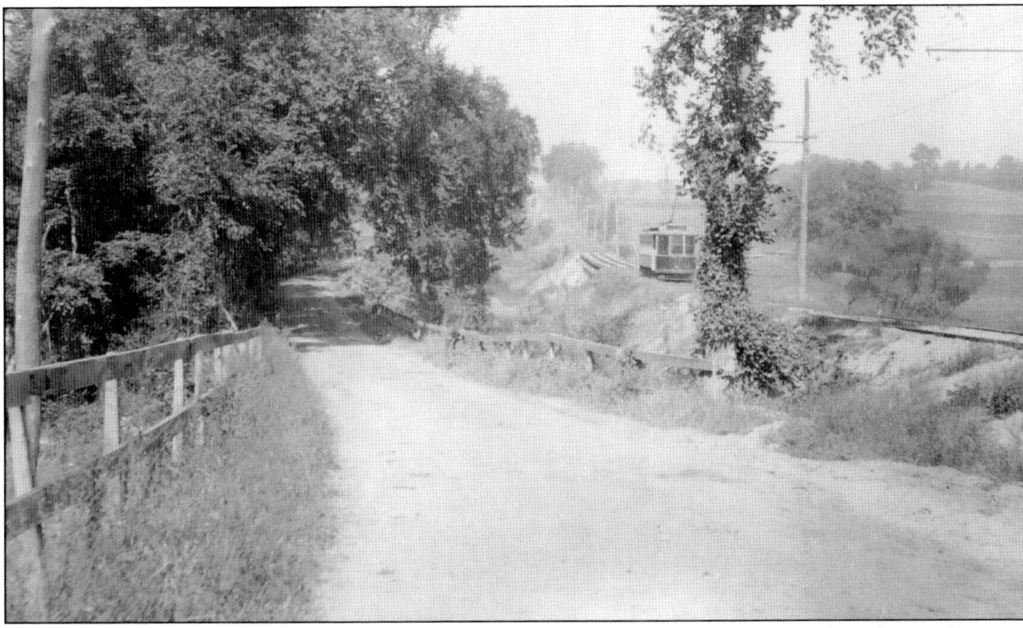

Today, Main Street stops abruptly a few houses north of the intersection with Sullivan Avenue, but until Route 5 was built in the early 1940s, Main Street continued over the Scantic River and met up with the road that is now Route 5. This photograph shows a trolley car crossing the Scantic River bridge. From 1895 until 1932, trolleys ran between Springfield, Massachusetts, and Hartford. (Hildred Raymond Collection, WMLM.)

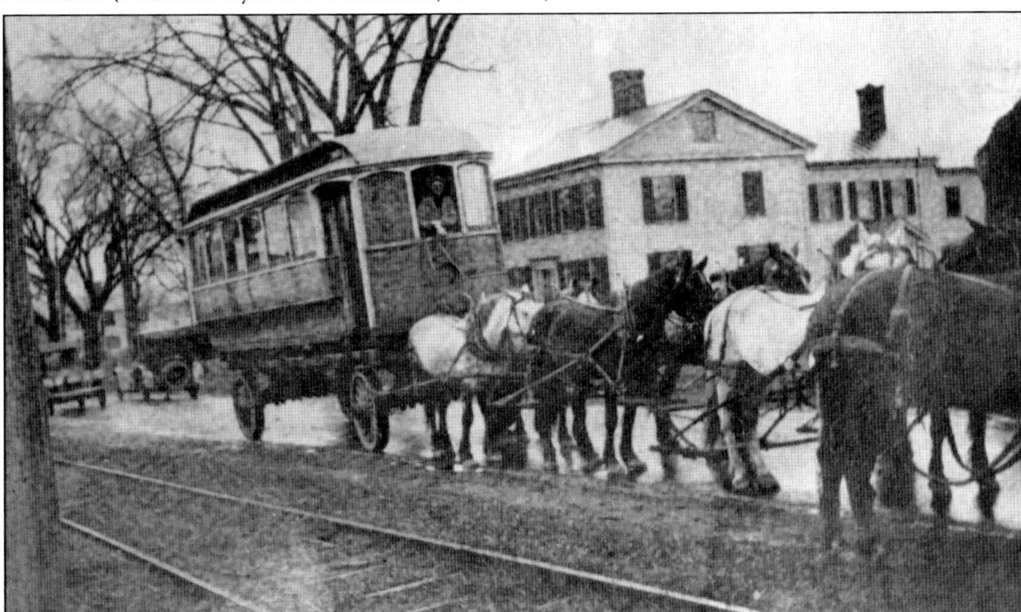

Tobacco farmer and teamster Edward Bancroft (1872–1954) refurbished and repurposed trolley cars. Charles Nielsen recalled: "Ed Bancroft [told me] during the winter instead of going down to Hartford and across the bridges . . . they would go directly over the frozen Connecticut River into Windsor. In those days the test of manhood amongst teamsters seemed to be who had enough nerve to be the last team across in the spring." (Ted Bancroft Collection, WMLM.)

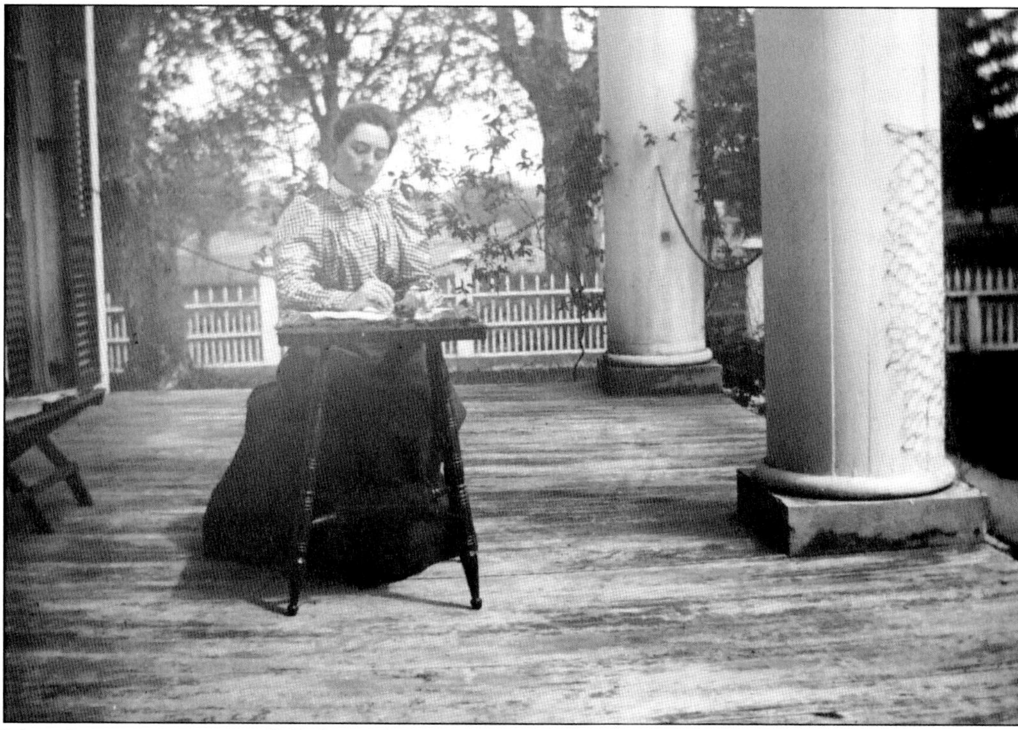

Mary Sperry sits at a small desk on the porch of 1837 Main Street when it was owned by William R. Wood. The house was built in 1815 by Epaphrus Bissell. Bob Raymond noted that "the property was always a working farm. Will Wood primarily farmed for a living. And . . . it was he who gave the library to the town." (Hildred Raymond Collection, WMLM.)

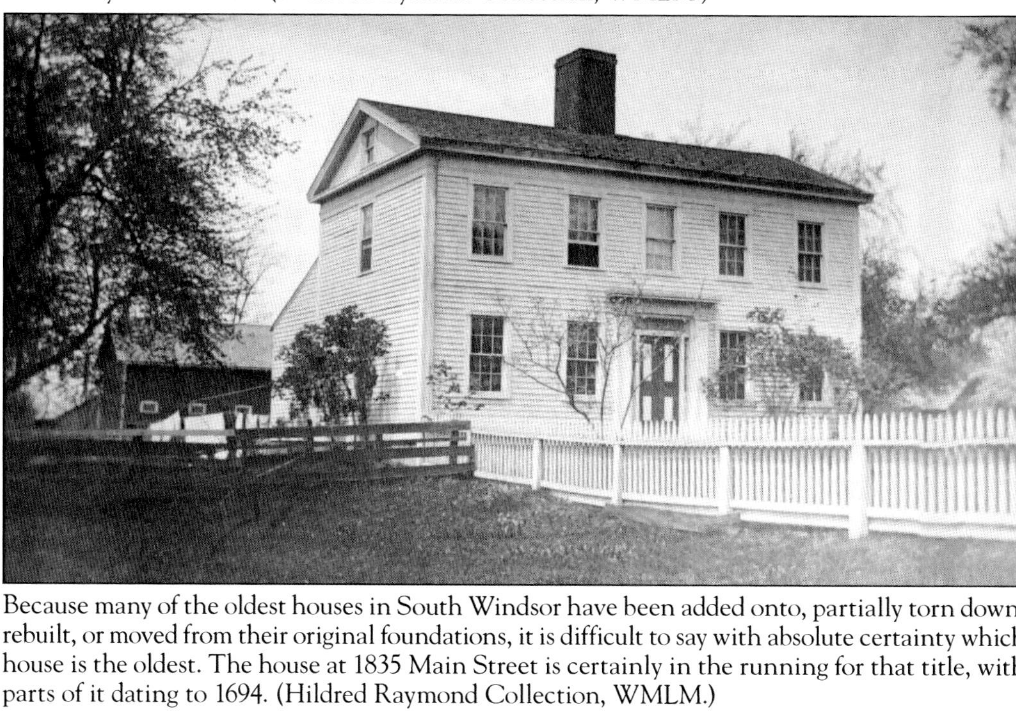

Because many of the oldest houses in South Windsor have been added onto, partially torn down, rebuilt, or moved from their original foundations, it is difficult to say with absolute certainty which house is the oldest. The house at 1835 Main Street is certainly in the running for that title, with parts of it dating to 1694. (Hildred Raymond Collection, WMLM.)

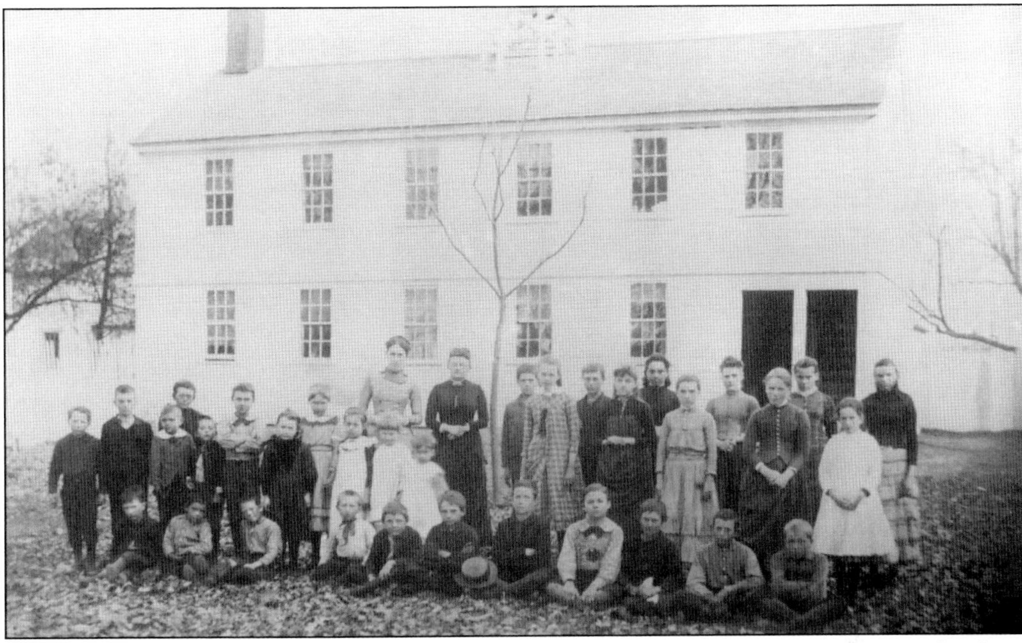

East Windsor Hill Academy was built in 1800 as a private, coeducational preparatory school and was located between what are now 1810 and 1828 Main Street. Professors from the Theological Institute of Connecticut taught there in the 1850s, and the academy closed in 1860. The building was used as a public school until it was torn down sometime around 1900. This photograph of students and teachers was taken in 1886. (SWHS.)

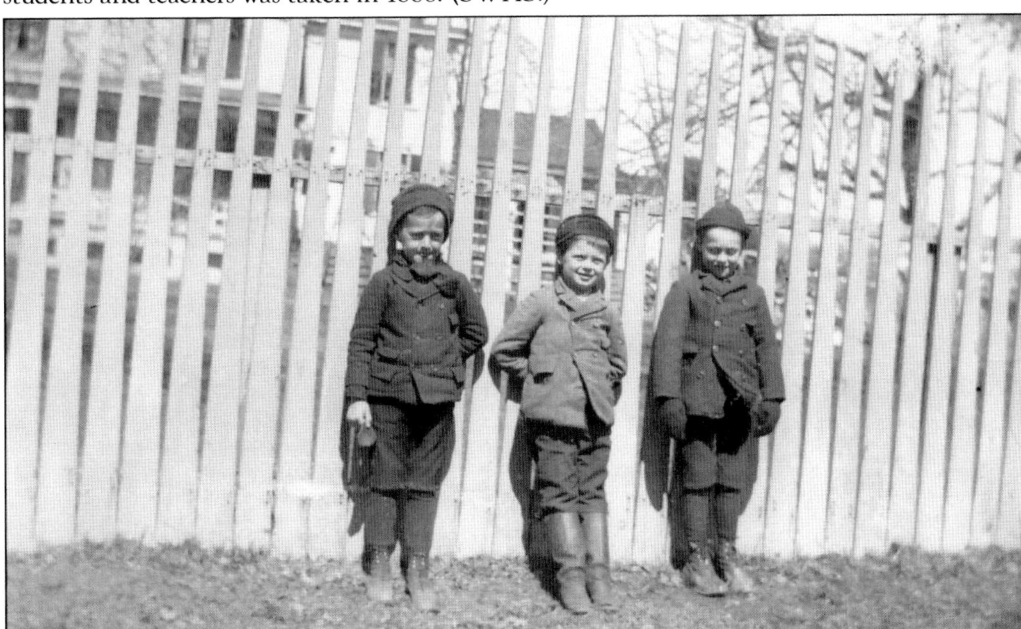

Three small boys stand against the East Windsor Hill Academy fence on a chilly day in the late 1890s. In the 19th and early 20th centuries, young boys wore short pants at all times of the year, pairing them with thick woolen socks in the winter to stay warm. Moving to long pants in early adolescence was a rite of passage. (Hildred Raymond Collection, WMLM.)

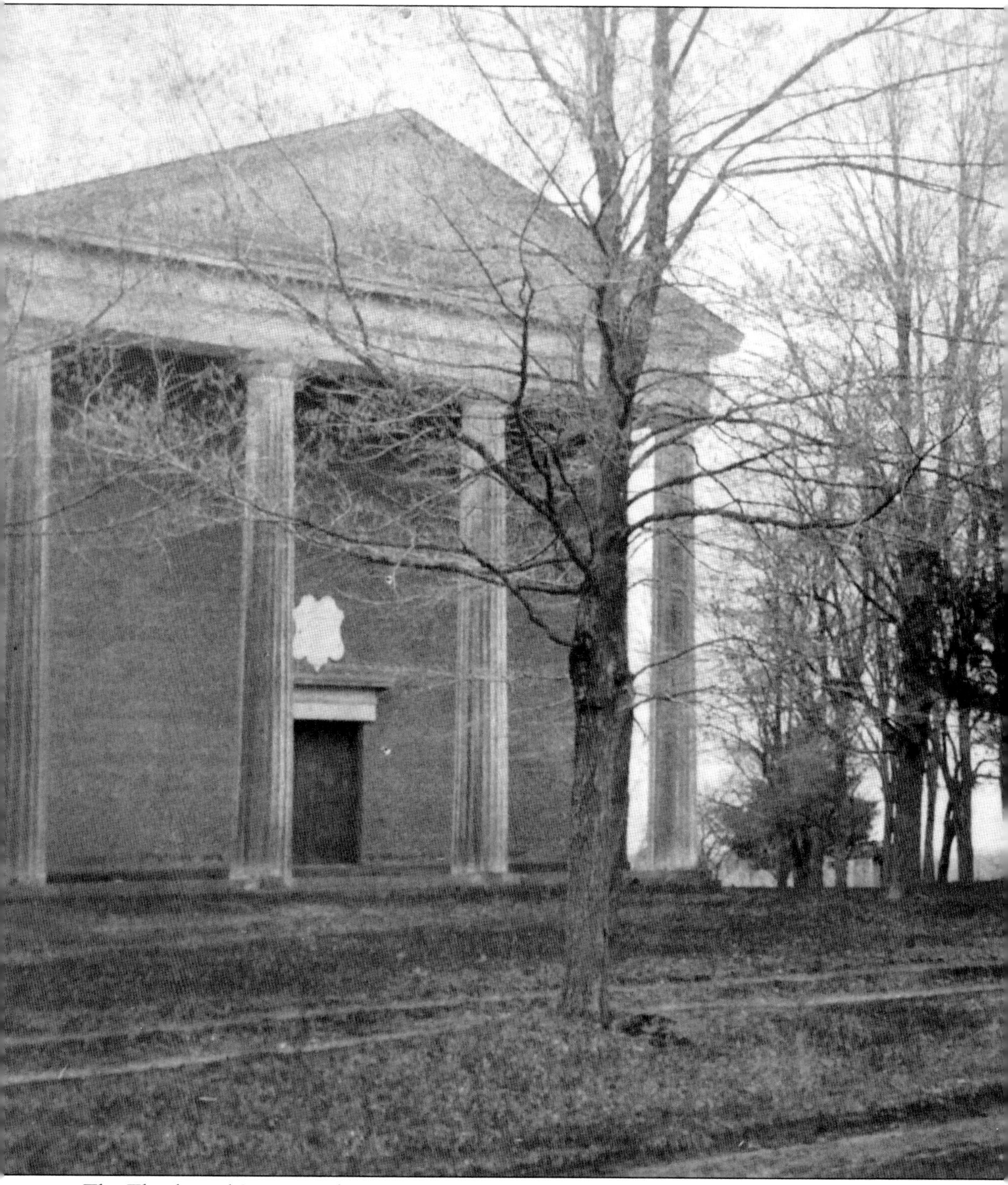

The Theological Institute of Connecticut at East Windsor Hill, also known as the Theological Seminary, was started in 1834 by Dr. Bennett Tyler as a more conservative alternative to Yale Divinity School. Students lived in the dormitory and classroom building at right and worshiped in the chapel building at left. Students at the Theological Institute were expected to work their bodies as well as their minds: each student was allotted a plot of land to farm, and there

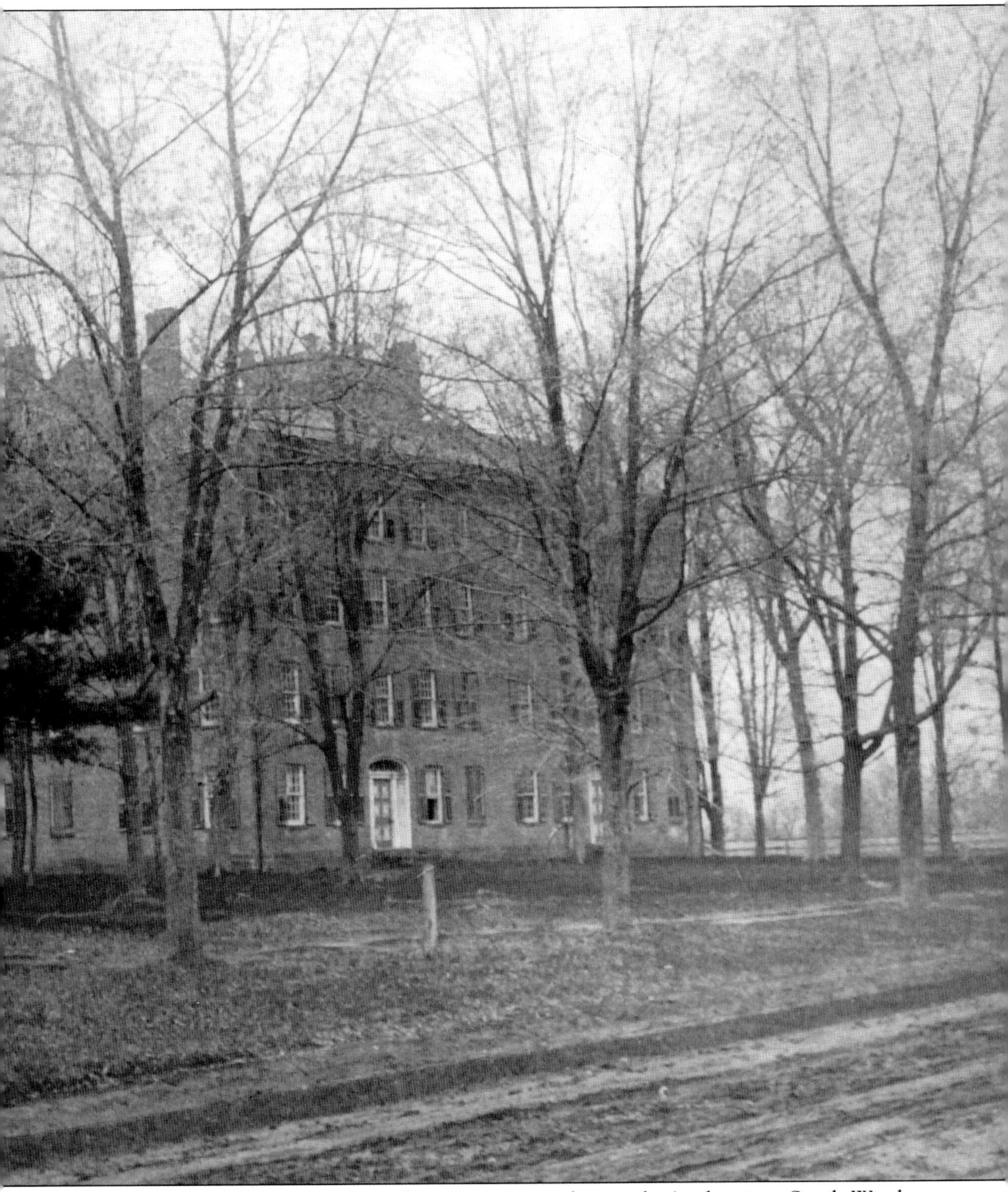

was a carpentry shop on-site where they were expected to work. At the time, South Windsor was considered a remote backwater, and the school had trouble attracting students. After only about 30 years in operation, the seminary relocated to Hartford, where it became the Hartford Theological Seminary. (WMLM.)

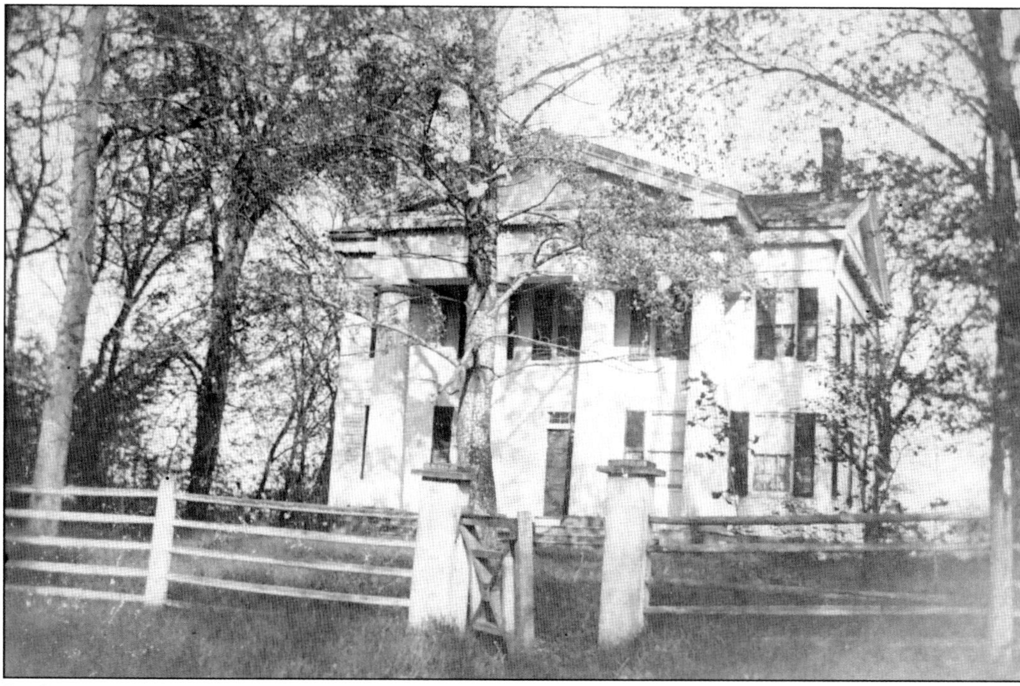

Built in 1834 for Dr. Jonathan Cogswell, an independently wealthy theologian who taught at the Theological Seminary without taking a salary, the Greek Revival mansion at 1752 Main Street is the only remaining building of the seminary. In 1844, Cogswell sold the house to the seminary, after which it became known as the Bennett Tyler House for the school's president, who took up residence there in 1844. In the 1920s, Augusta Graves and Mary Hovey owned the house and ran a tea room and antiques shop there called the Tea Tray. (Above, Hildred Raymond Collection; both, WMLM.)

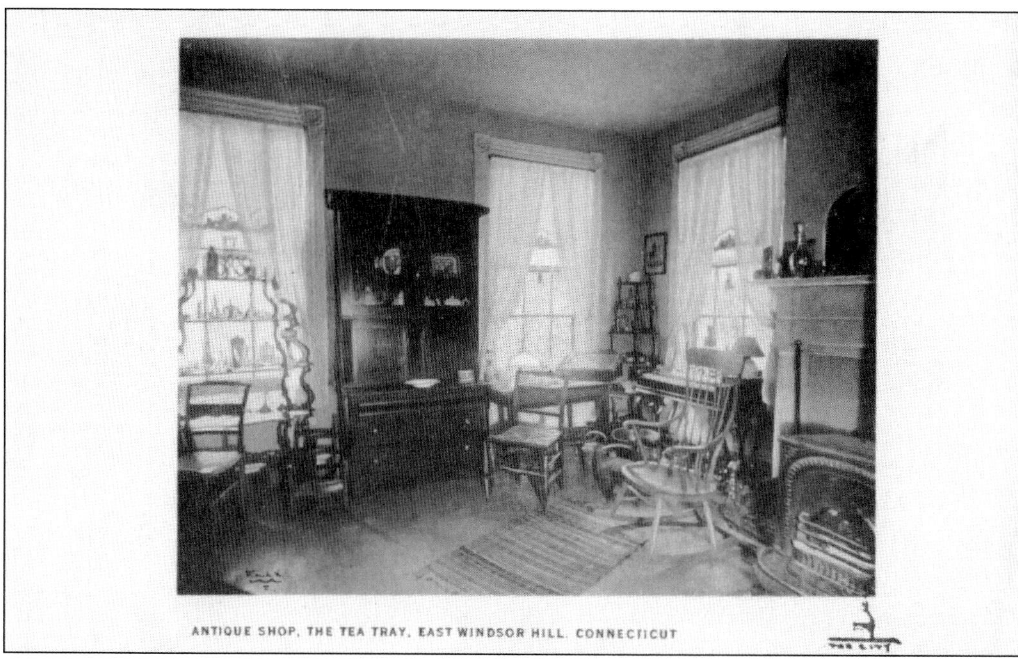

In a decidedly secular turn, the institute's chapel was used for a time as the Dixieland Nightclub, complete with strings of colored lights hanging from the portico, before it was torn down in the 1930s. The columns from the chapel were repurposed as the columns on the front of Ellsworth Memorial High School, which now houses the South Windsor School District administration. (WMLM.)

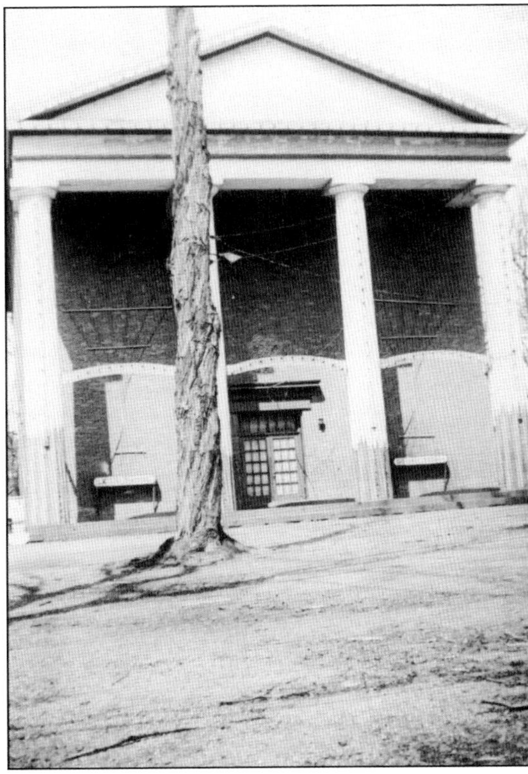

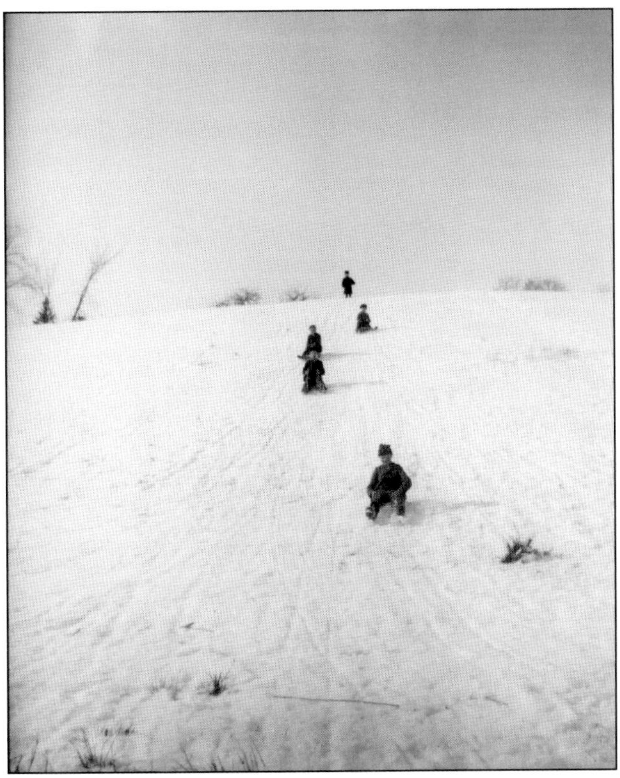

The hill behind the Theological Seminary (and later Ellsworth School) that sloped down to the Meadows below was a popular sledding site for many years, as these young boys could attest. Farther north on the same hill, one of the owners of 1891 Main Street used to keep a stash of sleds at her house for local children to use when they pleased. (Hildred Raymond Collection, WMLM.)

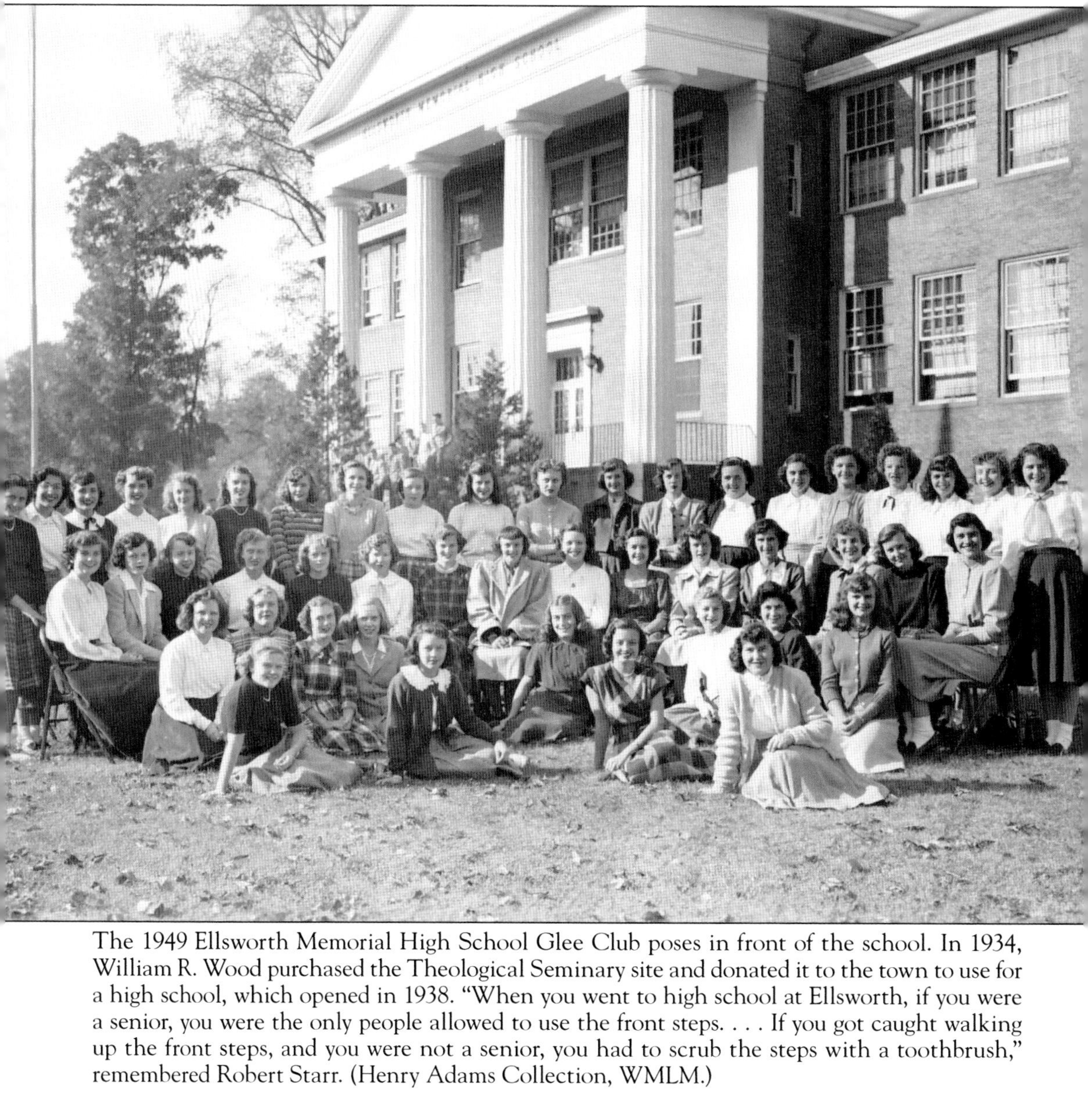

The 1949 Ellsworth Memorial High School Glee Club poses in front of the school. In 1934, William R. Wood purchased the Theological Seminary site and donated it to the town to use for a high school, which opened in 1938. "When you went to high school at Ellsworth, if you were a senior, you were the only people allowed to use the front steps. . . . If you got caught walking up the front steps, and you were not a senior, you had to scrub the steps with a toothbrush," remembered Robert Starr. (Henry Adams Collection, WMLM.)

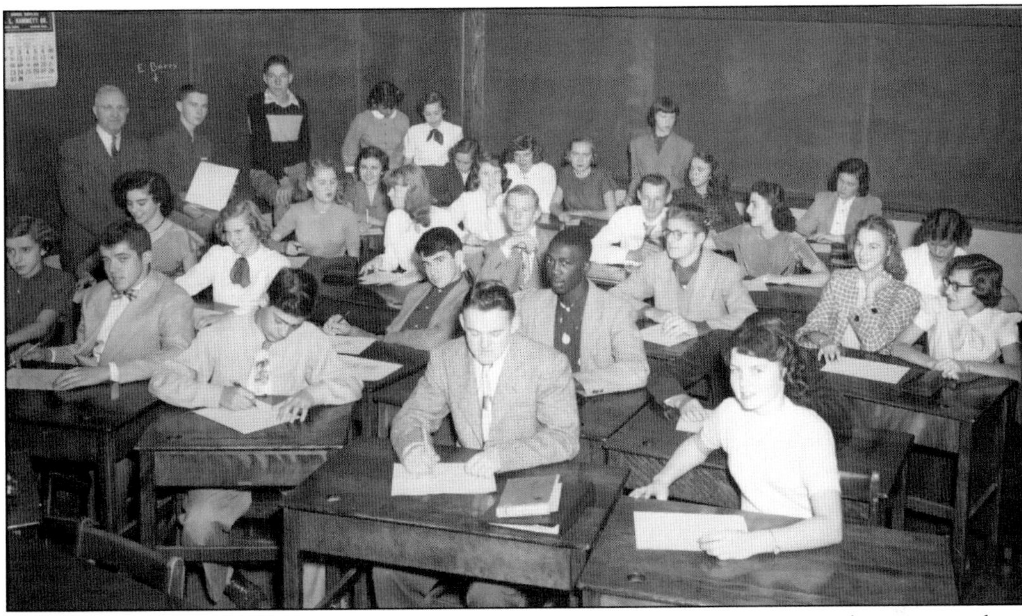

Noted painter Albertus Jones (1882–1957), who lived at 756 Main Street, taught art to students at Union School, Ellsworth Memorial High School, the Hartford Art School, and other colleges and public schools. In this 1951 photograph, Jones is the white-haired man standing next to the blackboard at left in an Ellsworth classroom. (Henry Adams Collection, WMLM.)

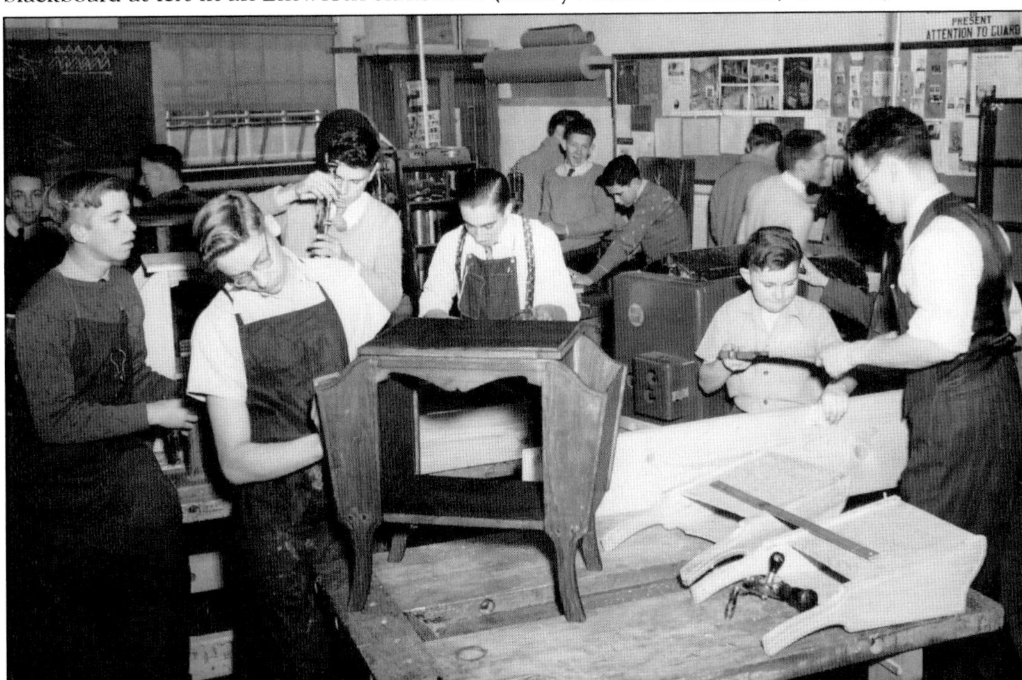

A 1948 woodshop class works on its projects. Ellsworth also offered machine shop and home economics classes. The school served as South Windsor's high school until 1962, when the new high school on Nevers Road opened. The building then housed middle school students until Timothy Edwards Middle School opened in 1968. (Henry Adams Collection, WMLM.)

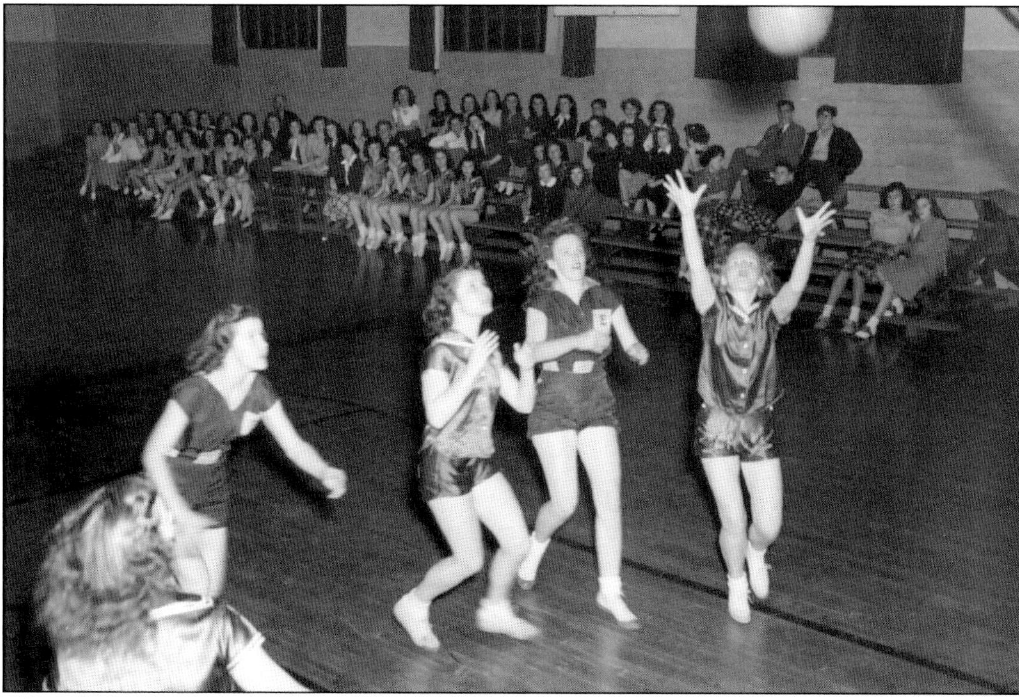

Above, the Ellsworth girls' basketball team plays a game against Stafford Springs, and below, the boys' team plays a game in 1951. Sally Edlund said: "We had winning basketball teams, because we had Coach Hugh Greer and many years we had state winning teams for our size school. And we went to as many basketball games as we could, because we didn't have a football team and it was school spirit." Hugh S. Greer coached for 10 years at Ellsworth, winning five boys' state basketball championships, before going on to coach the University of Connecticut men's basketball team. (Both, Henry Adams Collection, WMLM.)

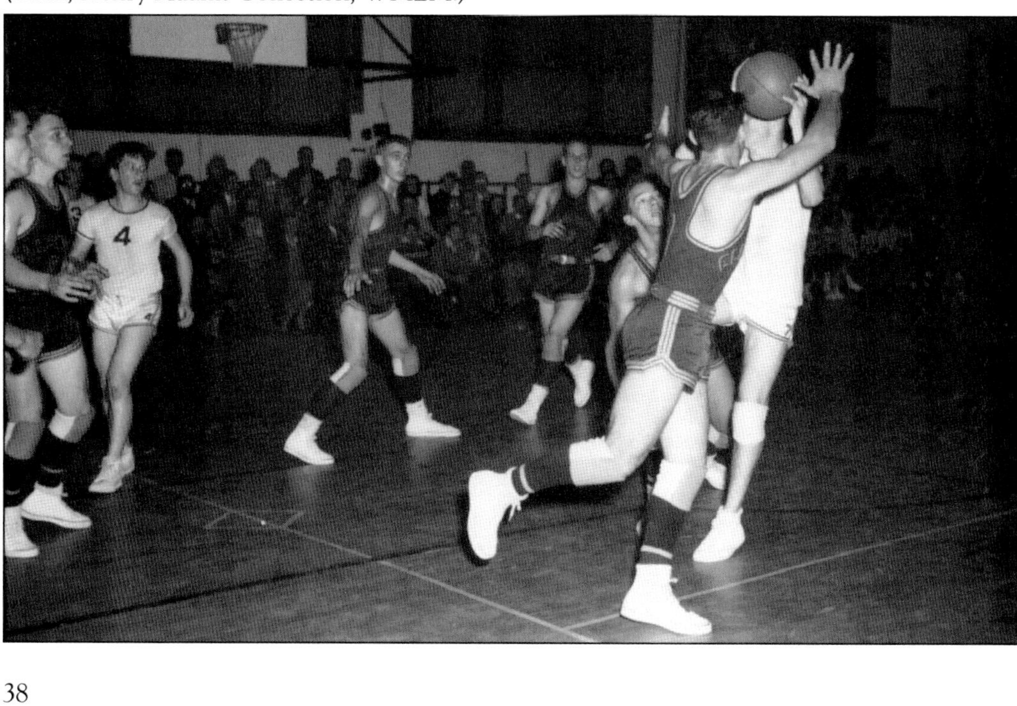

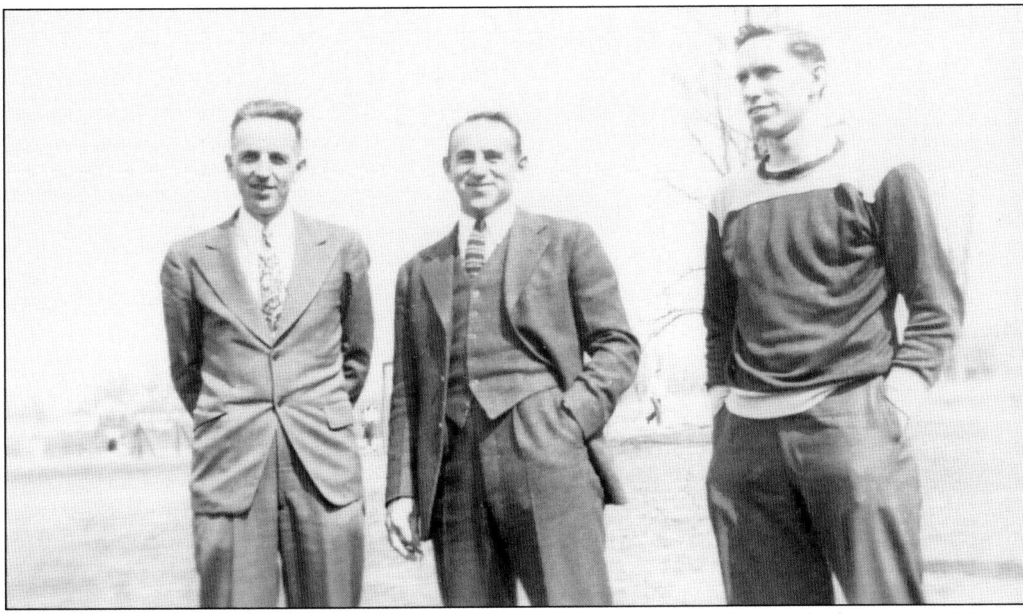

Ellsworth principal Henry Adams (left) pictured with teachers Mr. Horvath (center) and Albert Loeffler, was known as a strict disciplinarian. Ruth Bortolan recalled: "My brother got kicked out of school for two weeks for being with somebody who smoked a cigarette. My brother wasn't smoking the cigarette, but he was with somebody who was, so he got a two-week suspension." (Henry Adams Collection, WMLM.)

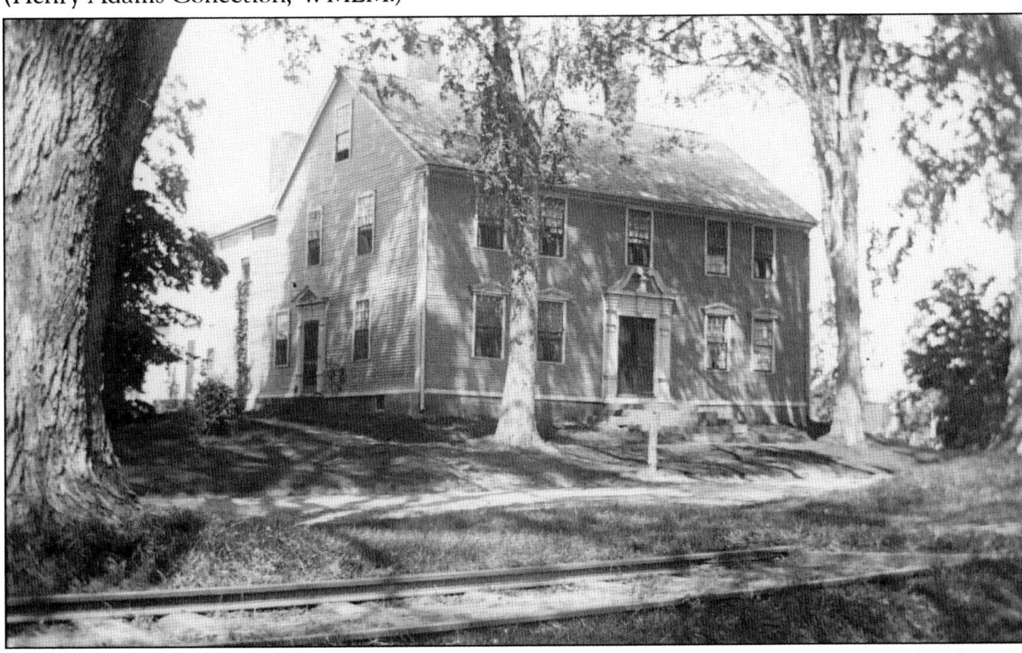

The house at 1653 Main Street was built around 1757 by Ebenezer Grant, who made his fortune in shipping: building boats and importing goods and sometimes slaves from the Caribbean. His most lucrative import was rum, which customers bought by the gallon. The house was a physical embodiment of its owner's success, with an ornate Connecticut River Valley door at the front. (Hildred Raymond Collection, WMLM.)

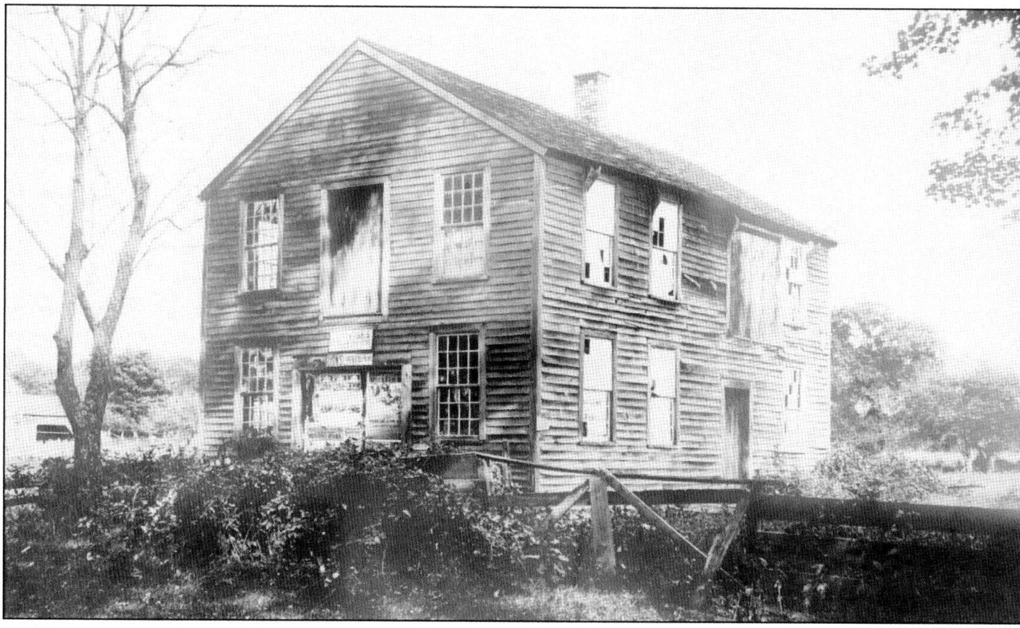

Joshua Risley bought 1648 Main Street around 1835 and opened a wagon shop next to the house. He built wagons, horse carts, and iron plows and employed some of his 13 children in the shop. Shown here in 1890, when the building was in disrepair, advertisements covered the walls, including one for asbestos paint and another for Hartford races with a $10,000 stake. (Hildred Raymond Collection, WMLM.)

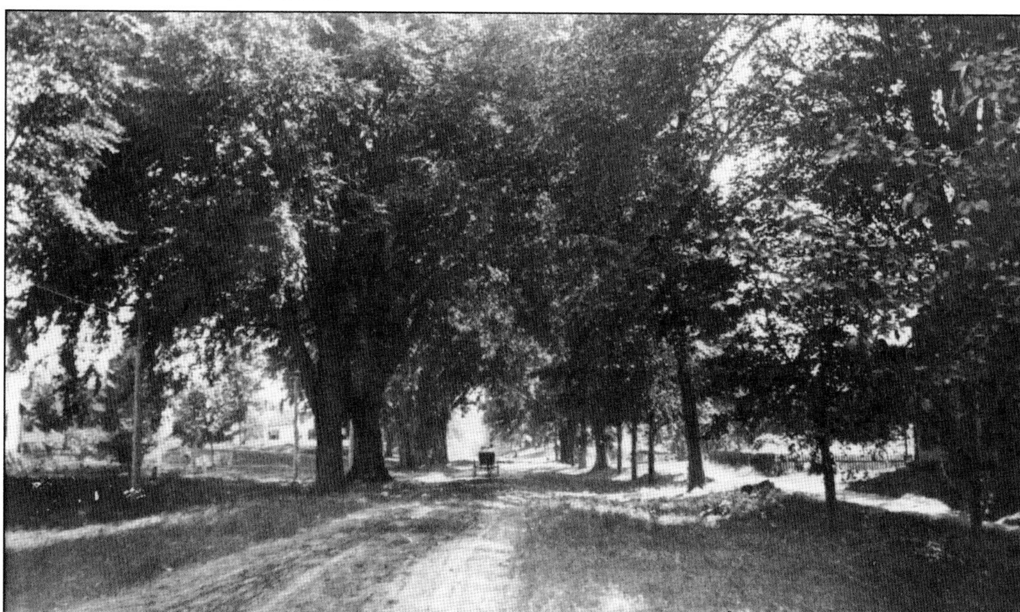

Main Street looked much different in the 19th century, before the road was widened to make room for trolley tracks in 1898 and paved in 1911. The street narrowly avoided being changed more drastically; it was initially designated as the path for Route 5, until the flood of 1936 inundated the street and state highway officials changed their minds. (Photograph by Herbert C. Newberry, Vibert family.)

Main Street used to be lined with arching elm trees that, according to local lore, were planted during the American Revolution by Hessian prisoners of war who were billeted in homes on the street. The trees shaded the street for about 150 years but were eventually felled between 1935 and 1955 by Dutch elm disease and hurricanes. This one stood just north of Wood Library. (Hildred Raymond Collection, WMLM.)

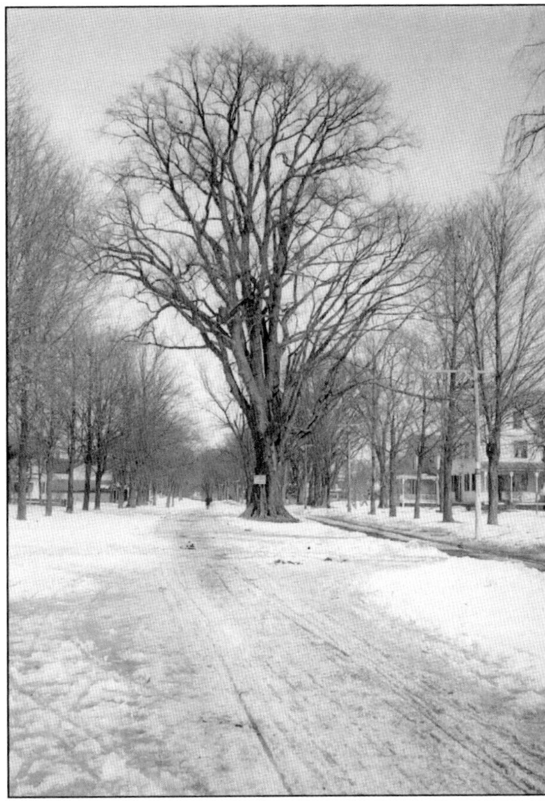

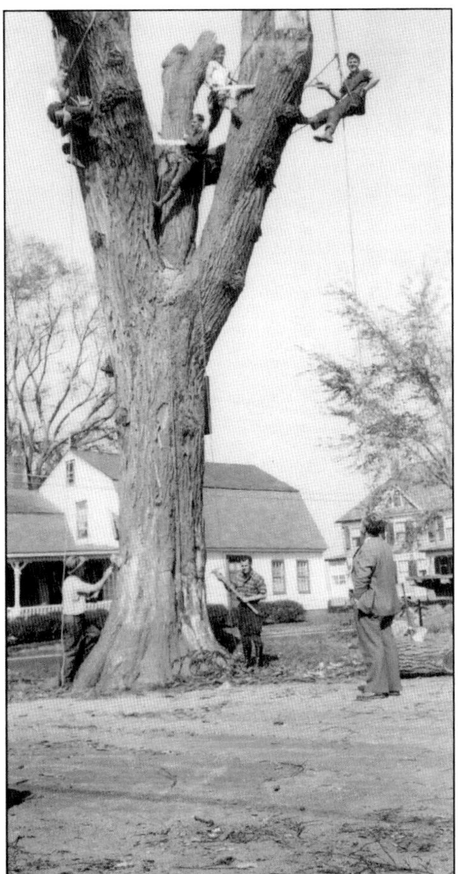

One of Main Street's massive elms was featured in the 1939 World's Fair in New York City. Sculptor Lawrence Tenney Stevens, with the help of Barney Daley and other local men, cut and carved the tree into a 60-foot sculpture entitled *The Tree of Life*. (Photograph by Barney Daley, Barney Daley Collection, WMLM.)

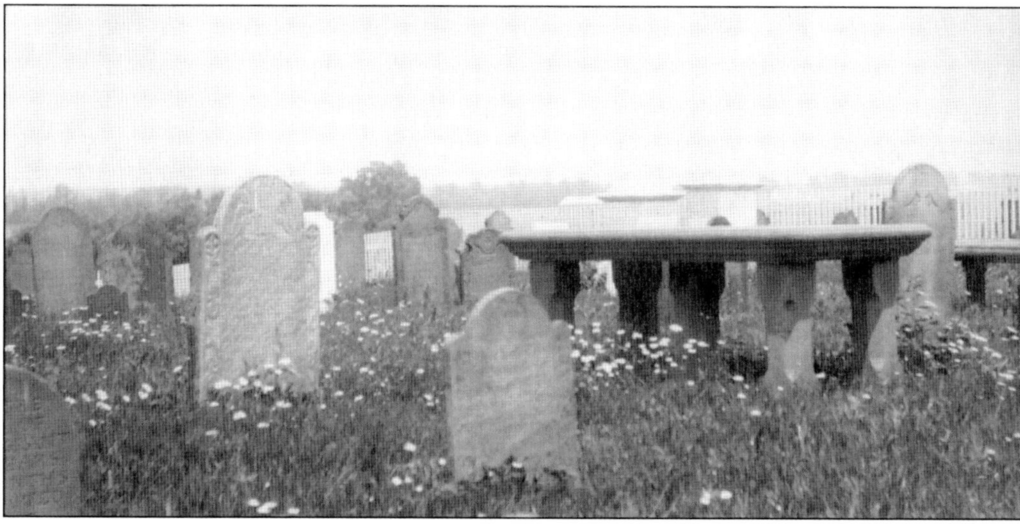

Timothy Edwards (1669–1758) and his wife, Esther Stoddard Edwards, have the two distinctive table monument–style gravestones in Edwards Cemetery on Main Street, also known as the Old Burying Ground or God's Acre. Timothy Edwards was the first minister in South Windsor and was the father of Jonathan Edwards, the famous fire-and-brimstone preacher who was a leading figure in the 18th-century Great Awakening spiritual revival. (Photograph by Edith S. Watson, WMLM.)

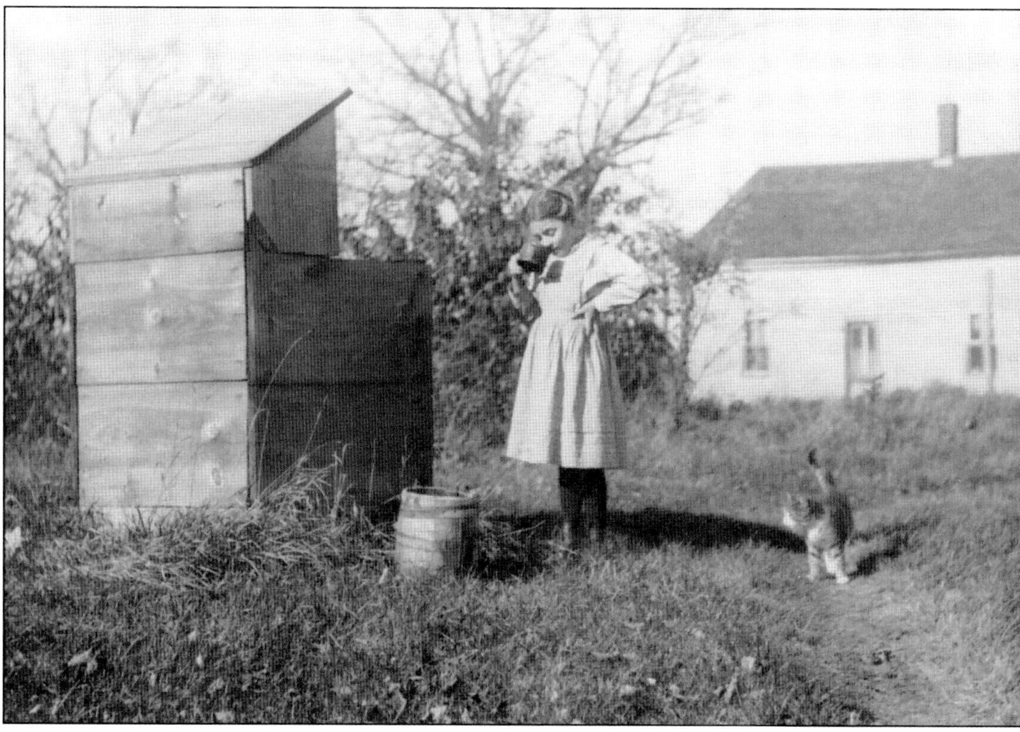

Rev. Timothy Edwards's house was torn down long ago, but there is a historical marker in front of 1414 Main Street at the site where it once stood. This photograph shows a young girl and her cat standing beside the well at the former site of the Edwards family home on East Windsor Hill. (Photograph by Edith S. Watson, WMLM.)

The First Congregational Church of South Windsor was established in 1694 when residents on the east side of the Connecticut River petitioned the Connecticut General Assembly for their own church so as not to have to cross the river to worship. The original meetinghouse was located just north of Edwards Cemetery. The third meetinghouse (shown in the drawing at right) was built in 1761 and stuck out into the street because the owner of the property behind the church refused to sell it to the congregation. It was moved back from the street around 1816 and demolished in 1845. In 1845, when South Windsor was incorporated, the congregation built the present church (below). (Right, drawing by Mary Janette Elmore, courtesy of Gary S. Pitcock; below, photograph by Herbert C. Newberry, Emma Bancroft Collection, WMLM.)

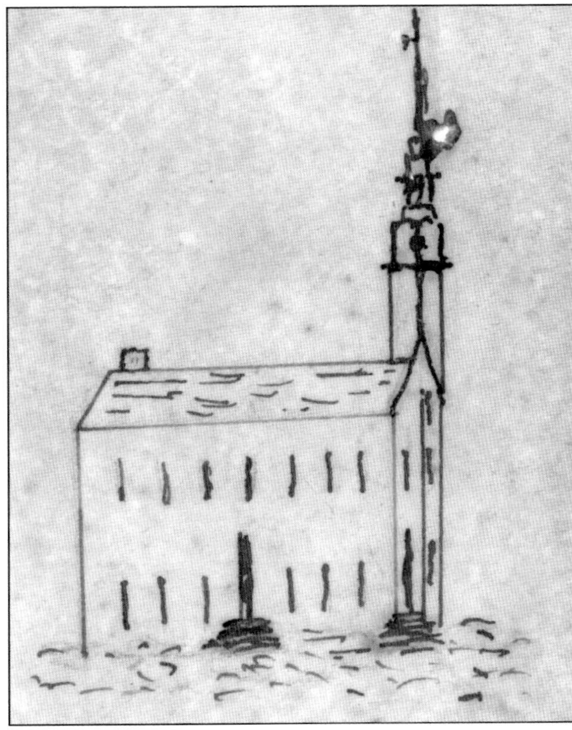

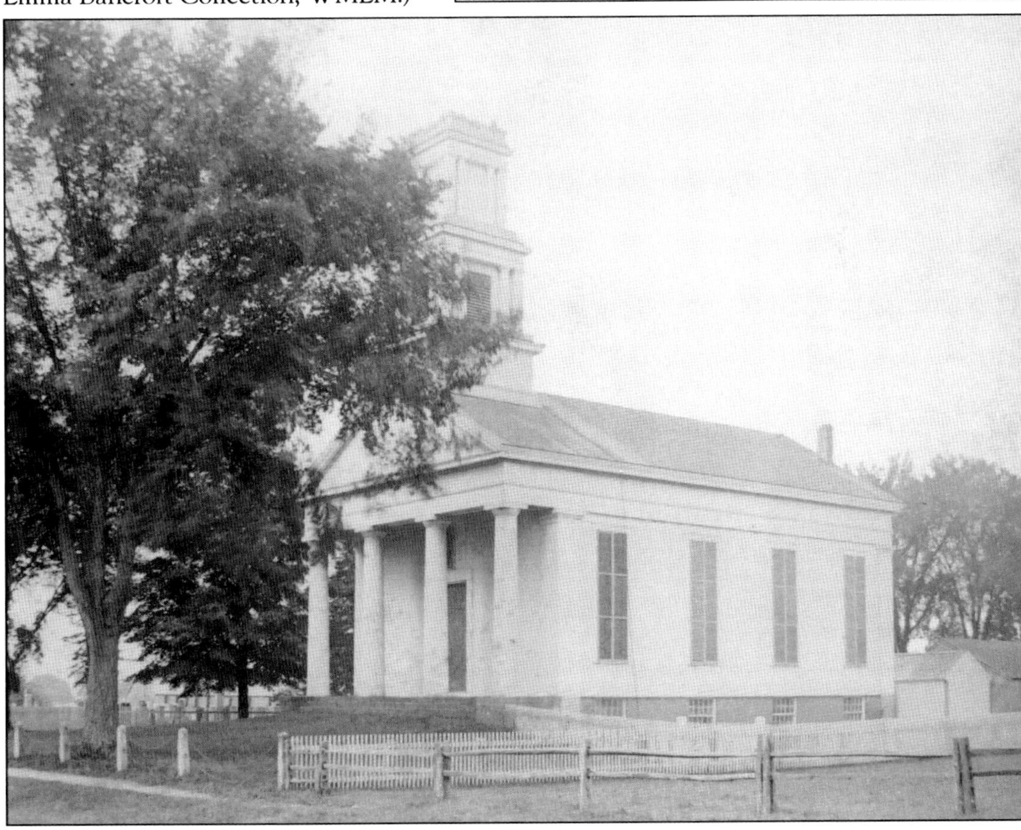

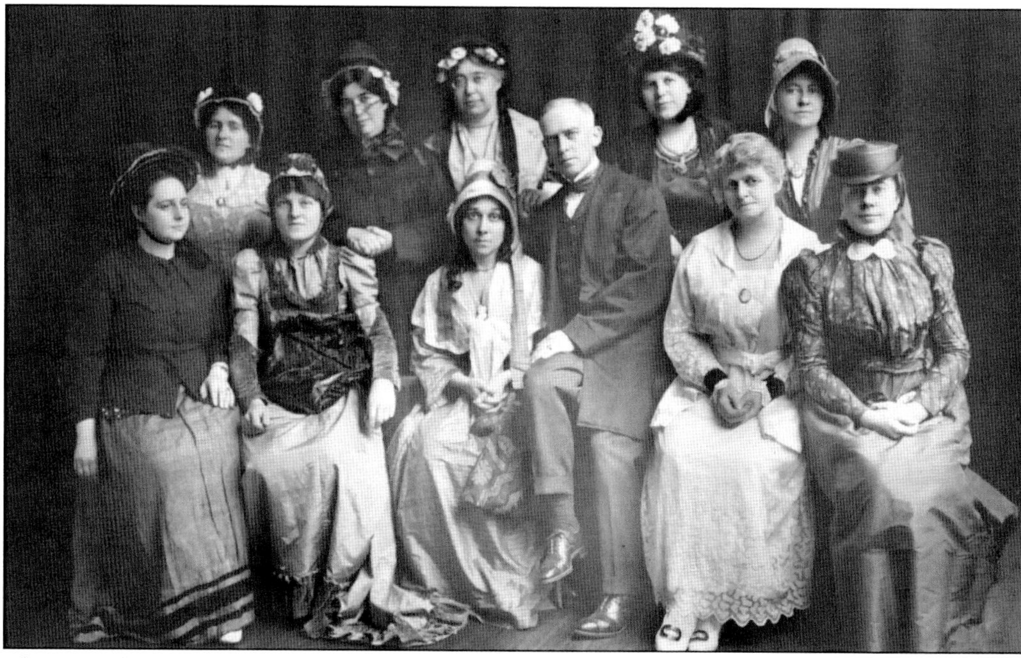

The cast of *The Old Peabody Pew*, which was performed by members of the First Congregational Church, poses for a photograph. *The Old Peabody Pew: A Christmas Romance of a Country Church*, by Kate Douglas Wiggin, was published in 1907 as a book and turned into a play by the same author in 1917. (Helen Pelton family.)

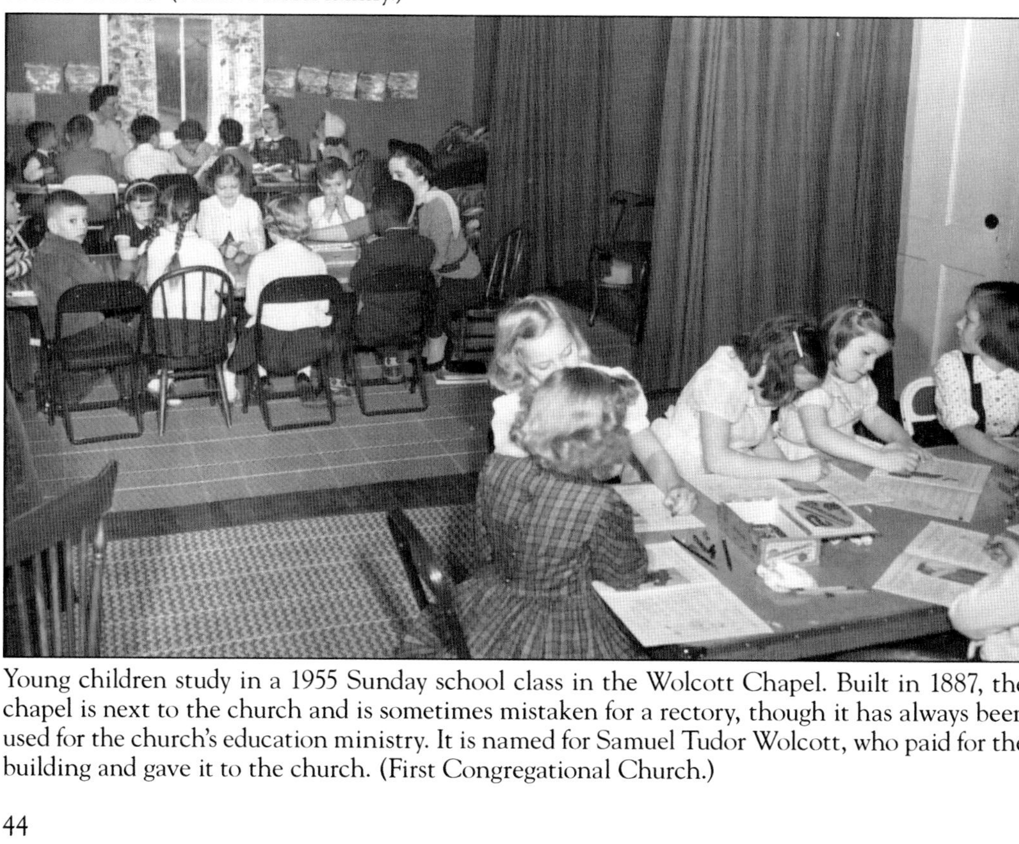

Young children study in a 1955 Sunday school class in the Wolcott Chapel. Built in 1887, the chapel is next to the church and is sometimes mistaken for a rectory, though it has always been used for the church's education ministry. It is named for Samuel Tudor Wolcott, who paid for the building and gave it to the church. (First Congregational Church.)

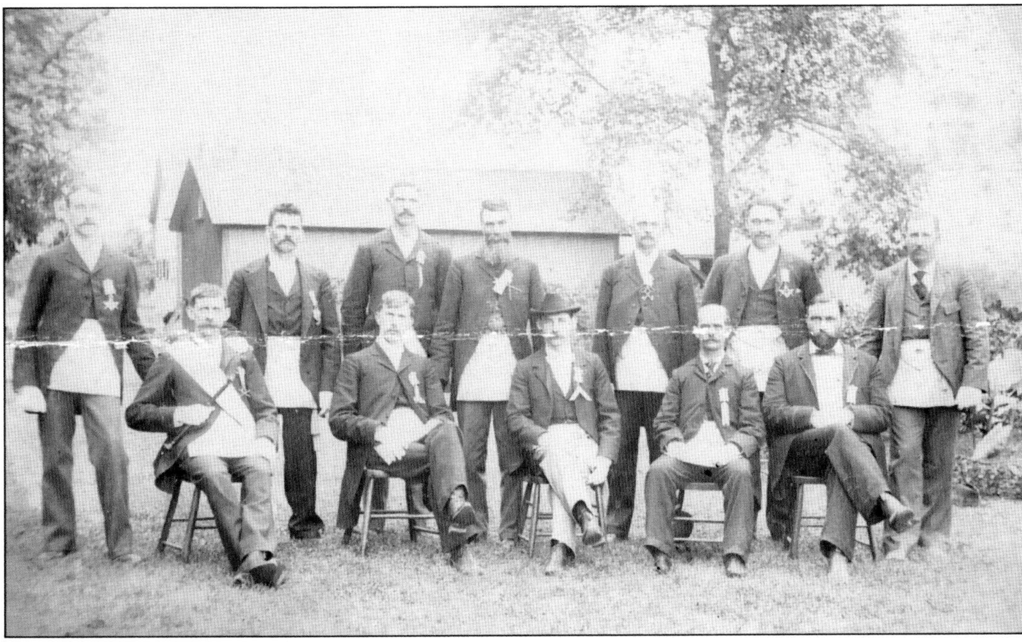

In the spring of 1872, Connecticut's Grand Lodge of Freemasons granted a group of South Windsor men the right to establish their own lodge, named Evergreen Masonic Lodge No. 114. This photograph, showing members in their ceremonial garb and medals, was likely taken shortly after the lodge was first established. (Edna and Norman Priest Collection, WMLM.)

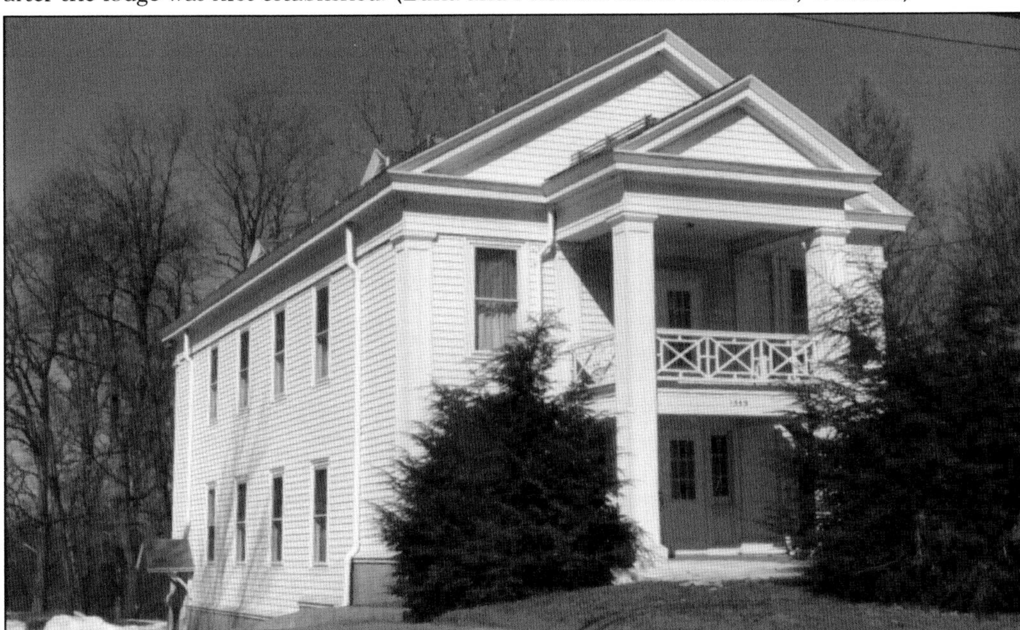

The two-story Greek Revival–style Evergreen Masonic Lodge No. 114 (now known as the Hartford Evergreen Lodge No. 88) was built in 1916, giving South Windsor Masons their first standalone building after years of meeting in schools and members' homes. The lodge, at 1559 Main Street, stands on the site of Rev. Timothy Edwards's first church on the east side of the river. (Historic Homes Files, WMLM.)

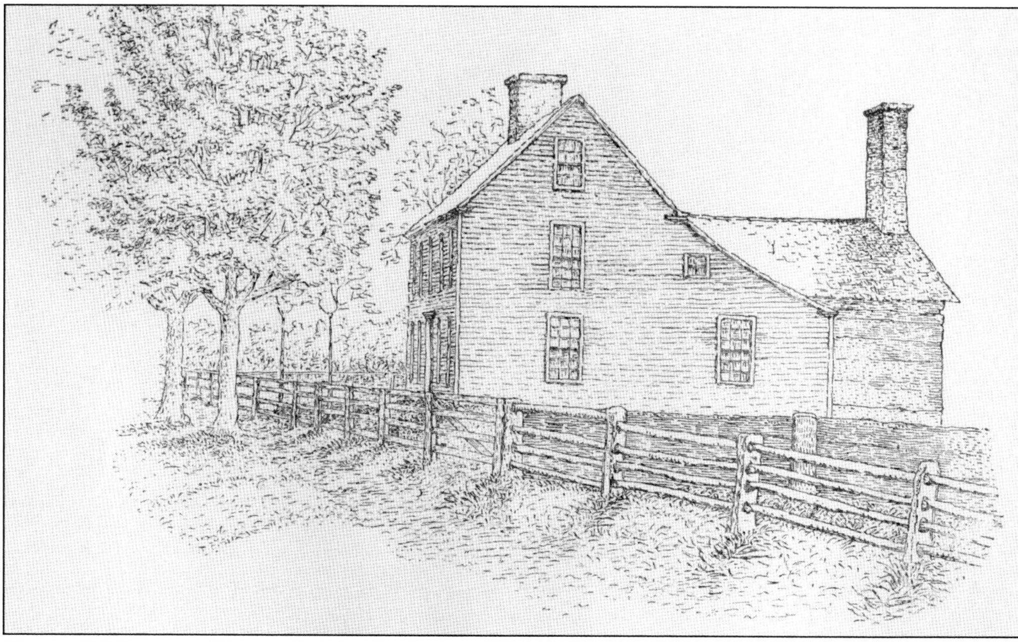

Simon Wolcott and his wife, Martha Pitkin Wolcott, both emigrants from England, settled in South Windsor in 1680 and built the house above. It was torn down several decades later, and some of the building materials were used in their son Henry's house. Simon and Martha's youngest son, Roger, served as Connecticut's colonial governor from 1751 to 1754. He built a house in 1704 (below) on the site of what is now 1169 Main Street. Governor's Highway, which ran next to the house, was given that name because of its proximity to his homestead. The house reportedly had murals painted on the plaster walls: dragons in one room and a scene of the Deerfield Massacre in another. These two etchings originally appeared in Henry Stiles's *History of Ancient Windsor.* (Both drawings by Erastus W. Ellsworth, WMLM.)

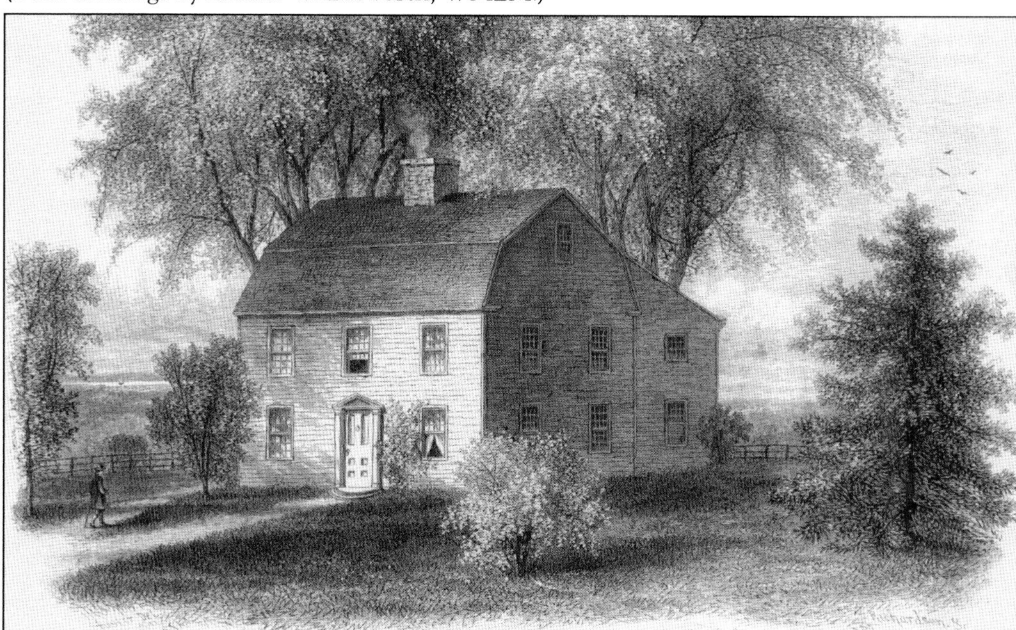

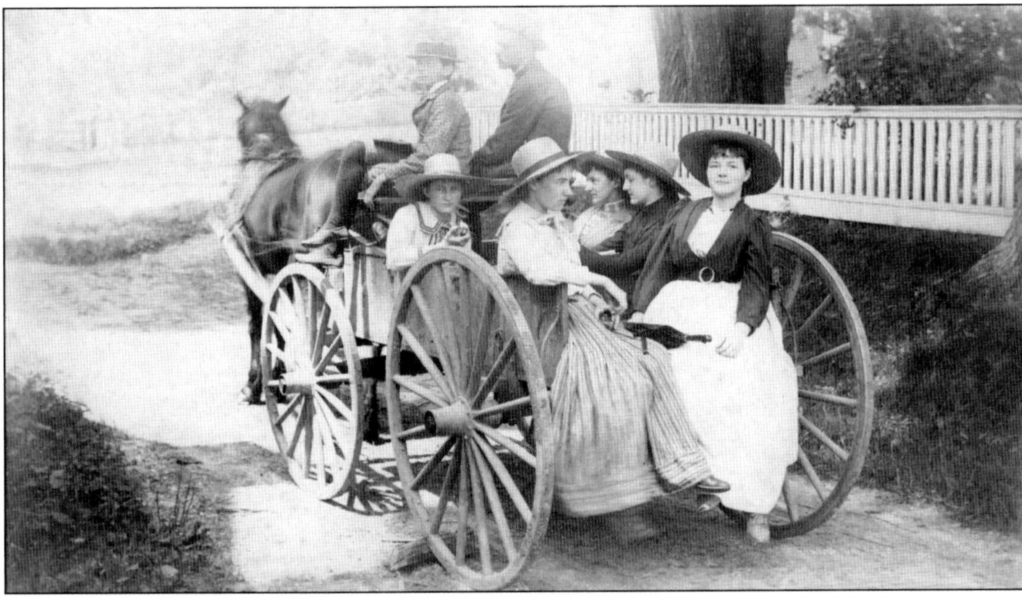

A group of young people head out for a Sunday afternoon ride in front of the Newberry house at 960 Main Street on the corner of Newberry Road, probably around the 1880s. This type of open wagon would have usually been used for hauling goods rather than people. (Roger Newberry Collection, WMLM.)

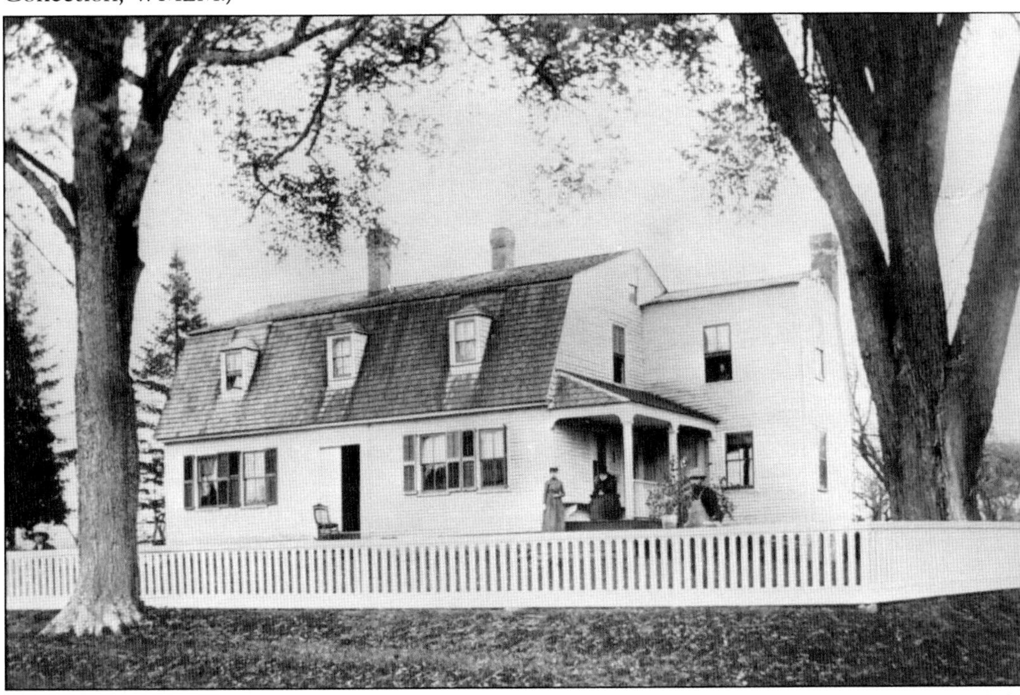

The gambrel-roofed house at 960 Main Street was built around 1785. From at least 1800 until the late 20th century, the house was owned by members of the Newberry family, and the road that runs along the right side of the property was named Newberry Road after the family. Dwight Newberry (1870–1969) was an avid ornithologist and donated his collection of mounted birds to Wood Library. (Vibert family.)

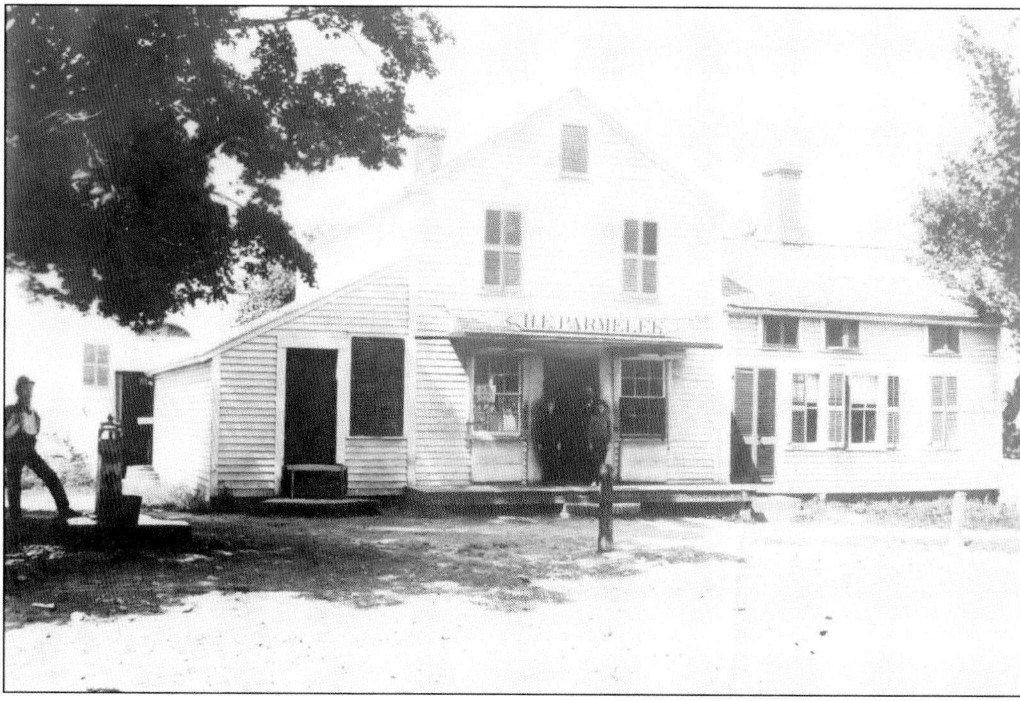

The building at 819–821 Main Street (above, around 1890; below, around 1950) opened as a store in 1855 and was operated over the years by members of the Foster, Parmelee, and Bossen families. Charles Nielsen said: "It was a store and a post office. . . . I don't know how anybody could hold that much merchandise in that small a space, but he did . . . the local farmers would congregate, and about nine o'clock was when the mail was supposed to have been sorted . . . you'd put the hired man to work, and then you'd go down to the store and sit around and shoot the bull with everybody else until the mail was sorted. Then you'd grab a handful of cigars, buy a handful of cigars, and go home." (Above, Hildred Raymond Collection, WMLM; below, WMLM.)

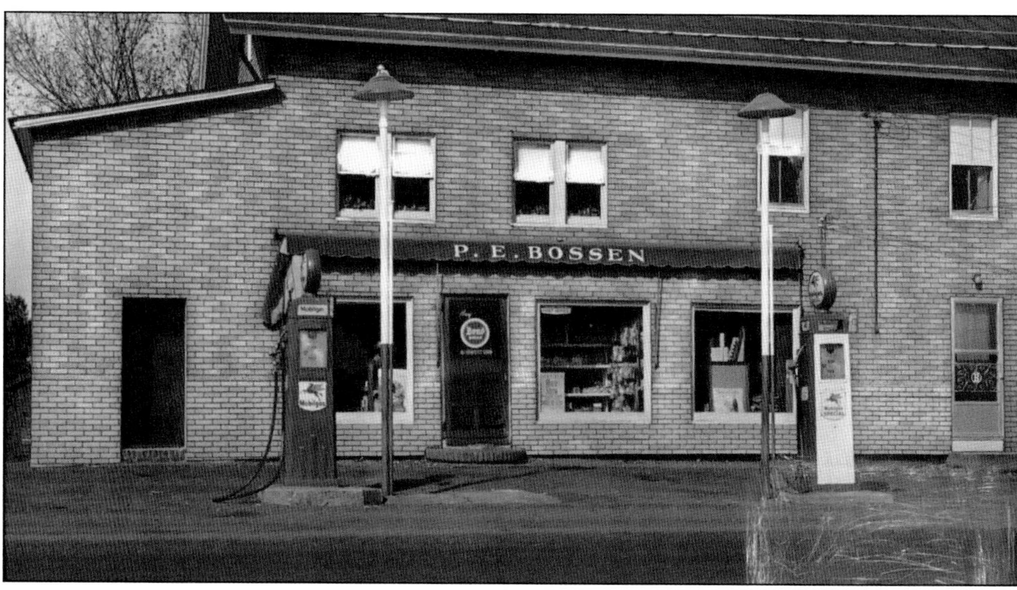

Children sit on a stone railing at the top of the stairs of the old South Windsor Town Hall around 1950. A large room on the top floor of the building was used for meetings, dance lessons, and recitals, while a room in the rear was used as the town court. The building was torn down in 1969, after the new town hall was built on Sullivan Avenue. (WMLM.)

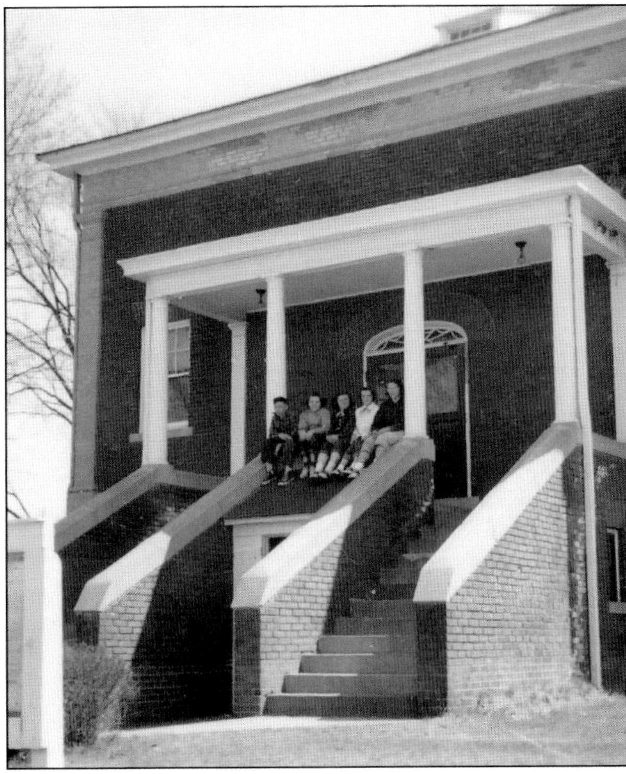

Main Street Baptist Church was built around 1873 and used as a church until 1900. From about 1938 to 1967, it was an American Legion hall. In 1967, it was sold to the town, which repurposed it as the South Windsor Community Hall, complete with a bowling alley in the basement. The building burned down in the early morning hours of October 7, 1973, and was not rebuilt. (Hildred Raymond Collection, WMLM.)

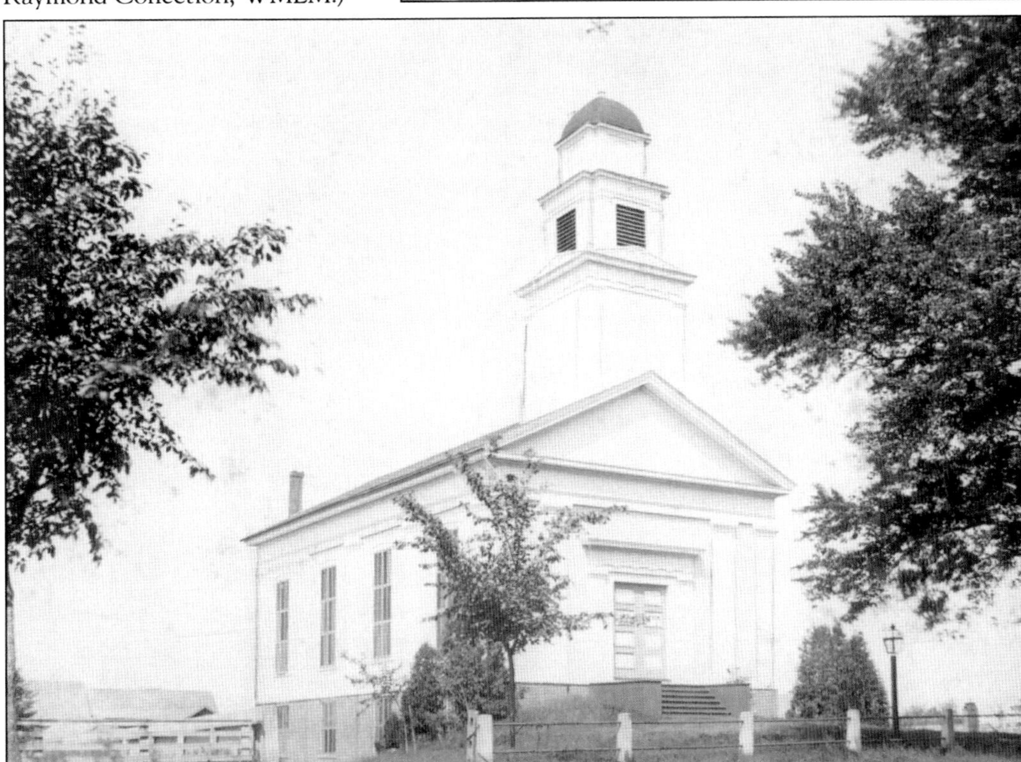

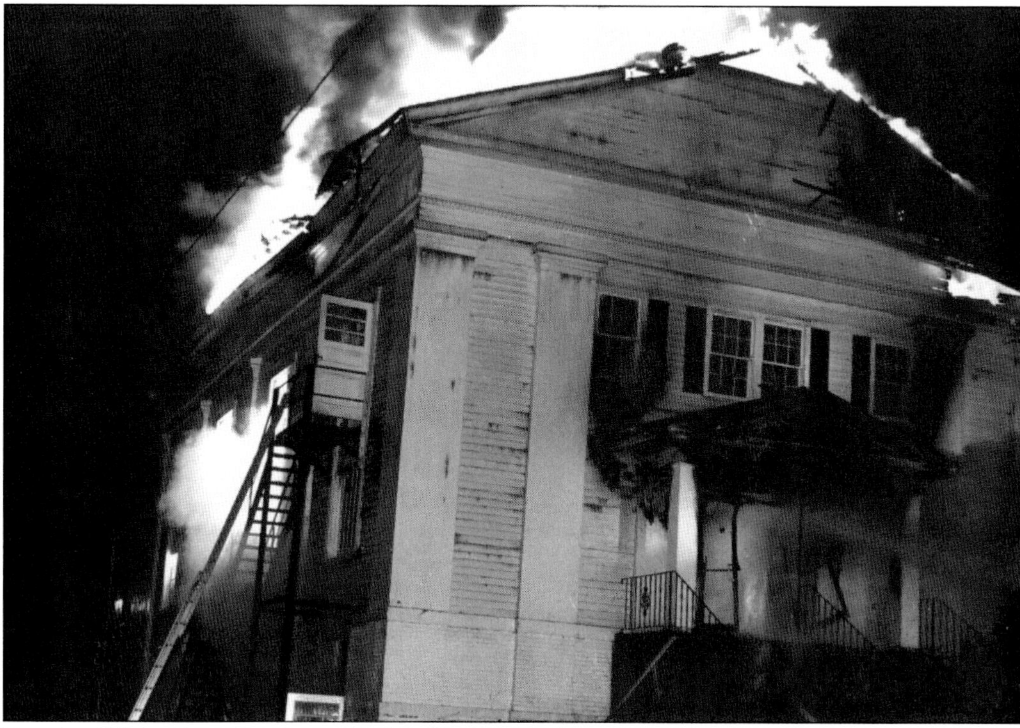

Fire chief Philip Crombie Sr. recalled: "About ten o'clock one night, we had gotten an alarm for a fire there. We got there, and the smoke is pouring out of the place. . . . It had been rented by a group of young people from Manchester. They were holding a party and a dance on the main floor. They were coming out as we arrived, and they were saving the beer keg, which was being carried out and set up across the street, whereupon they all still had their glasses and everything, and they were going to set up to watch the fire. . . . The lobby [was] all prefinished plywood, and the fire got into there and it exploded." (Above, Philip E. Crombie; below, Barney Daley Collection, WMLM.)

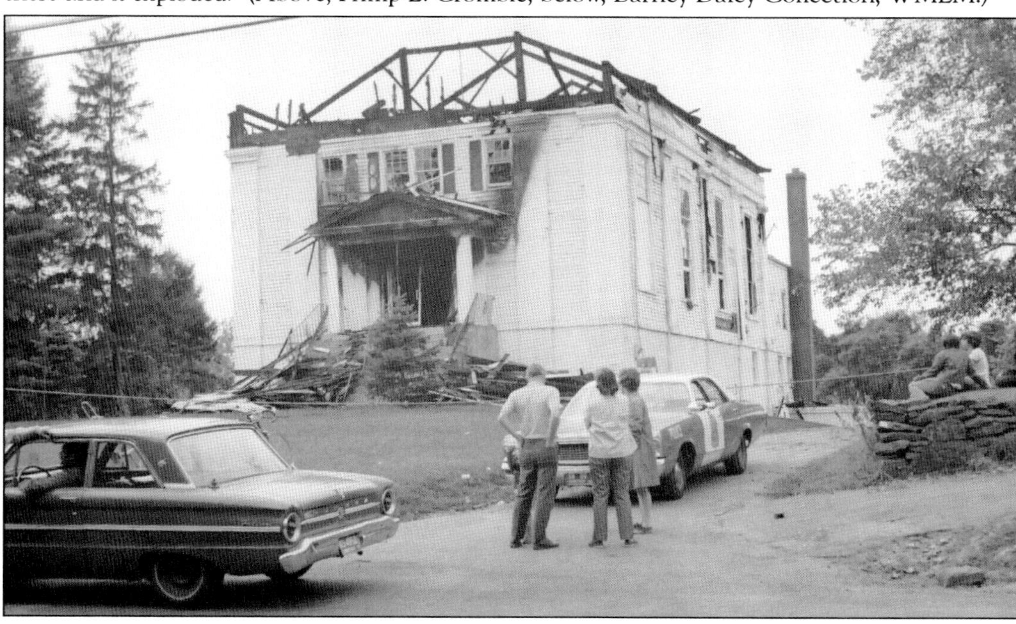

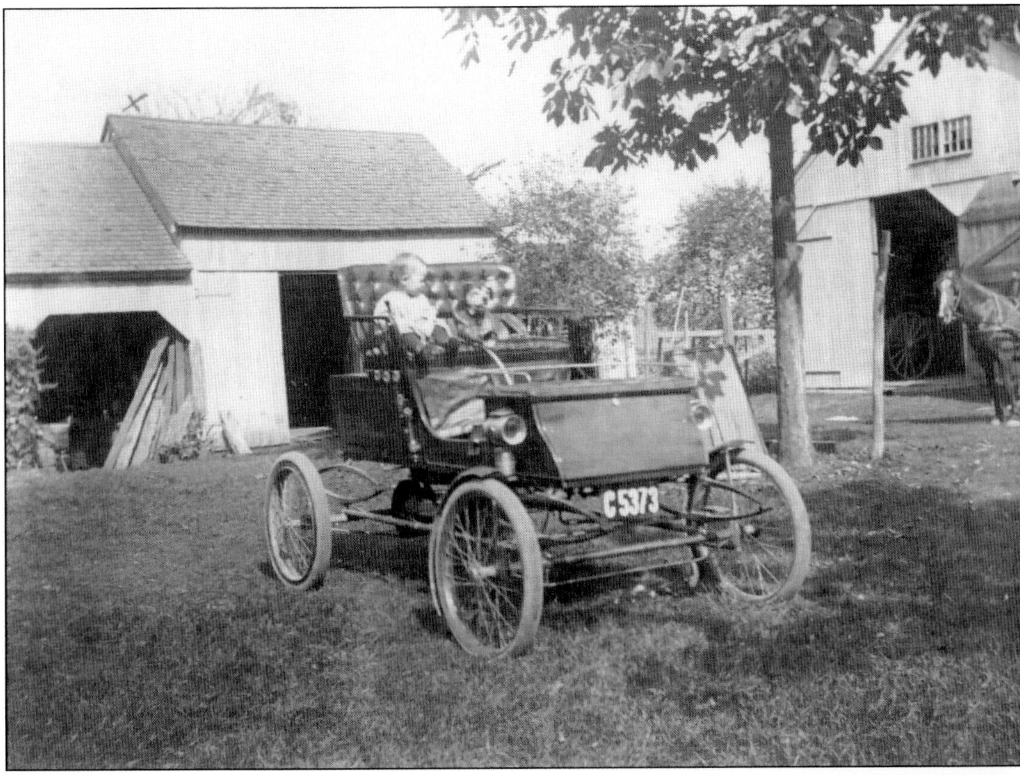

Toddler Hildred Sperry (see page 14) sits in her father Ellsworth Sperry's first car, a steam-powered Stanley Steamer, outside the house at 588 Main Street in 1910. The Stanley Motor Carriage Company, started by twin brothers Francis and Freelan Stanley, made cars from 1902 to 1927, but their high price and difficulty of operation eventually drove them from the market. (Hildred Raymond Collection, WMLM.)

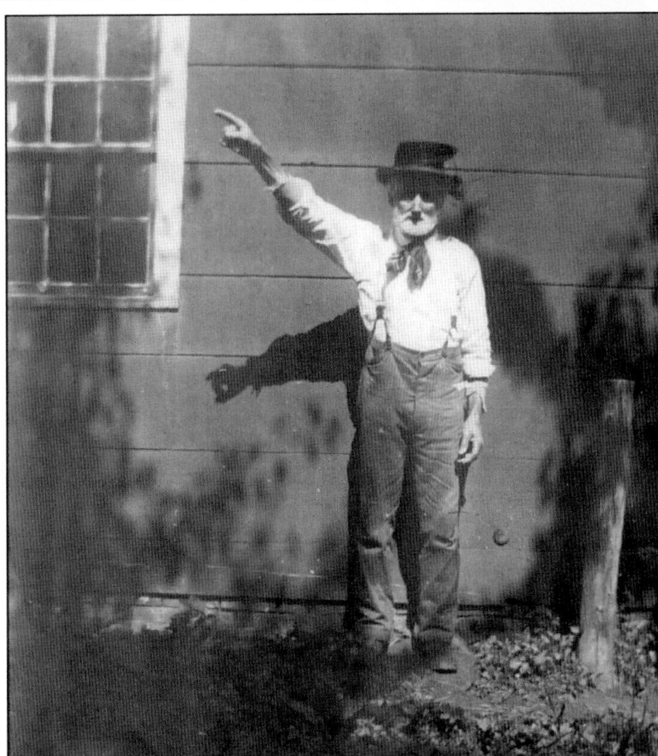

Human sundial Jake Strong and his shadow point in different directions. Strong (1827–1908) was a carpenter who built a barn at William R. Wood's house in 1898, at age 71, which is probably around when this photograph was taken. (Hildred Raymond Collection, WMLM.)

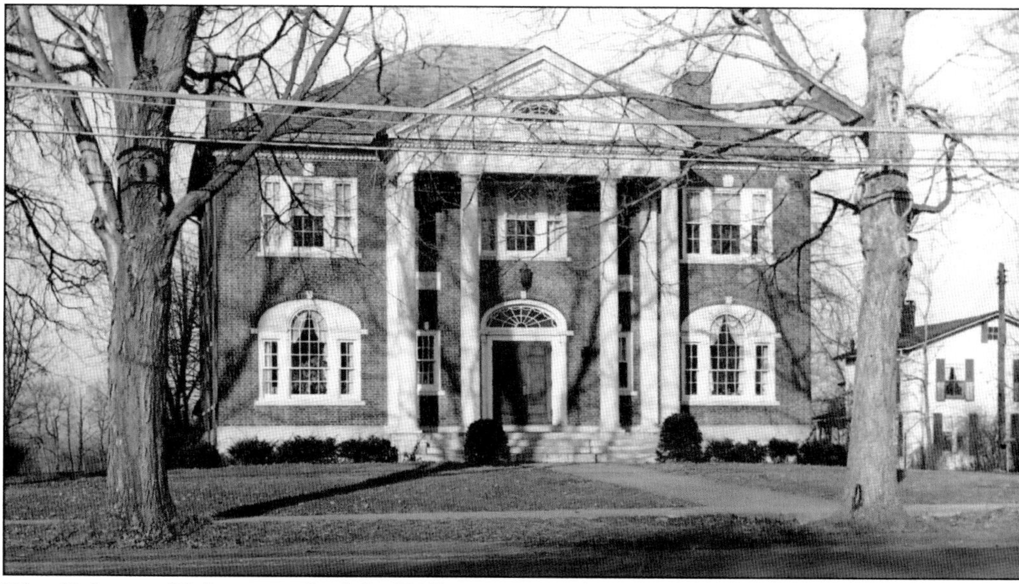

Wood Memorial Library was built by William R. Wood as a memorial to his parents, Dr. William Wood and Mary Ellsworth Wood. It opened in 1928 and was run as a public library until 1970, when the town closed it in favor of building a larger central library. In 1971, the Friends of Wood Memorial Library reopened it to the public. (Photograph by Ellsworth Fairbanks, Barney Daley Collection, WMLM.)

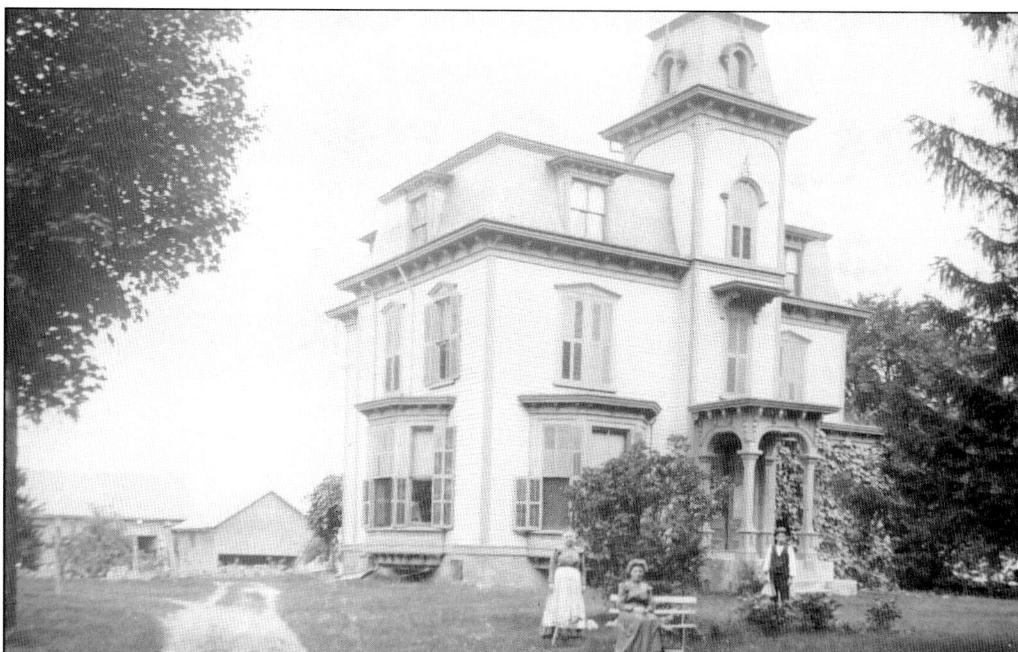

John Newberry King and his wife, Julia Ann Keeney King, were among the first tobacco farmers in South Windsor, a distinction that was quite lucrative for them. They built the French Second Empire–style house at 793 Main Street around 1873. This photograph of the house was taken in 1902 and shows the Kings' son Isaac White King, his wife, Ida Abbey King (seated), and another woman. (Vibert family.)

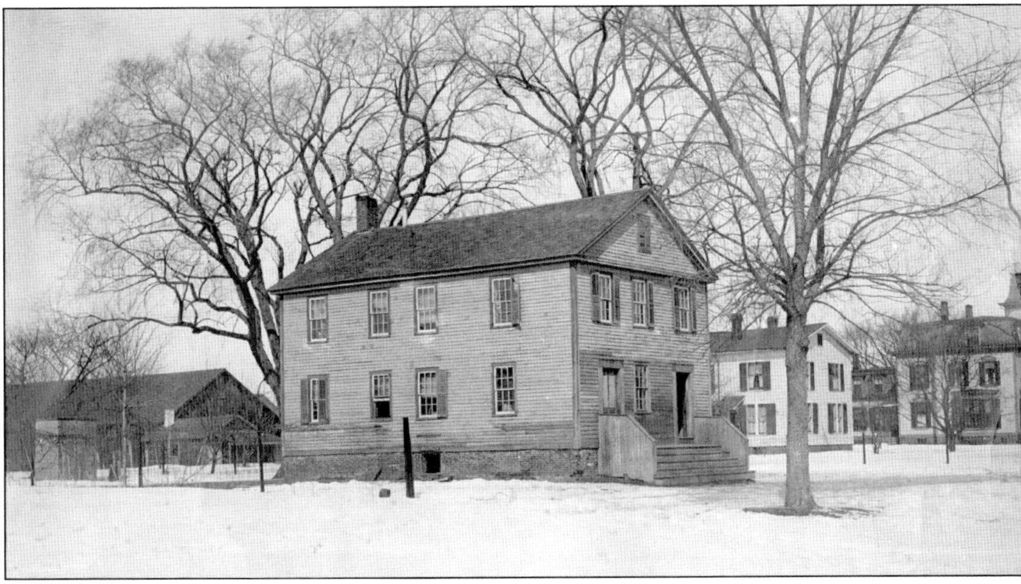

Originally a factory for brads (small metal fasteners), the building at the center of this image was later used as a public school. It stood on Main Street until the larger Union District School was built directly behind it. The brad factory building was then moved up Pleasant Valley Road, where it is now a multifamily house. (Hildred Raymond Collection, WMLM.)

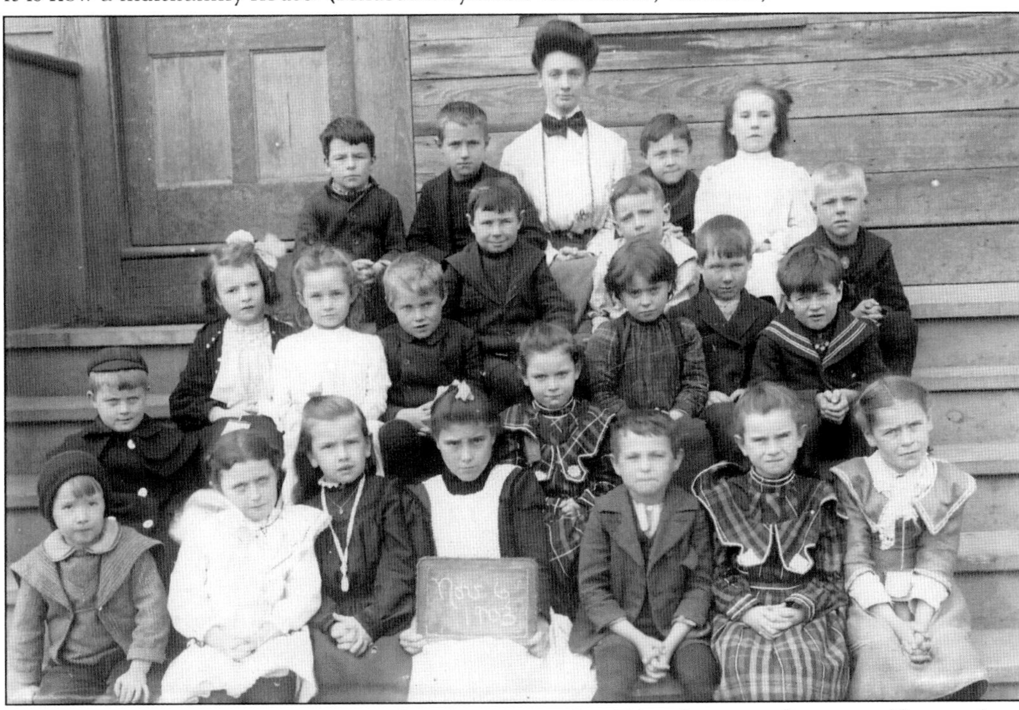

In this class picture taken on November 6, 1903, teacher Edna Jennings Sperry and her students sit on the steps of the District 3 schoolhouse, also known as the Brad Factory School. These were some of the last students to attend the District 3 school, and they would have been some of the first students in the new Union District School, which was built in 1905. (Hildred Raymond Collection, WMLM.)

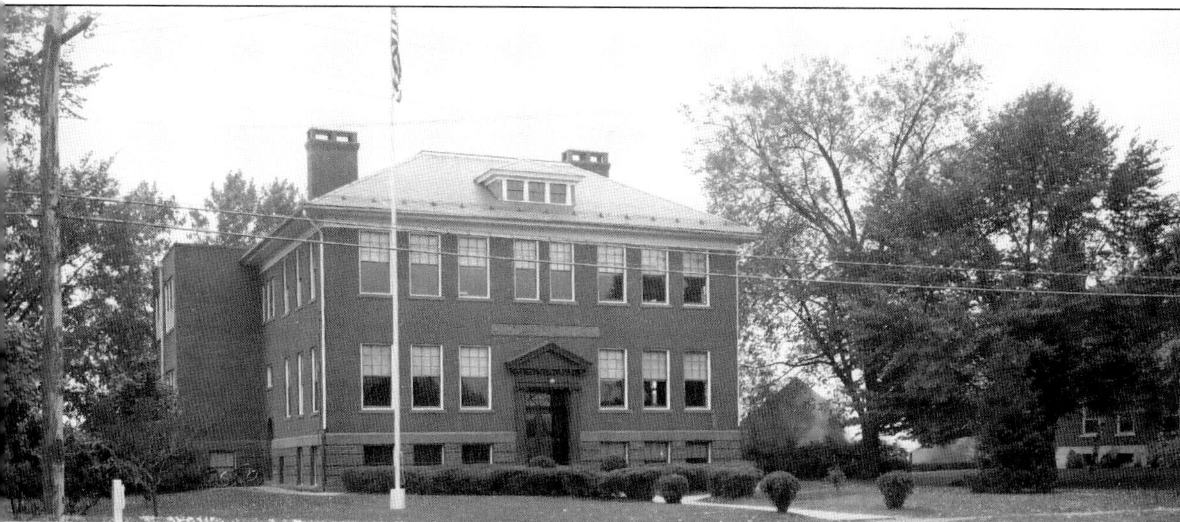

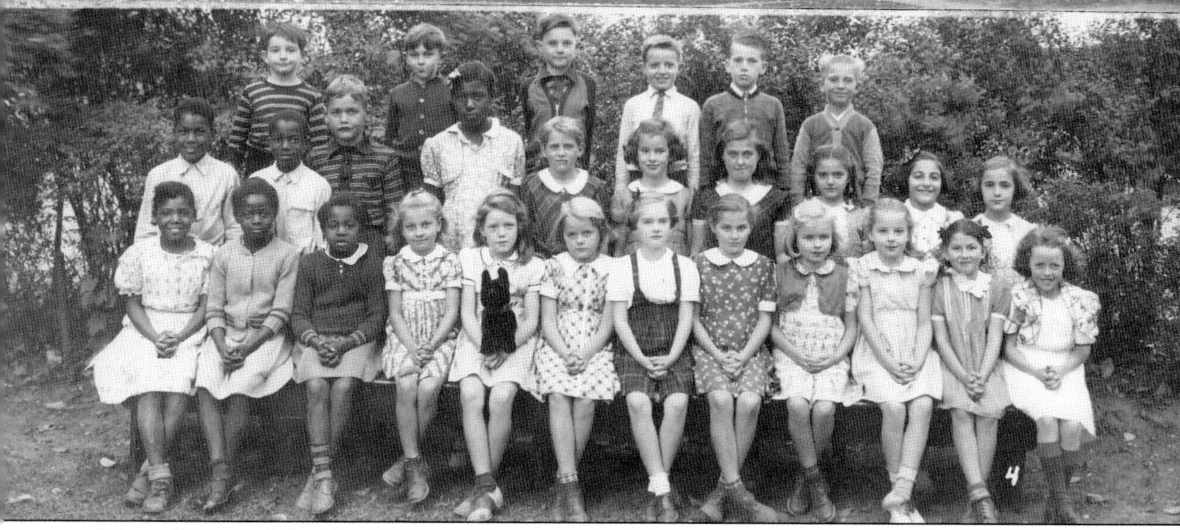

Union District School at 771 Main Street was built in 1905 and used as a public school until the late 1960s. Later, it housed the district administration offices and special education services, and in the 1980s, it housed a preschool. In 2007, after many years of vacancy, the South Windsor Historical Society purchased the building for $1. This photograph is from 1940. Joseph Vibert stated: "Originally, there were three rooms on the first floor. . . . A staircase on each side, and you went up the staircase and what later became the two front school rooms on the second floor were one big room. That's where they held the town meetings and so forth. There was a stage, the arch of which, I believe, is still there." (Margaret Busher Rybeck Collection, WMLM.)

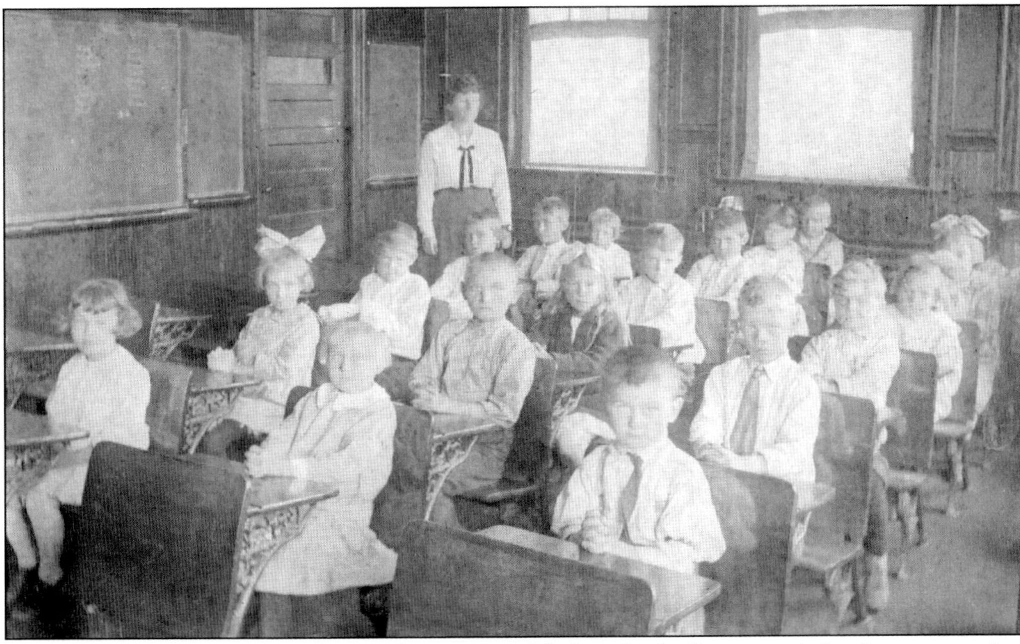

Union School had huge windows to let in natural light, which illuminated the classrooms when these students attended. "When Union School was built over here, I don't think it had running water even. . . . There was no electricity then, and without electricity you couldn't have an electric pump," Joseph Vibert recalled in his second oral history. (Hildred Raymond Collection, WMLM.)

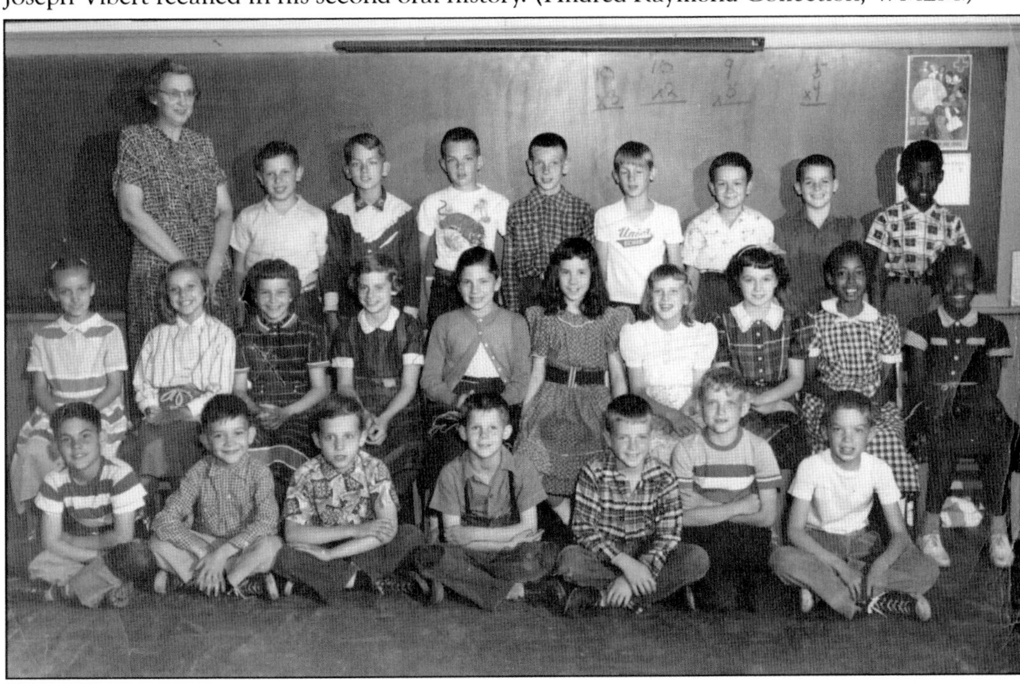

The Union School fourth-grade class of 1953 poses with teacher Josephine Couch. Bob Raymond noted that the "7th or 8th grade teacher was also the principal of the school. We had a janitor, Deke Fairbanks . . . that was the entire staff for eight grades of school: eight teachers and a janitor to keep the place under control." (Bonnie Enes.)

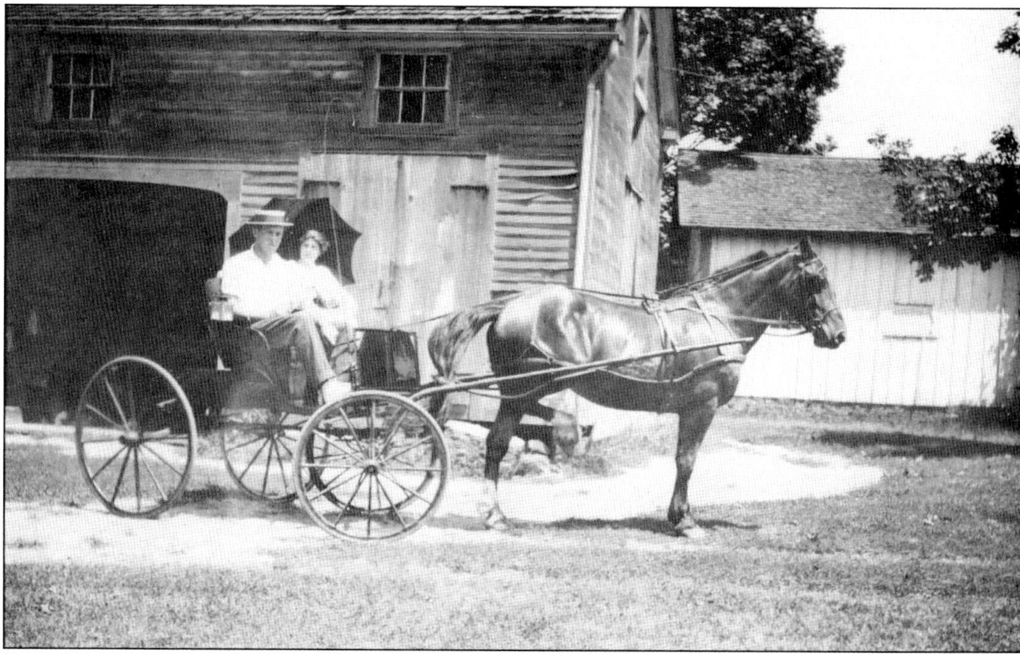

Husband and wife Albertus and Eva Jones sit in a horse cart. The Joneses built their house at 756 Main Street in 1882. "Albertus Jones used to come over and out of the goodness of his heart teach art to the kids at Union School. I always loved it when we had art because he taught us how to draw," Ruth Bortolan said. (Vibert family.)

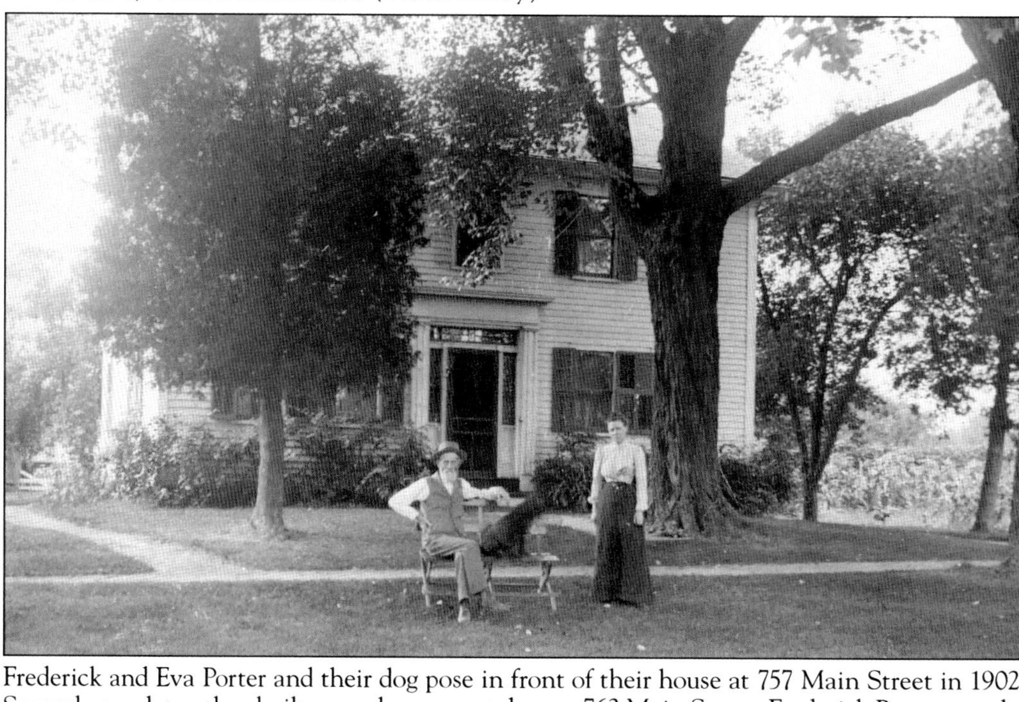

Frederick and Eva Porter and their dog pose in front of their house at 757 Main Street in 1902. Several years later, they built a new house next door at 763 Main Street. Frederick Porter was the town tax collector and had his office in the back of the house. (Photograph by A.W. and G.E. Howes Photographers, Hildred Raymond Collection, WMLM.)

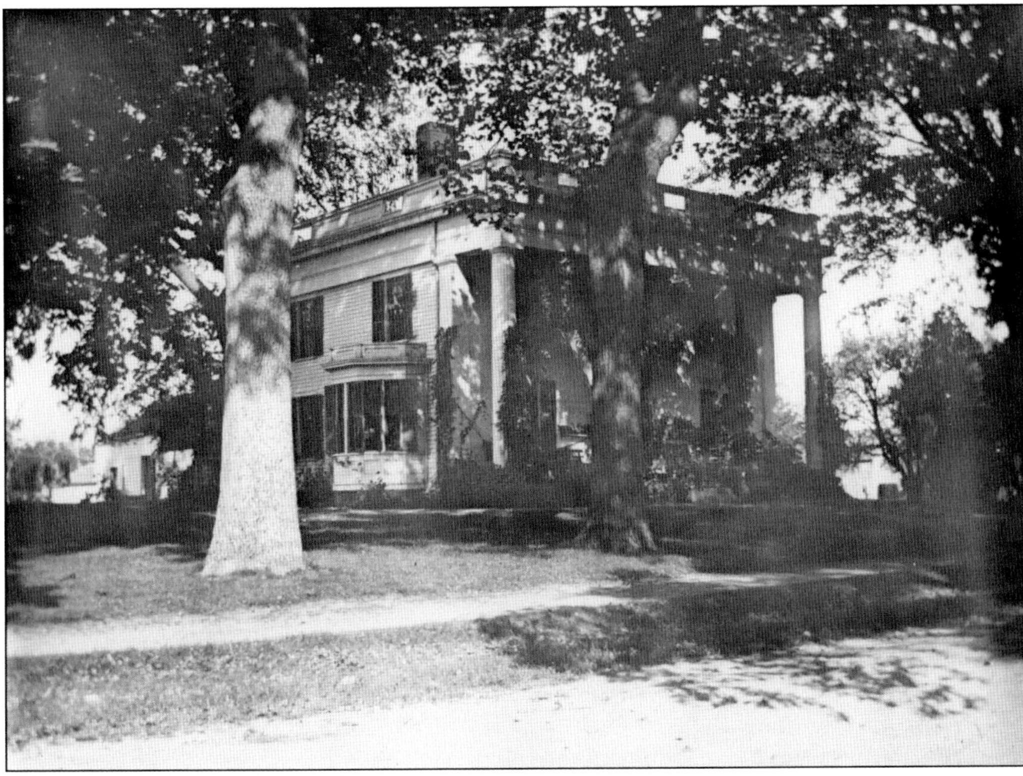

The house at 695 Main Street was built around 1730 by Samuel Wolcott, a descendant of Roger Wolcott, the famous colonial governor of Connecticut who a century before had lived only about a mile south. In the 20th century, the home was owned by J.E. Shepard Jr., who developed a new machine-made cigar binder from pieces of tobacco leaves, eliminating the need for leaves to be perfectly intact. (Hildred Raymond Collection, WMLM.)

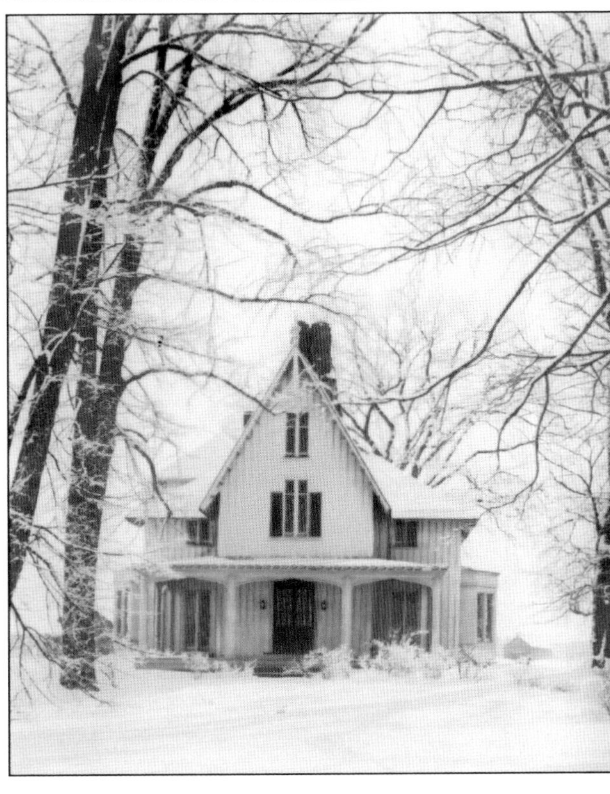

Charles Green entered the US Navy at age 13 and retired in 1867 at age 55 with the rank of commodore. He built a 16-room Gothic "cottage," called the Ponderosa, at 660 Main Street in 1851. The house was designed by renowned architect Alexander Jackson Davis and has seen no major structural changes since it was first built. (Shepard family.)

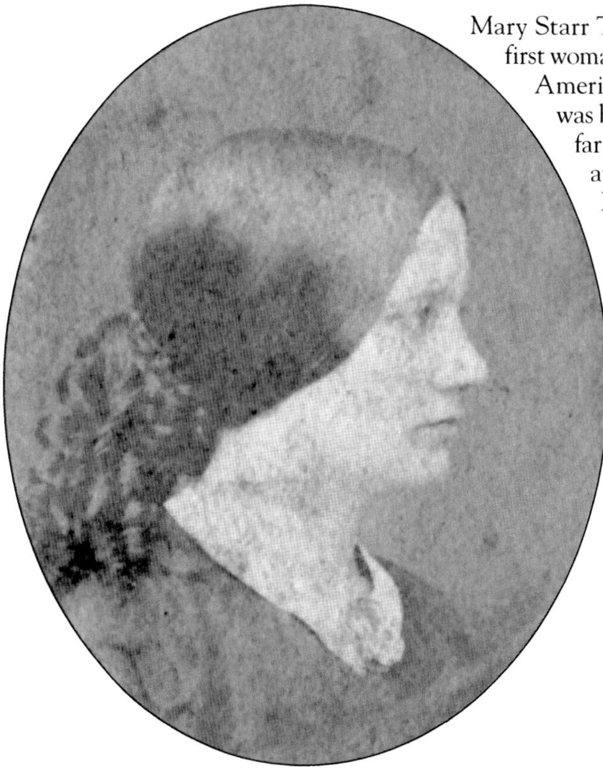

Mary Starr Tudor (1840–1917) was South Windsor's first woman physician and one of the first women in America to graduate from medical school. She was born at 621 Main Street and managed the farm there for much of her adult life. In 1892, at age 52, she graduated from the Women's Medical College of Philadelphia. She returned home and practiced medicine from her house until shortly before her death in 1917. (Hildred Raymond Collection, WMLM.)

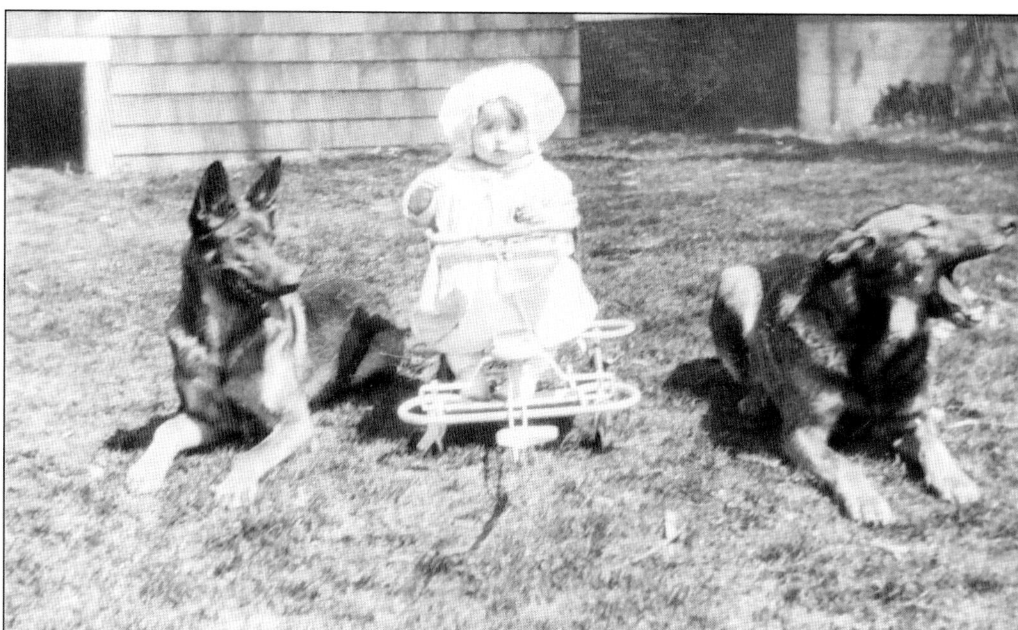

One-year-old Charlotte Andross, photographed here in 1931, looks like a baby doll in her stroller in her grandmother's yard at 246 Main Street, flanked by German shepherds Prince and Wolfie. Andross and her parents lived next door at 244 Main Street. (Andross and S.R. Collins Family Collection, WMLM.)

Three

Sullivan Avenue and Wapping

If Main Street was the original nexus of colonial-era South Windsor activity, the Wapping area was not far behind. The settlement of Wapping, named for a district in London, was formed approximately three miles east of the Connecticut River and beyond the reach of the original South Windsor land grants mentioned in the previous chapter. There were households in the Wapping area (which was originally called Bissell Farms) by 1700, and the first house was most likely at the spot where Troy Road meets Sullivan Avenue.

As with most colonial American communities, the central social organization of people's lives in Wapping was the church. Wapping residents grew tired of trekking miles by horse each Sunday to go to church on Main Street. In those days, before the separation of church and state, residents had to petition the colonial legislature for the right to organize a parish. They were turned down several times, but approval was finally granted in 1765 to hold services in Wapping during the winter months. Several years later it was extended to a year-round parish.

In the 20th century, as the small businesses, schools, and town hall on Main Street closed, Wapping took over as the center of activity, particularly around the Five Corners, where Sullivan Avenue, Buckland Road, Ellington Road, and Oakland Road met. Part of Ellington Road was diverted in 1993 to make the intersection safer, changing the five corners to four.

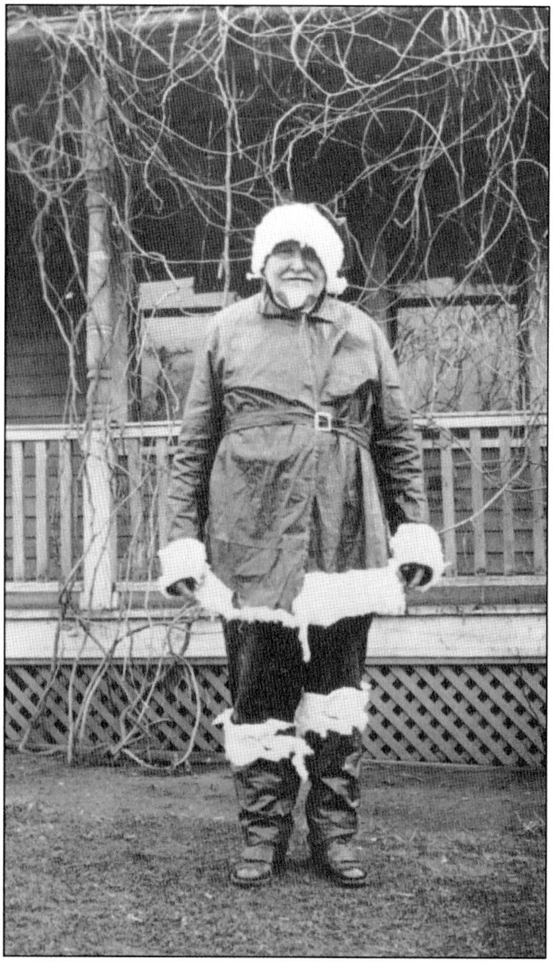

The road that led from East Windsor Hill to Wapping Center was known as the Wapping Road until the late 1930s, when it was renamed to honor Morris D. Sullivan. Sullivan (1848–1935), an Irish immigrant who lived near the intersection of Hillside Drive and Sullivan Avenue, was nicknamed "the Mayor of Wapping." Every Christmas, he dressed as Santa Claus for a children's party at the Wapping Community House. (SWHS.)

Around 1811, town blacksmith Increase Clapp (1783–1859) built the brick house that stands at the corner of what are now Sullivan Avenue and John Fitch Boulevard. The iron rings set into the walls of the jail cells in the Bissell Ferry Tavern (see page 12) were forged by Increase Clapp. (Hildred Raymond Collection, WMLM.)

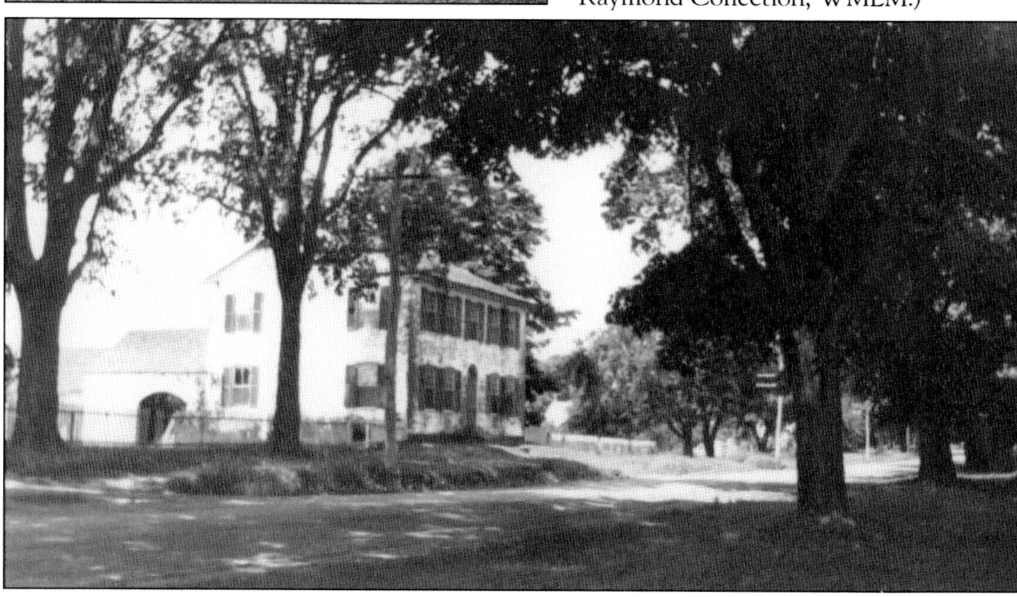

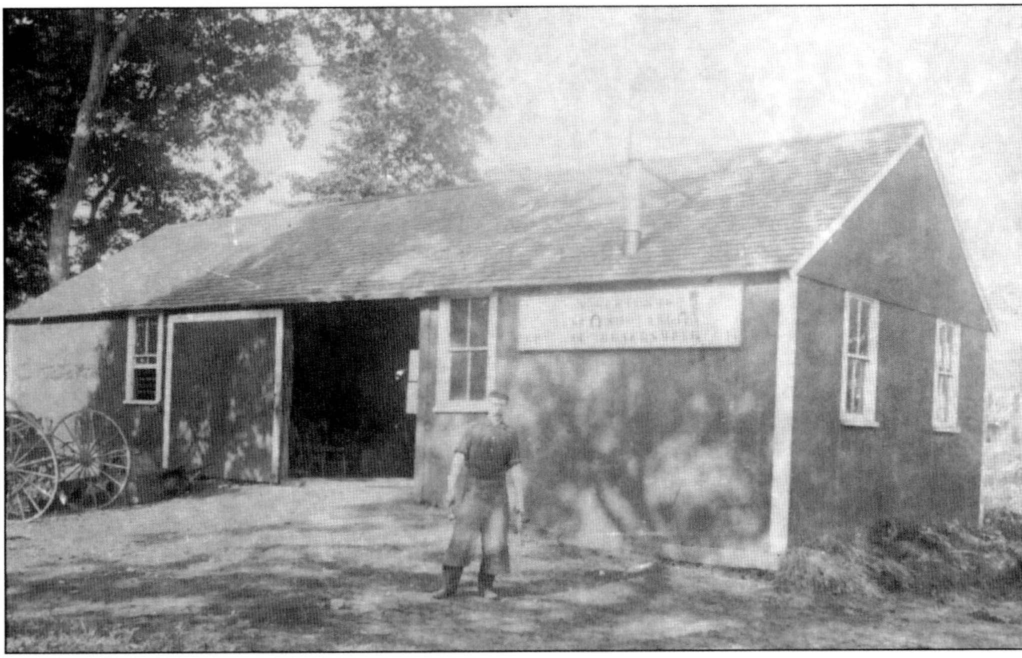

James Crickmore and his young family emigrated from England to South Windsor in 1895, and he soon started operating a blacksmith and wagon-making shop at approximately 233 Sullivan Avenue. Given its proximity to the Increase Clapp house, it may be that Crickmore took over Clapp's old forge. The Crickmore shop, now demolished, is shown from the outside (above) and inside (below), with James Crickmore standing near his forge. Unlike blacksmiths of earlier centuries, Crickmore would have worked primarily on small repairs and shoes for horses and oxen rather than on larger-scale fabrications. (Both, Hildred Raymond Collection, WMLM.)

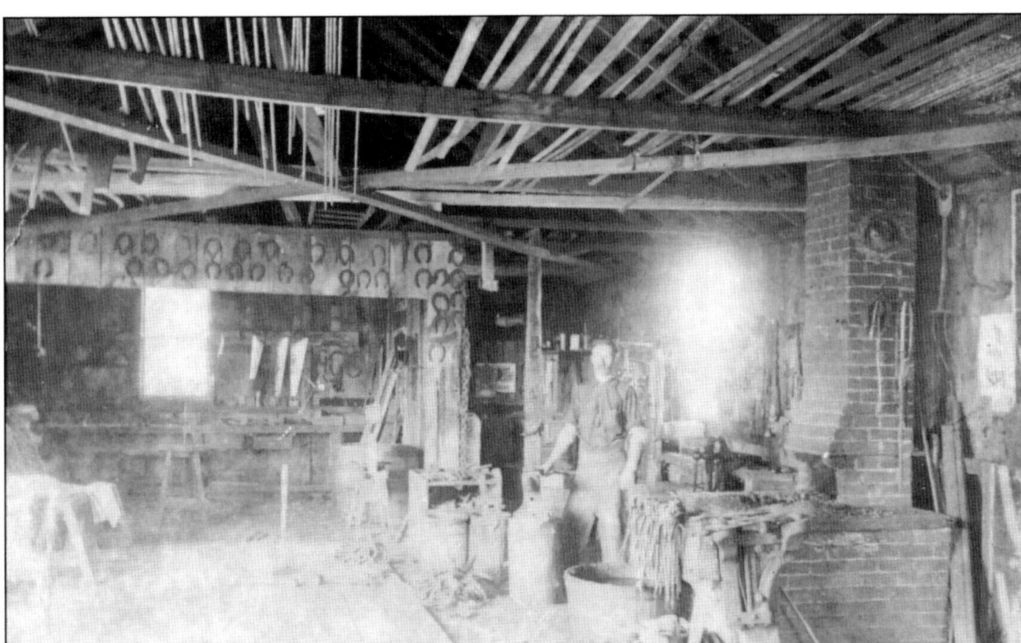

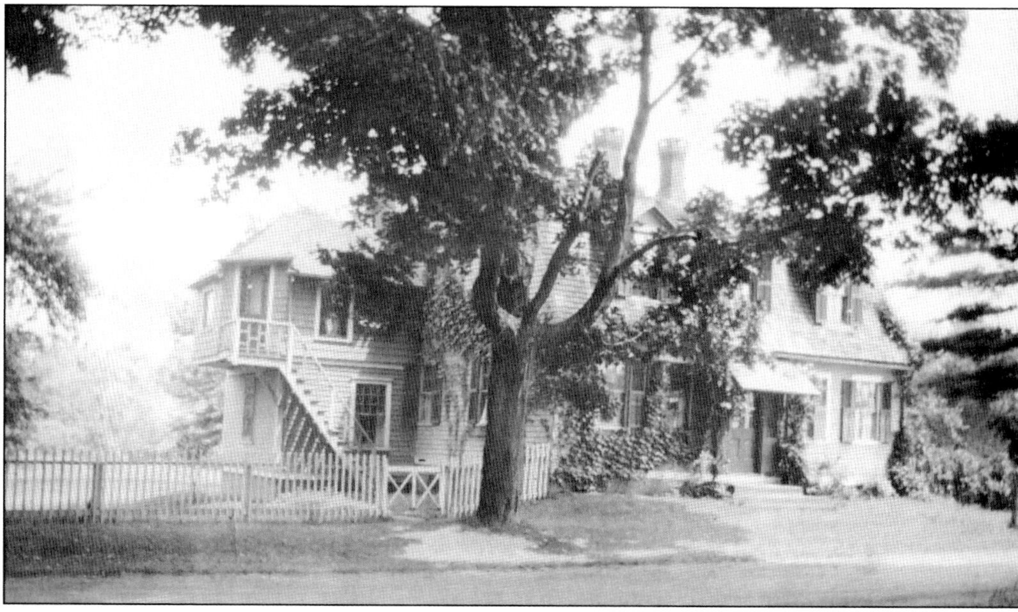

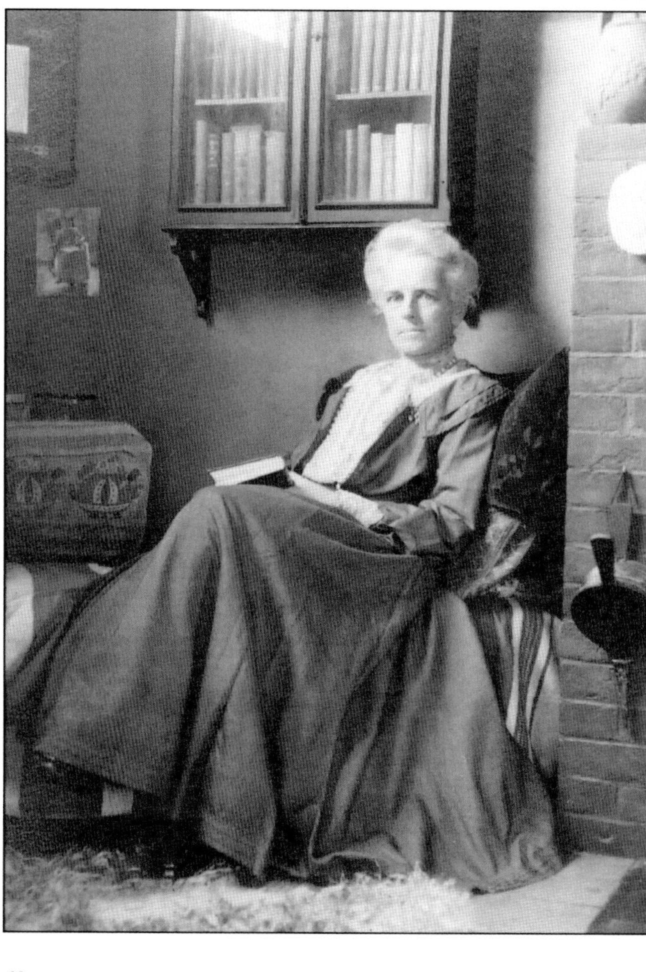

Wild Acres, on Sullivan Avenue, was the home and studio of sisters Amelia and Edith Watson. Amelia was a noted watercolorist and Edith a widely published photographer (five of her images are in this book). Before the Watson sisters took ownership of the house and christened it Wild Acres, it was owned by their parents, Reed Watson and Sarah Bowles Watson. The home was torn down in the 1950s, and the site is now an industrial park. (Hildred Raymond Collection, WMLM.)

Amelia Montague Watson (1856–1934), seated at her studio in Wild Acres, was a professional painter who taught at the Hartford Art School. She illustrated the 1896 edition of Henry David Thoreau's book *Cape Cod* and provided cover art for several other books. Many of her watercolors of South Windsor houses and landscapes hang in Wood Memorial Library. (Photograph by Edith S. Watson, WMLM.)

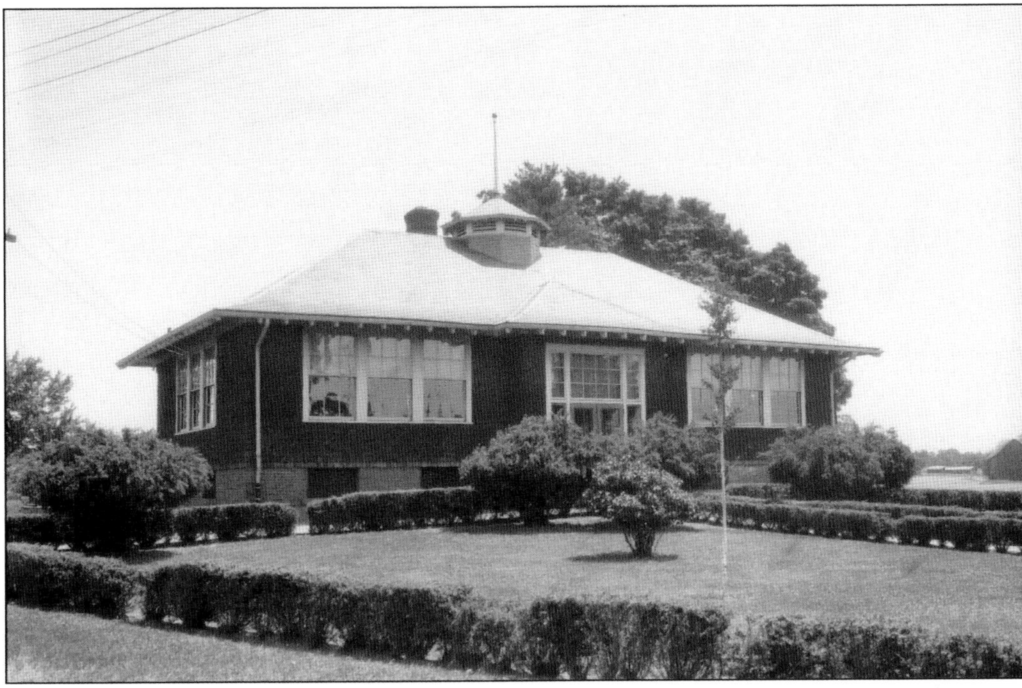

The two-room Rye Street Schoolhouse, close to the East Windsor line, was not strictly part of East Windsor Hill and not quite part of Wapping. The school building, which is now a private residence at 14 Windsorville Road, sits on a triangular lot in the fork between Rye Street and Windsorville Road. Above, the Rye Street School is shown in 1933. Below, teacher Arline Miller Bidwell (far right) stands with her class of first through fourth graders in 1923. The fifth through eighth grades would have been taught in the other room. (WMLM.)

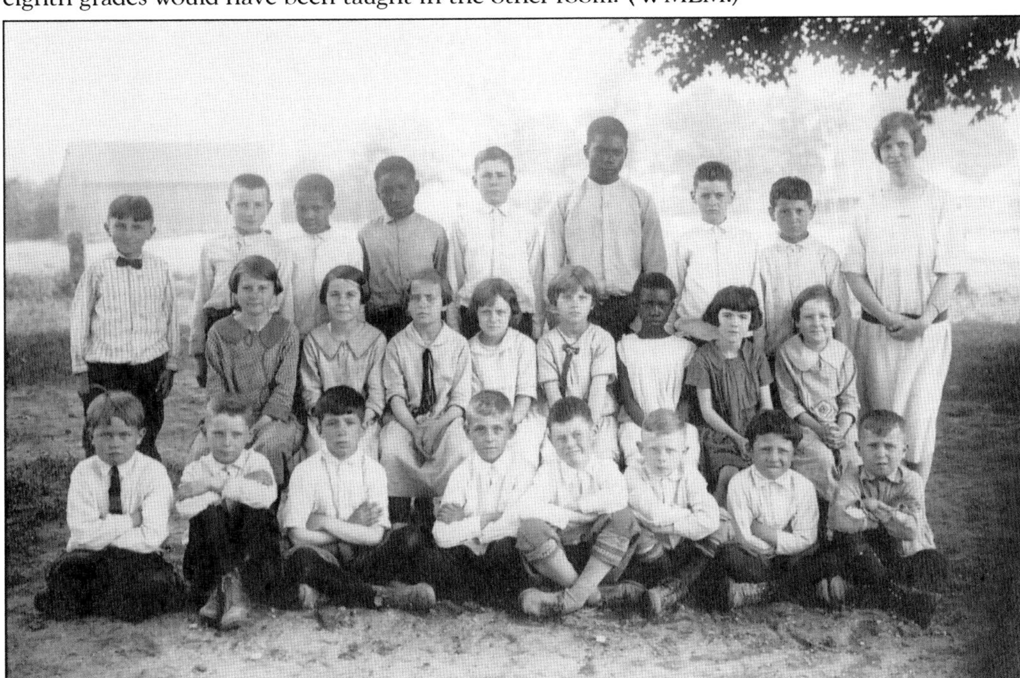

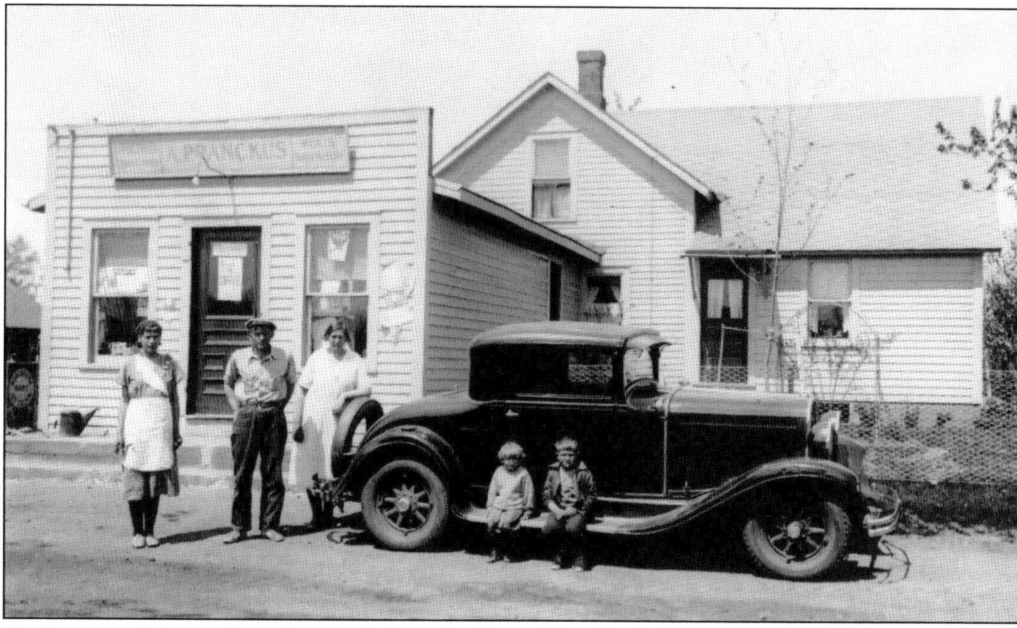

Anthony and Anna Pranckus and their children Julia (far left), Amelia, and John (on running board) pose in front of their grocery store at the corner of Troy Road and Sullivan Avenue. Shown here sometime in the early 1930s, the Pranckus family were part of South Windsor's sizeable Lithuanian American immigrant community. (Sherwood Waldron Collection, WMLM.)

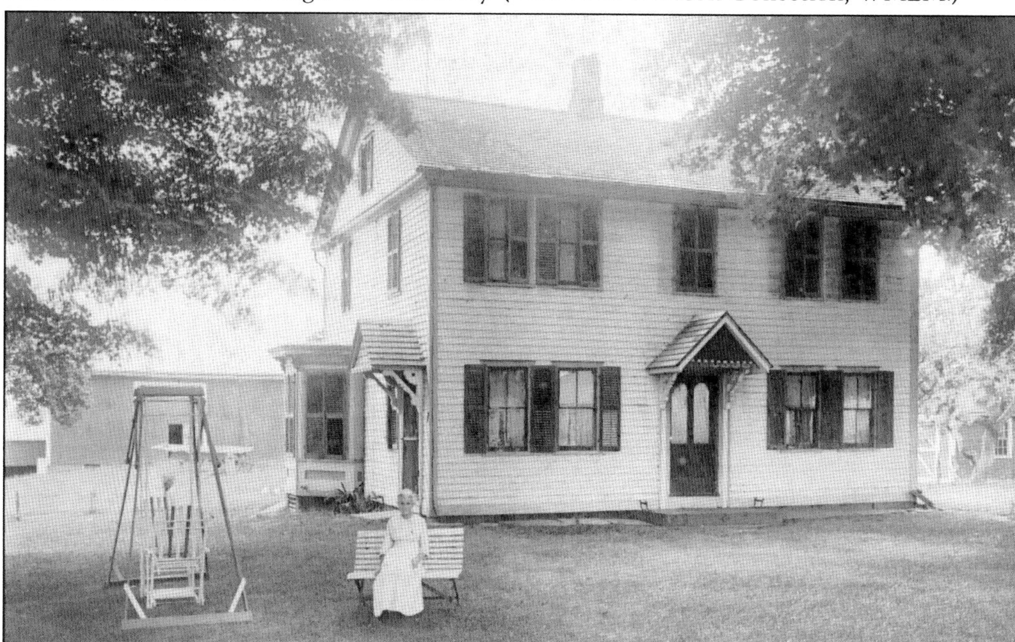

Lawrence Stoughton built the farm house at 1407 Sullivan Avenue in 1823, and the property stayed in the same family (albeit with different last names) until 1998, when the town of South Windsor purchased the property after the death of Edna Priest, the final owner. This photograph likely shows Abbie Hills Priest, Edna Priest's mother-in-law, around 1900. (Edna and Norman Priest Collection, WMLM.)

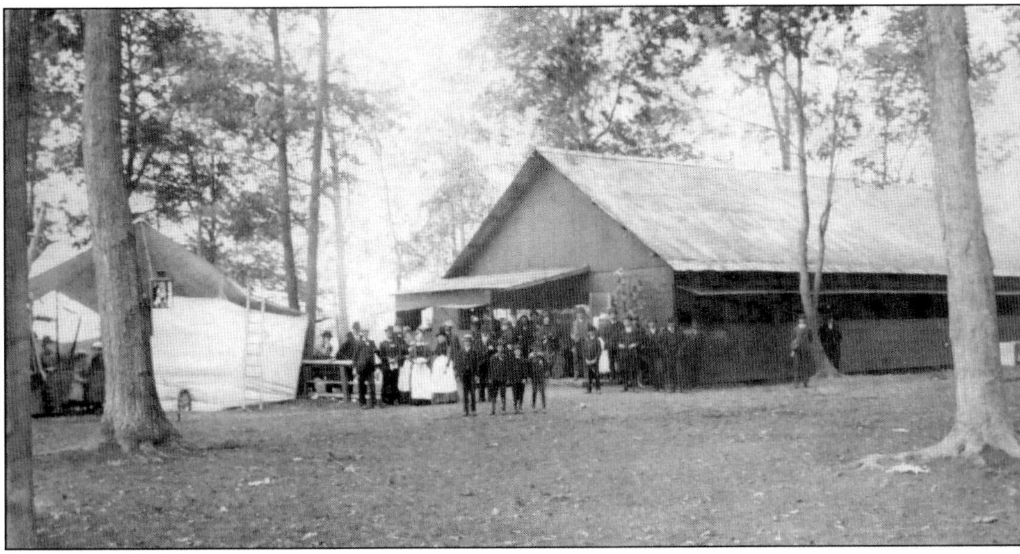

In 1877, Wilbur Hill opened Hills' Grove, a dance hall, food pavilion, and picnicking site, in the woods at 1407 Sullivan Avenue. People would drive to Hills' Grove in wagons for picnics during the day and square dances at night, when they would dance in the unheated hall. The Wapping Fair and other events were held here until the dance hall burned down in the early 1950s. (SWHS.)

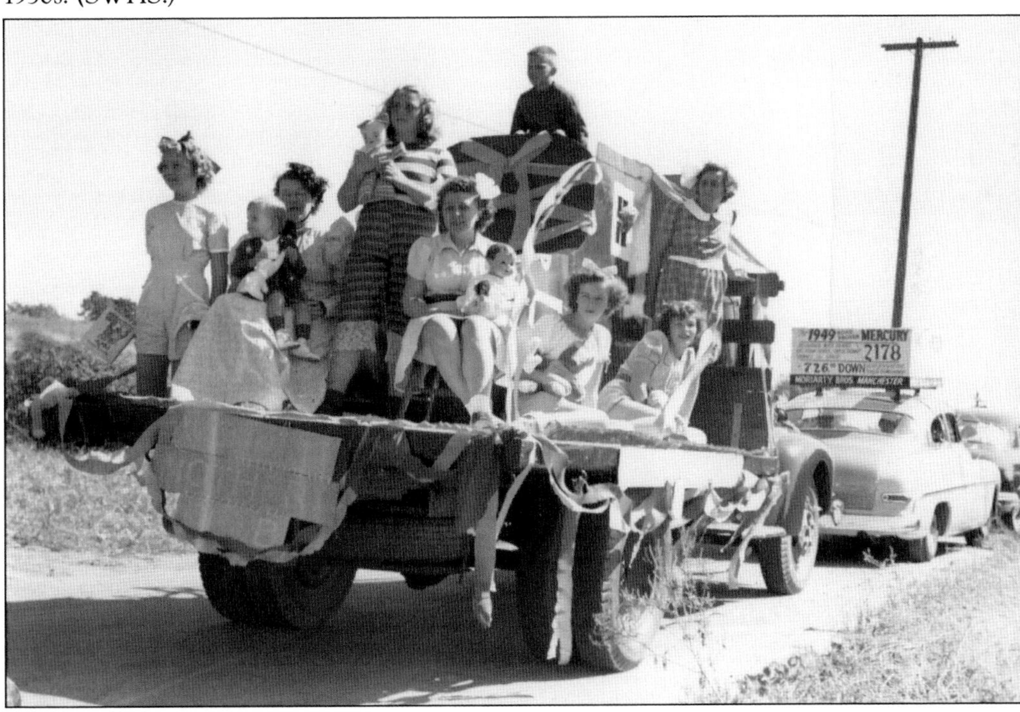

Started by the Wapping Grange Association, the Wapping Fair has been held annually since 1892, with the exception of a few years during the Great Depression. The fairgrounds have changed location several times, but for many years, the fair was held at Hills' Grove. This photograph shows the Wapping Mothers' Club float in the 1949 Wapping Fair parade. (Foster Wapping Fair and Wapping Grange Collection, WMLM.)

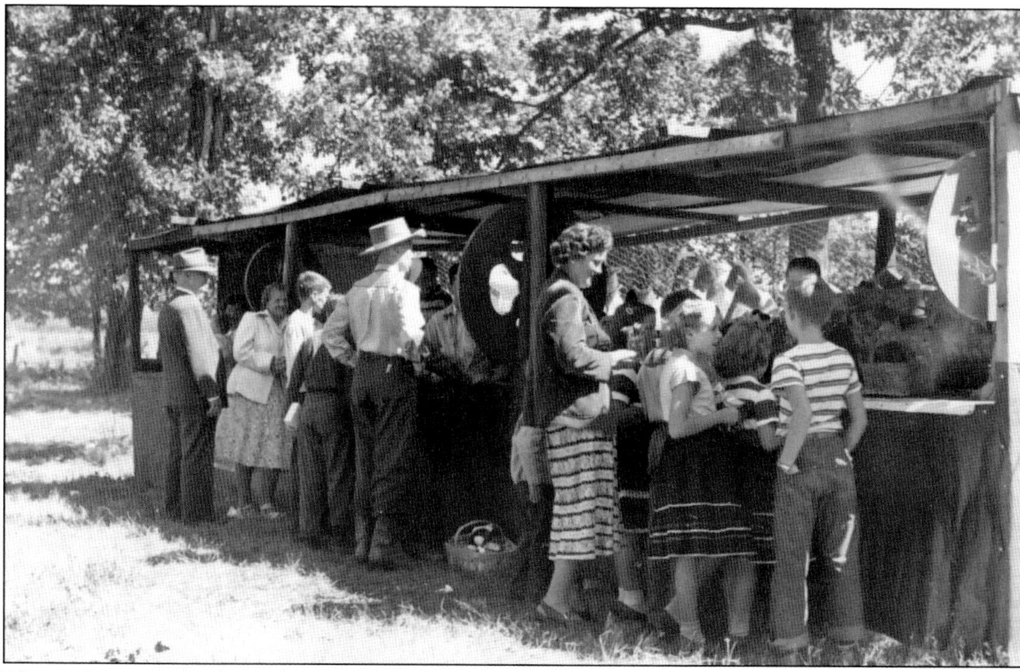

These photographs from the 1949 fair show food and games stalls (above) and a young boy with his prize cow (below). Like all country fairs, the Wapping Fair has always featured food, games, and contests to judge produce and livestock. The fair was the celebratory, symbolic end to the farming season, and as such was a huge event. Terry Files recalled: "Of course when we had the fair, they used to shut Sullivan Avenue off right there . . . they shut the street right down for the Wapping Fair. Couldn't very well do that today, you know?" (Both, Foster Wapping Fair and Wapping Grange Collection, WMLM.)

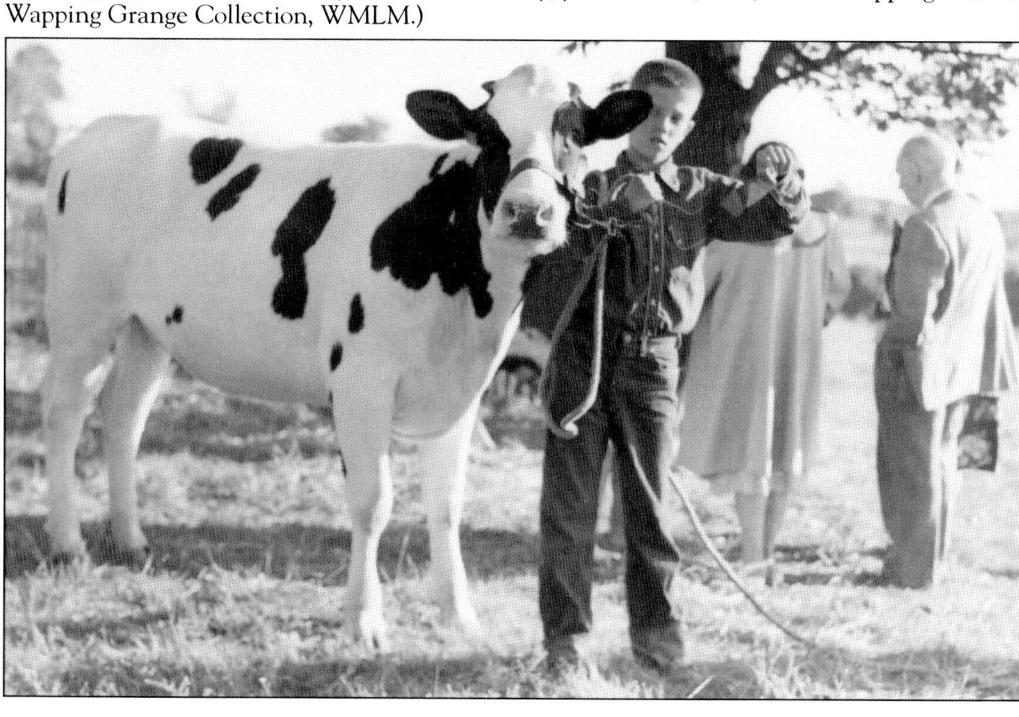

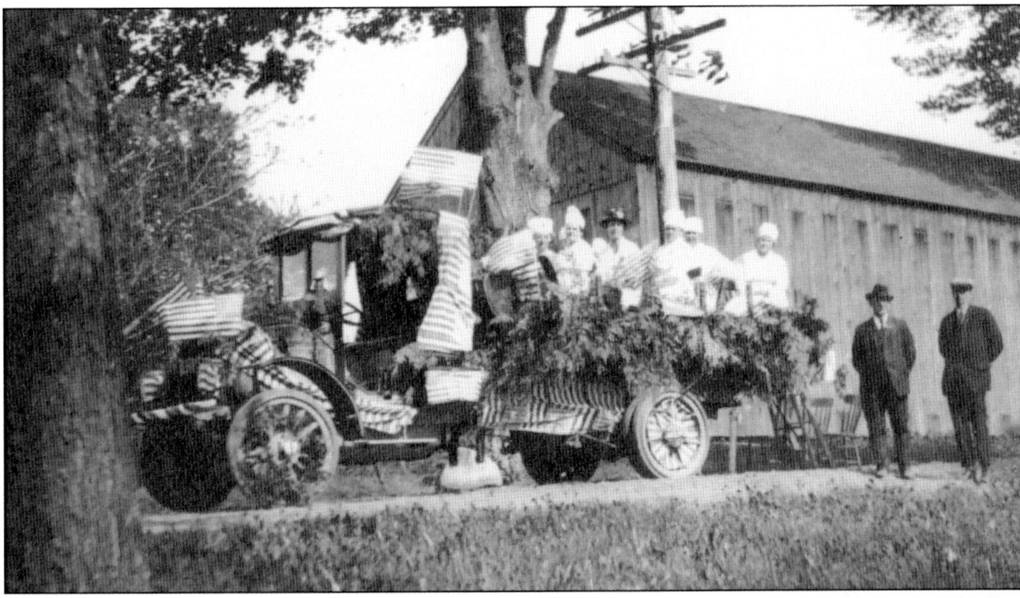

Wapping Fair parades weren't the only parades at Hills' Grove. This Decoration Day parade float was photographed around World War I near Hills' Grove, where the parades ended at that time. Begun in 1868 in the aftermath of the Civil War, Decoration Day was established as a day to decorate the graves of the Civil War dead and is now celebrated as Memorial Day. (SWHS.)

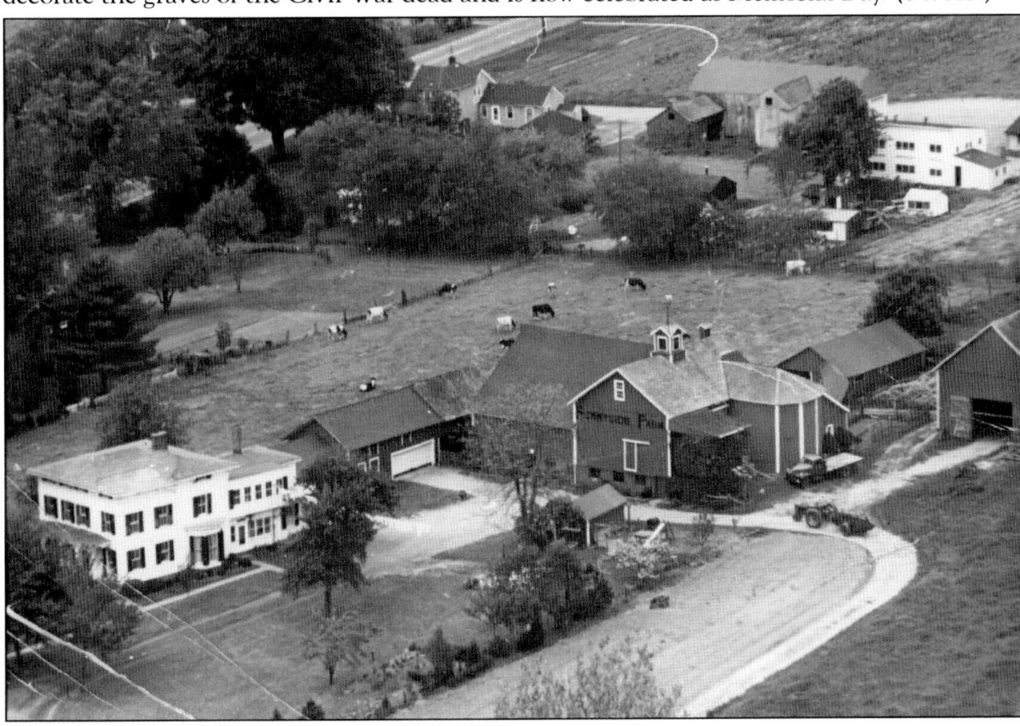

This c. 1960 aerial photograph shows Asher Allen Collins's white house and Sunnyside Farm in the foreground and Leslie Collins's poultry farm in the background. The large white house at left, which faces Sullivan Avenue at 8 Collins Lane, was built in 1869. The Collins family grew crops and raised dairy cows at Sunnyside Farm. (Andross and S.R. Collins Family Collection, WMLM.)

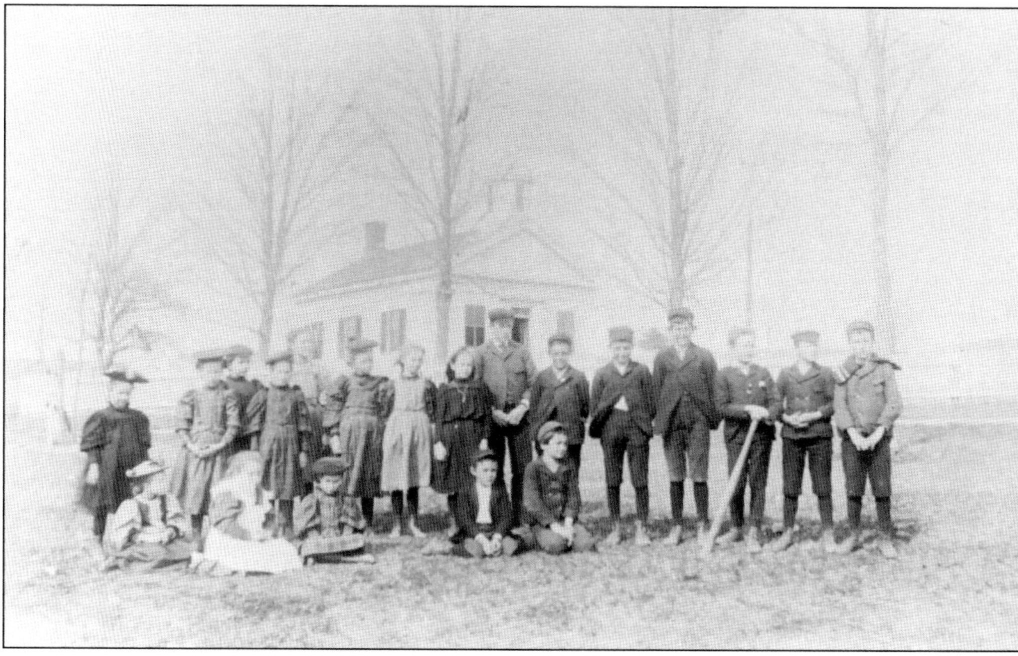

The District 8 schoolhouse, also known as the Old North School, still stands, albeit in a different spot from where it was built. Now at 1271 Sullivan Avenue, it previously stood on the opposite side of the road, on the Collins family farm. After the school closed, Asher Allen Collins moved the building across the street to house farm workers. The schoolhouse is shown above with the class of 1900 and teacher Howard Hamilton. Below, around 1910, a group of students stand with their sleds around the school doors. (Above, Andross and S.R. Collins Family Collection, WMLM; below, Collins family.)

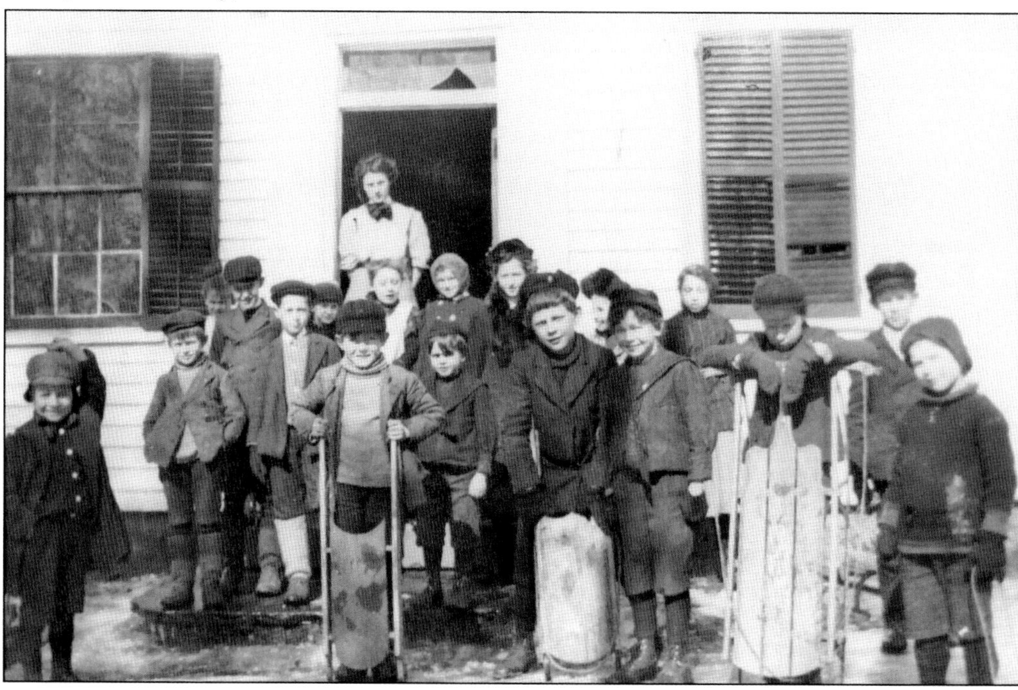

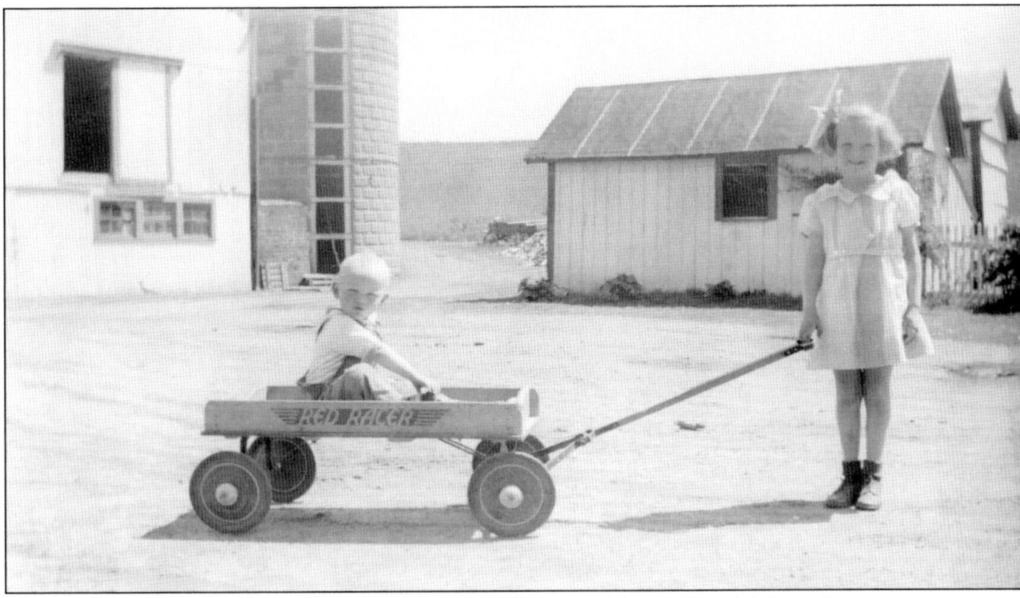

Cynthia Collins Waldron pulls her brother George Walter "Buddy" Collins in a wagon at Sunnyside Farm. She recalled: "My brother and I walked many, many times from Pierce Road all the way down. My father had pastures, and we'd walk the cows home. And can you imagine today walking twenty-five cows up that street, crossing Sullivan Avenue? I just can't imagine." (Collins family.)

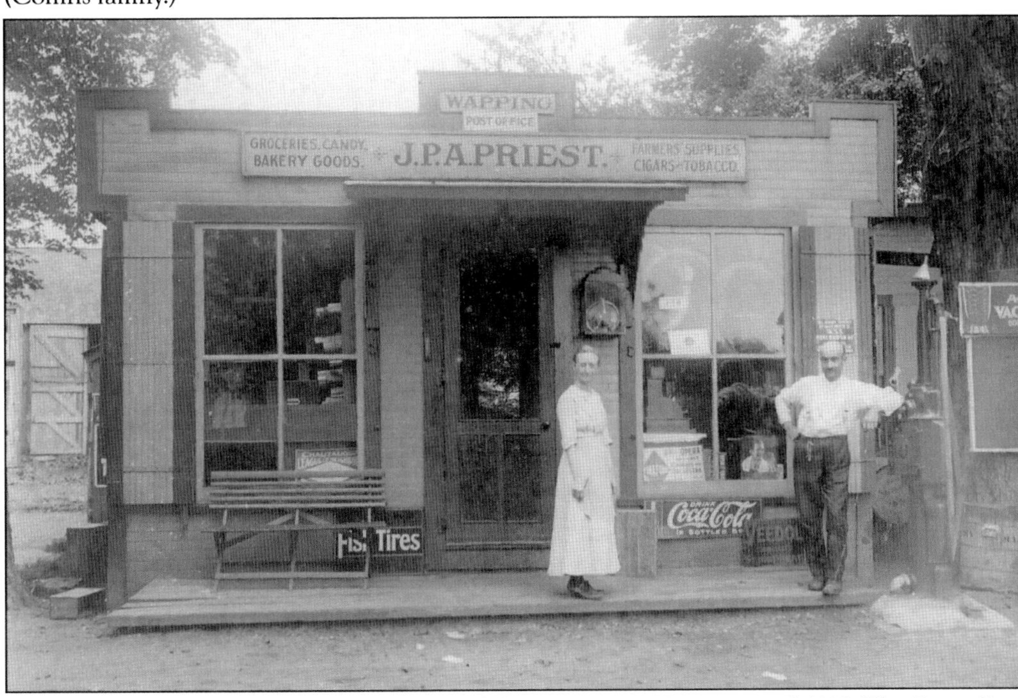

Lillian Grant and Paul Priest stand in front of the J.P.A. Priest Store around 1910. The Priest Store was a combination general store and post office on Ellington Road in Wapping Center from the late 19th century until it closed in 1925. The building was later used as a probate office until it was torn down in the middle of the 20th century. (Edna and Norman Priest Collection, WMLM.)

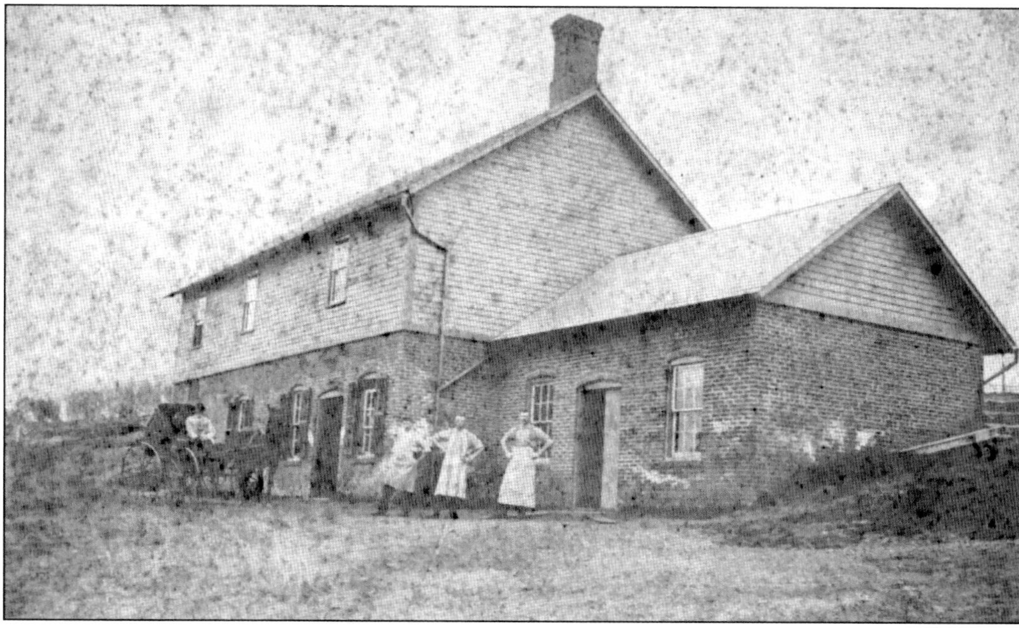

The Wapping Creamery Company operated from about 1883 to 1929. Shown here around 1890, the creamery collected milk from local dairy farms and churned it into butter that was then sold to stores around the region. During Prohibition, the building was processing another liquid—in 1930, authorities discovered a 1,500-gallon illegal still inside. Today, the creamery building is a private residence at 74 Felt Road Extension. (WMLM.)

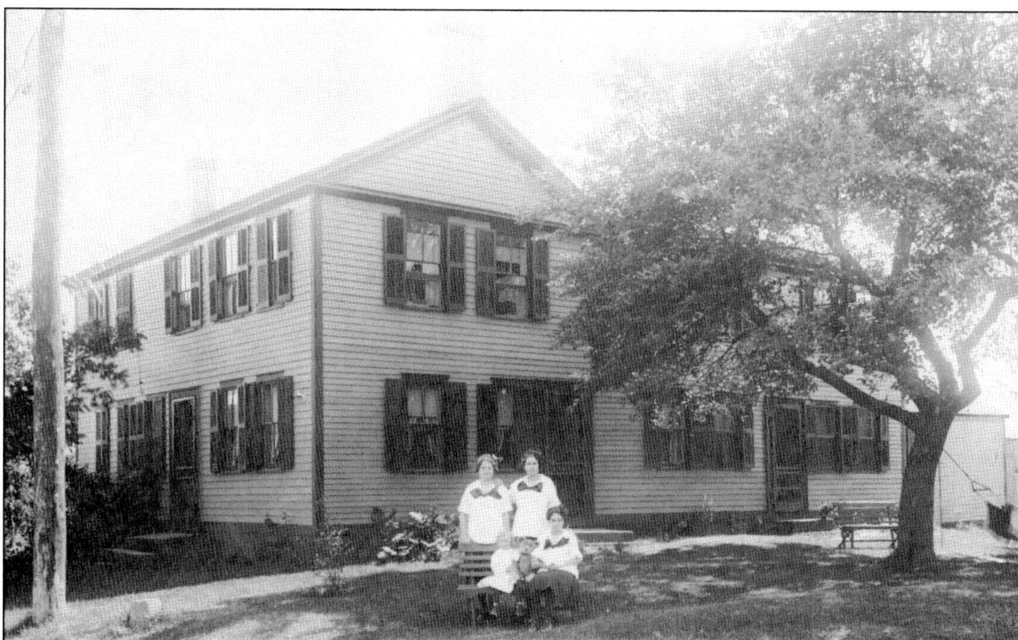

Shown here around 1900, the house at the corner of Buckland and Ellington Roads in Wapping Center was built by Samuel Grant. At one time, the house was a stagecoach stop, and it even had a ballroom on the second floor. Judd and Marge Files were the last owners of the house, which burned down in August 1954. (Collins family).

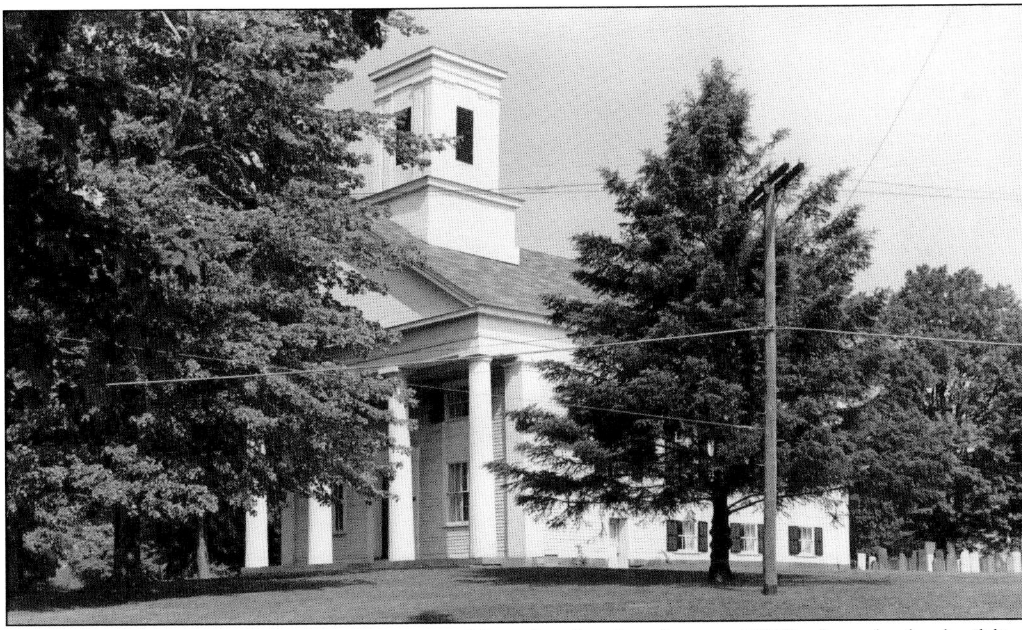

The bones of the Wapping Community Church of today date to 1800, though the building has seen several rounds of major renovations since then. It was built as a joint meetinghouse for Congregationalists and Methodists, though each group held separate services. In 1833, the Methodists built their own church, but the two reunified in 1936 to form the Wapping Community Church. (Photograph by Ellsworth Fairbanks, Barney Daley Collection, WMLM.)

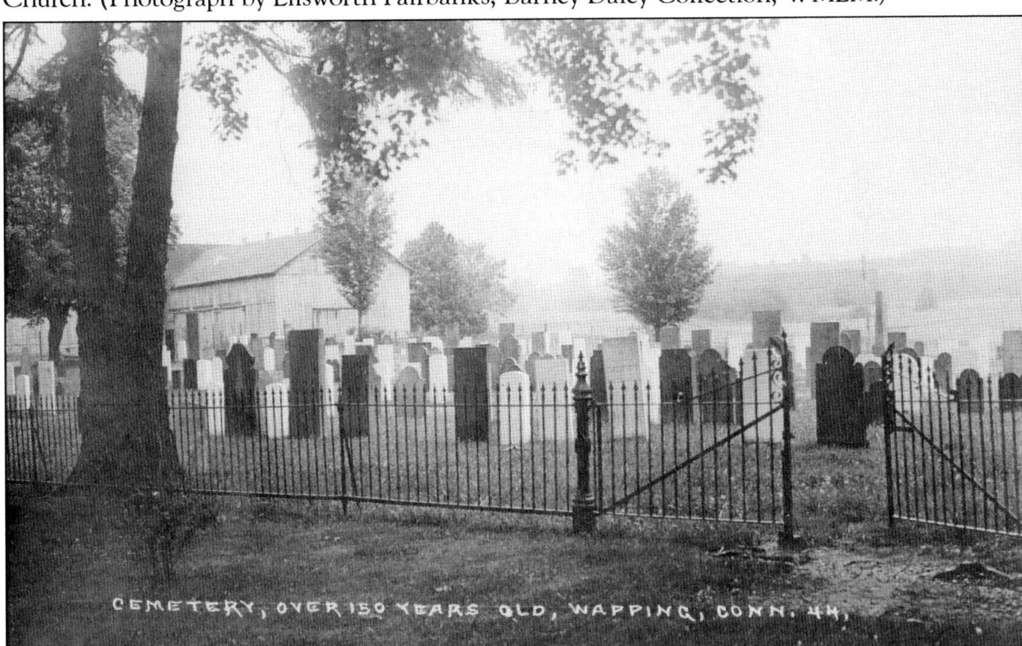

The Old Wapping Cemetery behind Wapping Community Church, shown here around 1915, was drastically revamped by New Deal workers in the 1930s. Charles Nielsen stated that the Works Progress Administration "pulled up all the stones and piled them in a pile, graded the cemetery, and then just put the stones back wherever they thought they ought to be." (Collins family.)

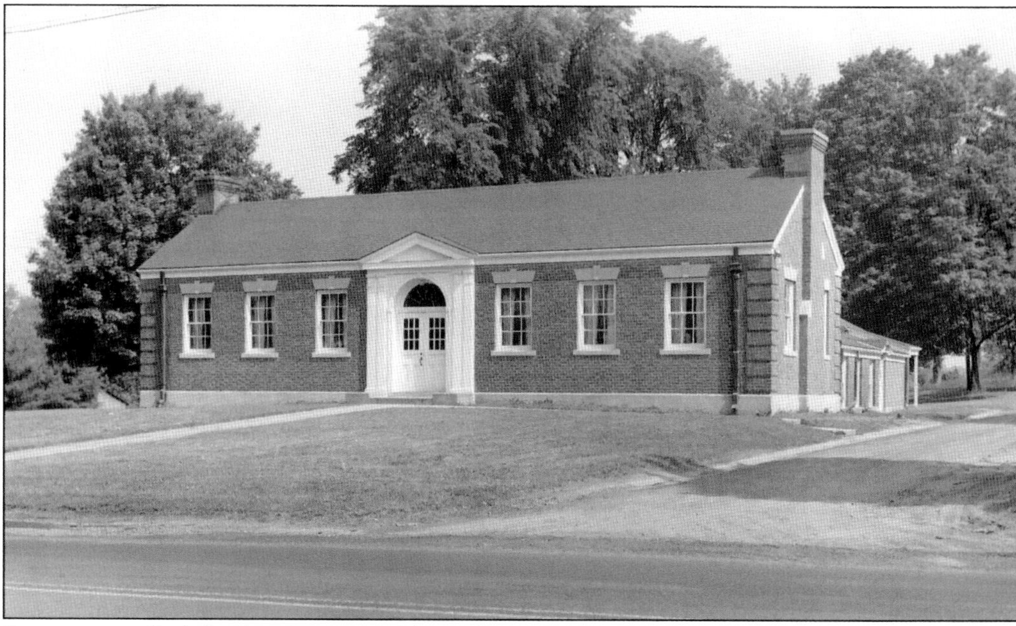

Sometimes called the Dorchester Building, the Wapping Community House was built in 1932 to commemorate the Wapping Methodist Church that burned down, with a plaque made from the brass of the old church bell. A true community center, the building has hosted Boy Scout troop meetings, basketball games, police training, school lunches, and more over the years. (Photograph by Ellsworth Fairbanks, Barney Daley Collection, WMLM.)

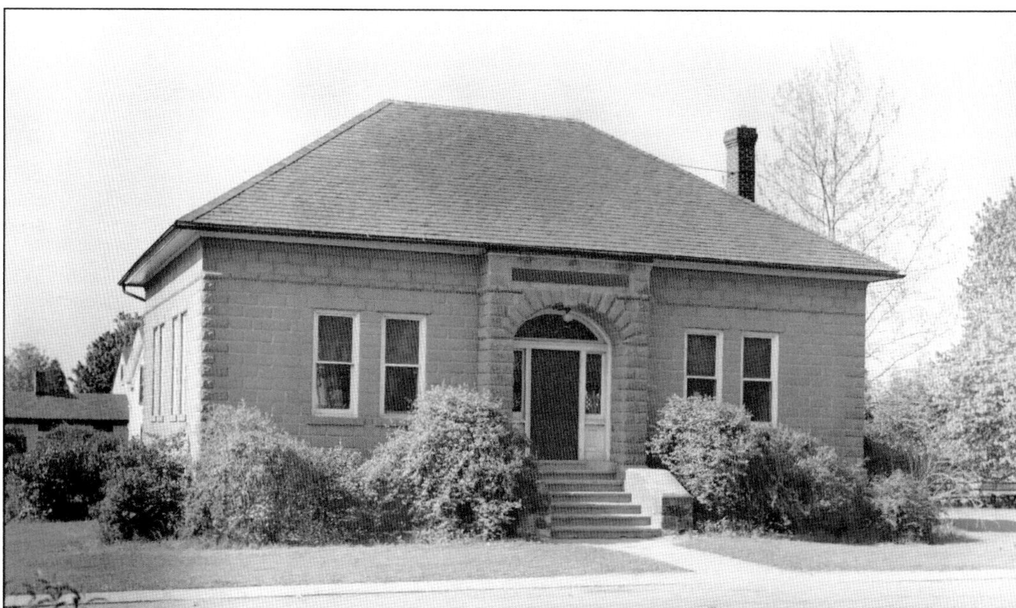

Sadd Memorial Library was built in 1906 by H.W. Sadd and was the first public library building in South Windsor. In the early 20th century, it was the meeting place of South Windsor's Chautauqua Circle, an organization that promoted adult continuing education. The library closed in the 1960s, and the building is now used as private offices. (Photograph by Ellsworth Fairbanks, Barney Daley Collection, WMLM.)

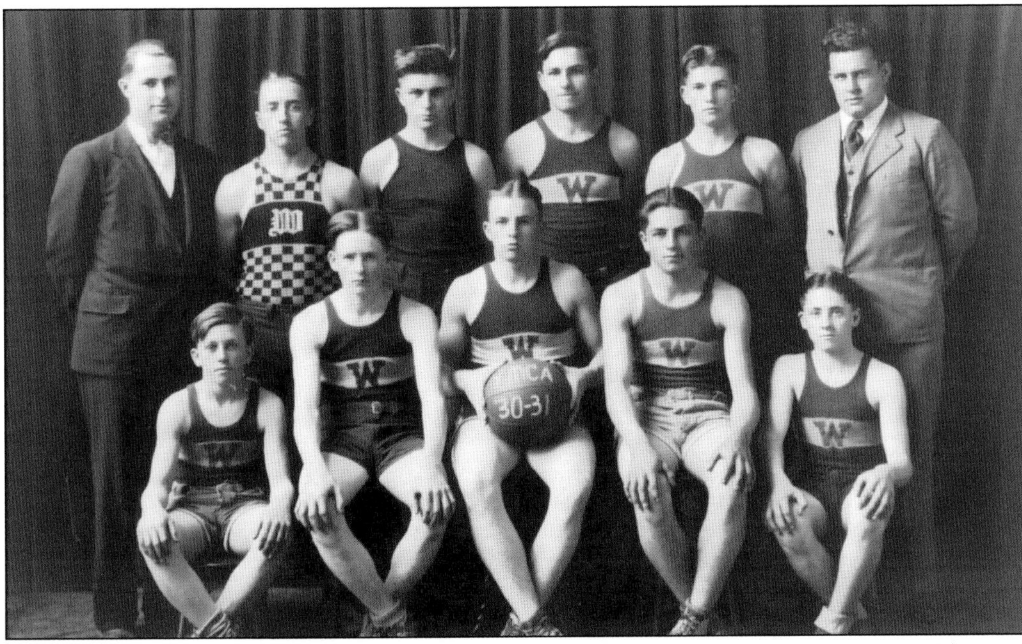

Although it is no longer in existence, the Wapping YMCA was the first Young Men's Christian Association in Hartford County, founded in 1919. The group organized camp expeditions for South Windsor youth as well as basketball teams and regular get-togethers. This picture shows the 1930–1931 YMCA Uncas basketball team, named for a Mohegan sachem who allied with the English during the Pequot War and King Philip's War. (Wapping YMCA Collection, WMLM.)

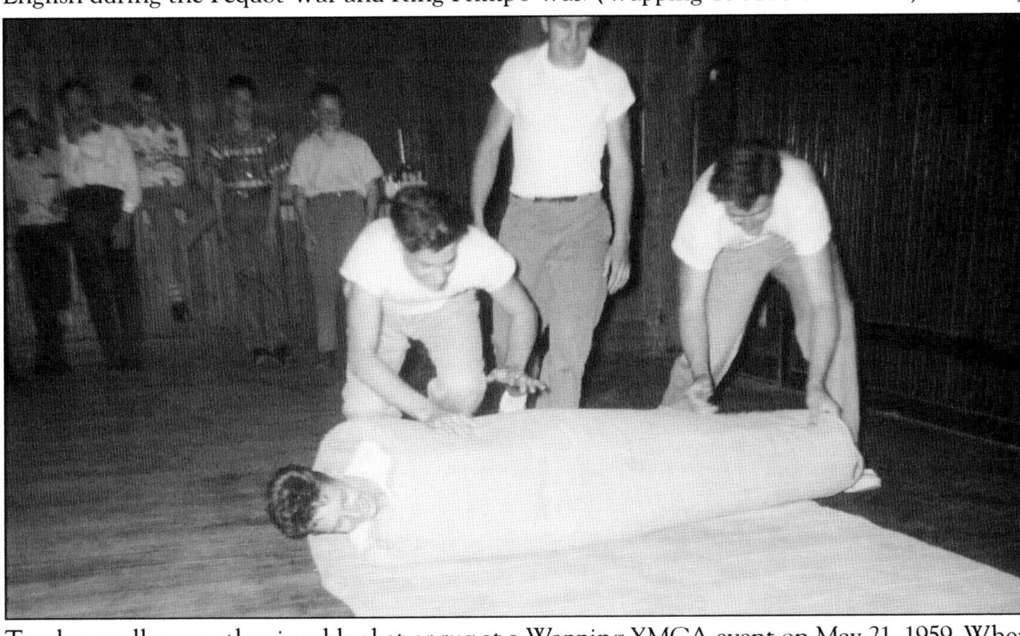

Two boys roll up another in a blanket or rug at a Wapping YMCA event on May 21, 1959. When it was first organized, the Wapping YMCA held weekly meetings at the Wapping Methodist Church, then later at the Wapping Community House. From 1919 until around 1940, the YMCA only included men and boys, but in later years, girls were included as well. (Wapping YMCA Collection, WMLM.)

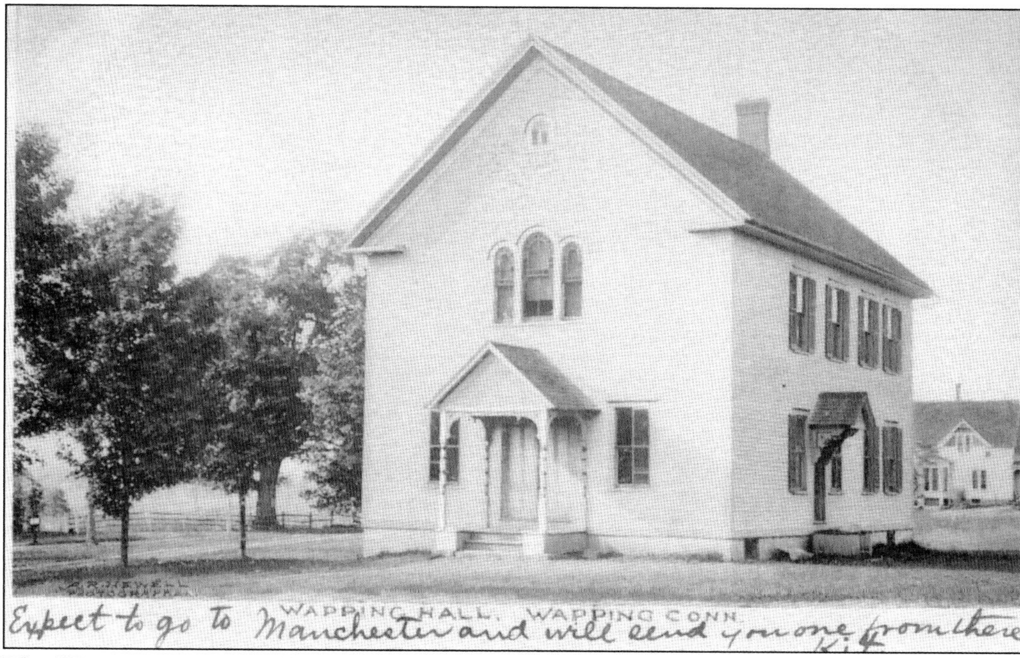

The Wapping Grange Hall, pictured above around 1900, was built as a meeting hall for South Windsor's community agricultural organization. For a handful of years, it housed Wapping's short-lived high school, but the building was added onto and reopened as the Wapping Grammar School. Wapping Grammar School opened around 1915, pictured below. The building was torn down in 1972, and the site is now a parking lot. "It was two gigantic stories with the third story—believe it or not—they used to play basketball up there on the third floor. . . . You didn't make any high passes because technically speaking, if you jumped up, you could touch the roof," recalled Sherman Collins. (Above, photograph by A.R. Newell, WMLM; below, WMLM.)

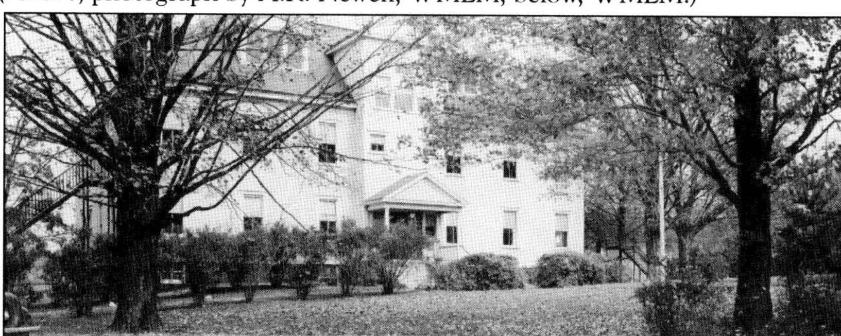

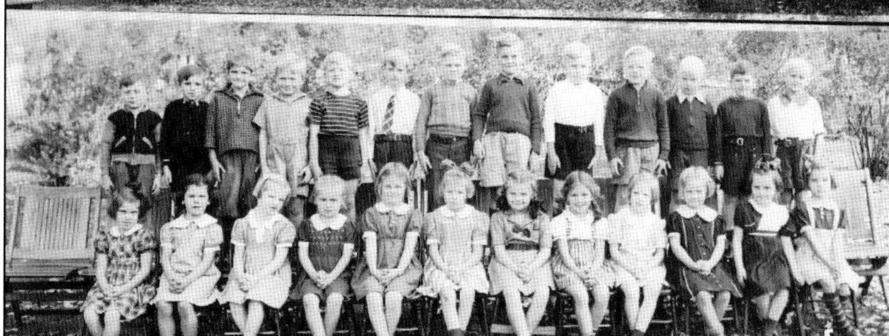

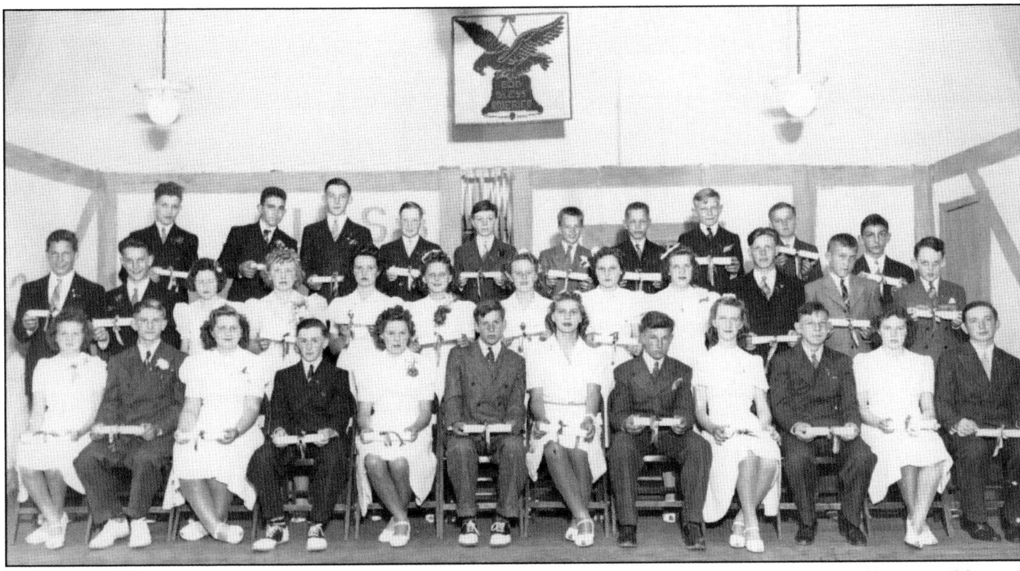

The 1942 Wapping Grammar School eighth-grade class sits at its graduation. "Well, my girlfriends and I used to take a lunch and go down to the brook behind the school . . . we would put our feet in the brook in the hot summer, or we would just sit there and eat our lunch. That was the highlight of the day," said Janet Prior. (Henry Adams Collection, WMLM.)

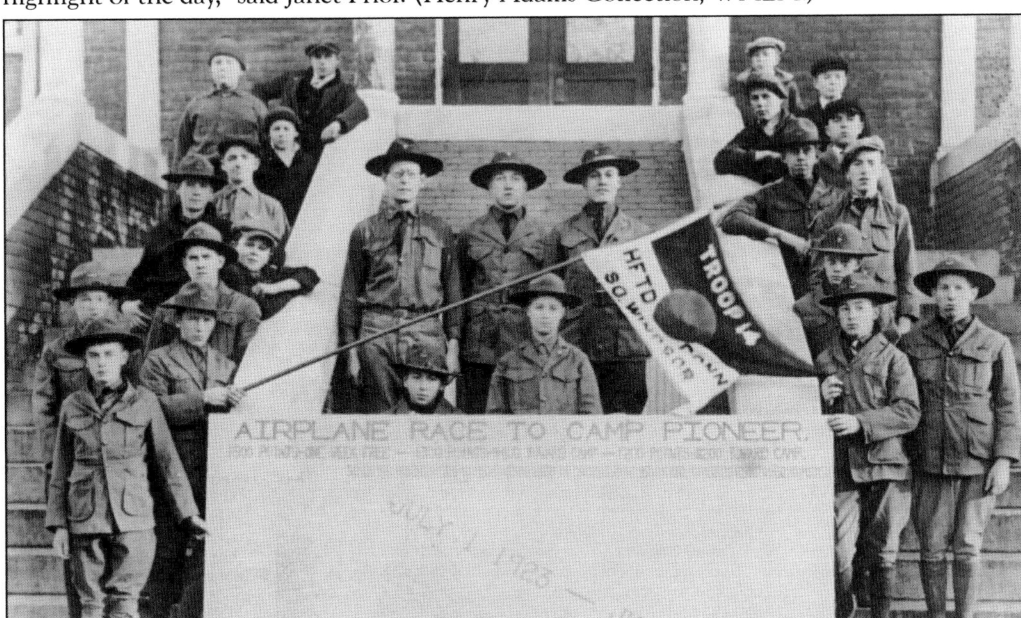

Boy Scouts hold a banner that reads "Airplane Race to Camp Pioneer" in 1923 or 1924. In later years, Scouts met at the Wapping Community House. Fred Edlund noted: "I got into Scouts in 1940 and I remember when we went to summer camp at Camp Pioneer [during World War II]. Gee, we even had to take rationing books with us, coupons; you had to bring so many coupons for sugar so you could go to camp." (WMLM.)

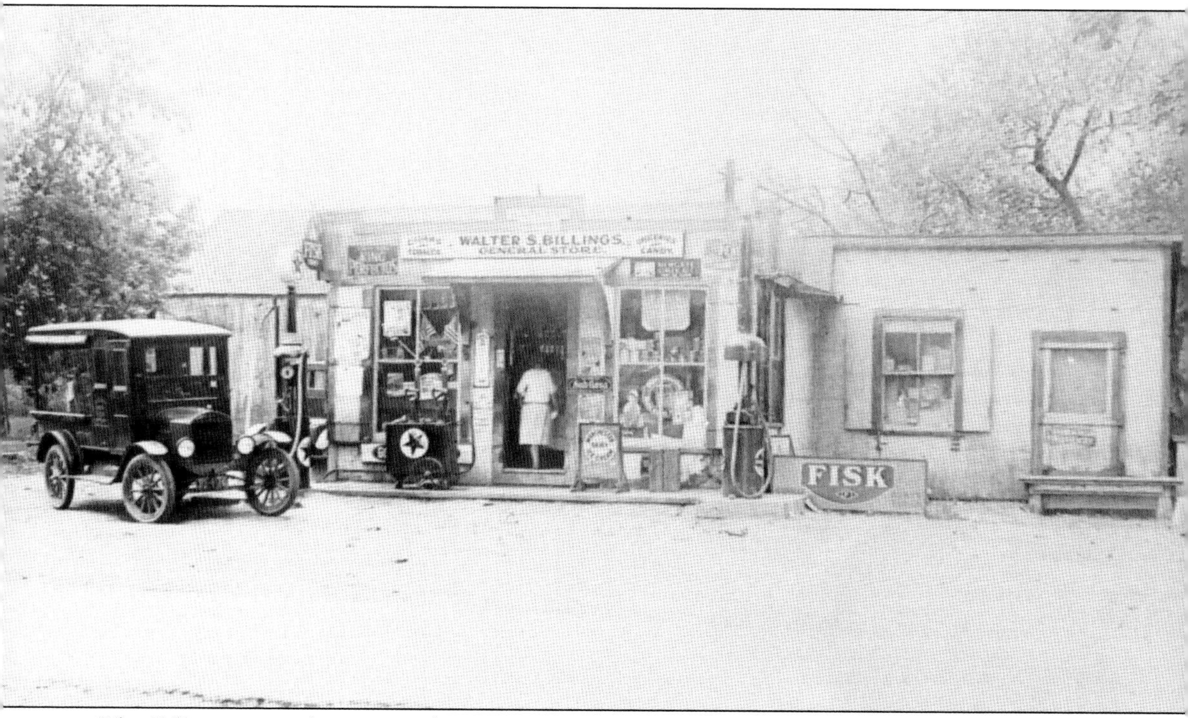

The Billings general store stood near Wapping Grammar School. Francis Peter "Butch" Carney said: "I was two years older than my brother Tom. When Tom went to school, he somehow had a little change and he went to Billings' store—he had recess at a different time than I had but—going to do something nice for his brother, he bought an ice cream cone and he came back to the school and he came into the room where I was and, 'Is my brother here? Well here's his ice cream cone.' Well the teacher said something about we're having class. 'Well he could eat it later,' my brother said. [My teacher said,] 'Oh Francis you might as well eat your ice cream cone.' " (Courtesy of SWHS.)

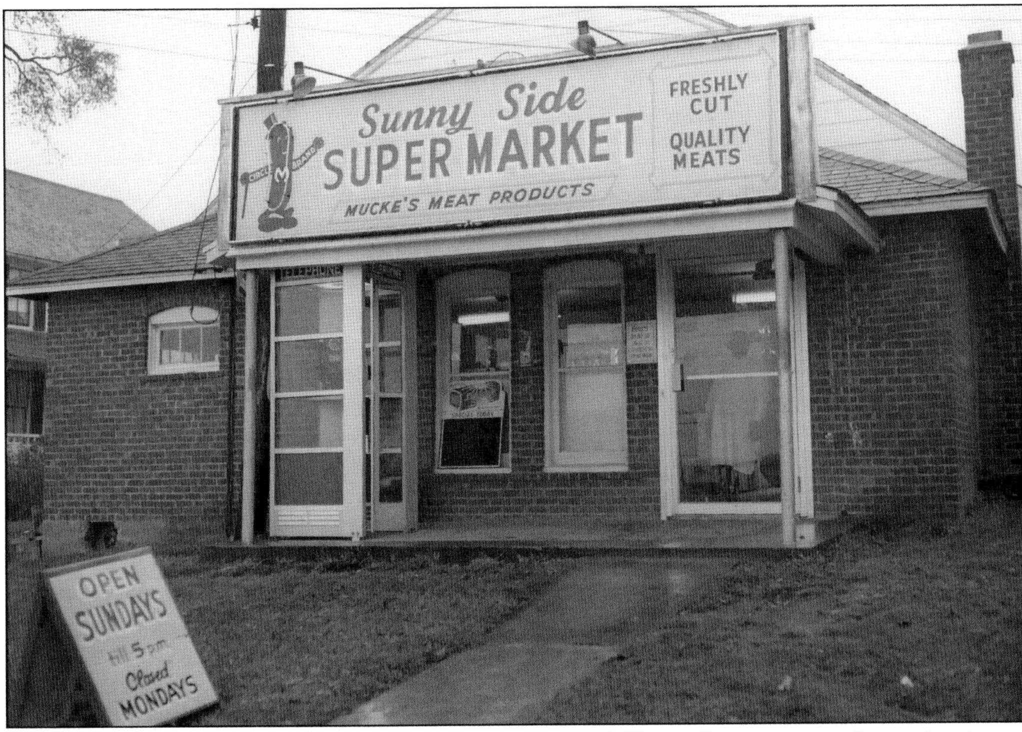

Frank and Helen Petraitis owned Sunnyside Market on Sullivan Avenue across from what is now Geissler's Plaza. Shown here in the late 1940s or early 1950s, the store was well known for its selection of penny candy and for the butcher shop where Frank Petraitis made his own sausage. It was one of the only shops open on Sundays, and children stocked up on candy after church. (Henry Adams Collection, WMLM.)

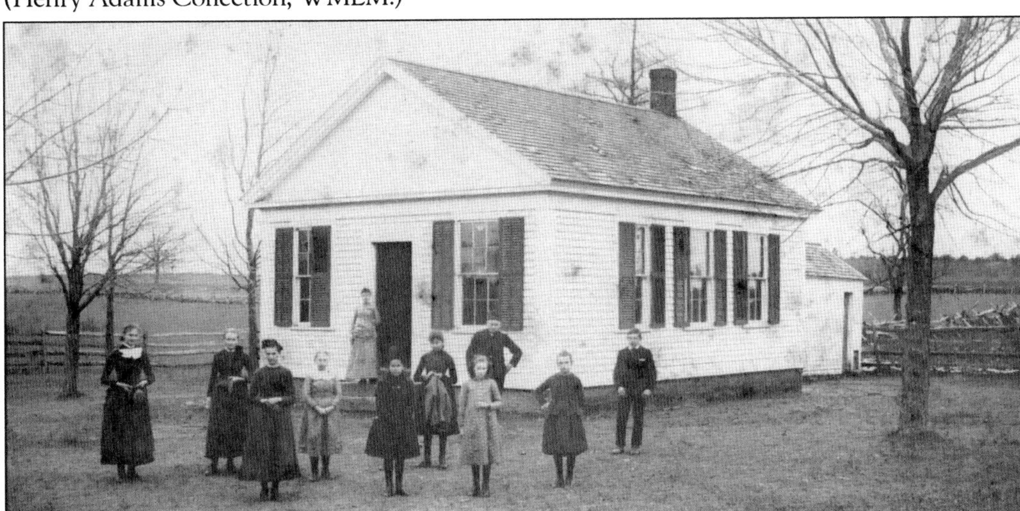

The Dart Hill Road schoolhouse, also known as the District 9 schoolhouse, was built in 1860 and replaced a previous schoolhouse on the same site. The 1860 building, shown here around 1870, was a small, one-room structure near the intersection with Niederwerfer Road and served as a school until Wapping Grammar School opened. It still exists as a private residence, with significant additions. (Frank Niederwerfer.)

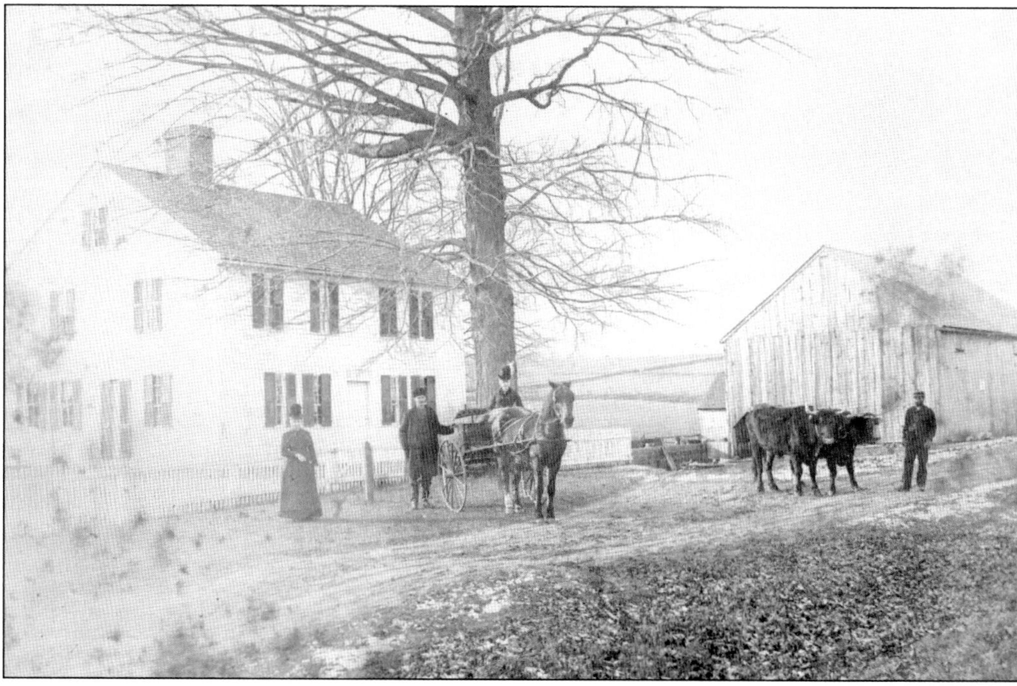

In the fall of 1885, Albert C. Dart bought a house and farm on what is now called Dart Hill Road. The following year, he married Hattie L. Skinner and moved her, her mother Harriet Dart Skinner, and her grandmother Merion Walker Dart to live with him. This photograph shows (from left to right) Harriet, Albert, Hattie, and Sam Chappel around 1886. (Frank Niederwerfer.)

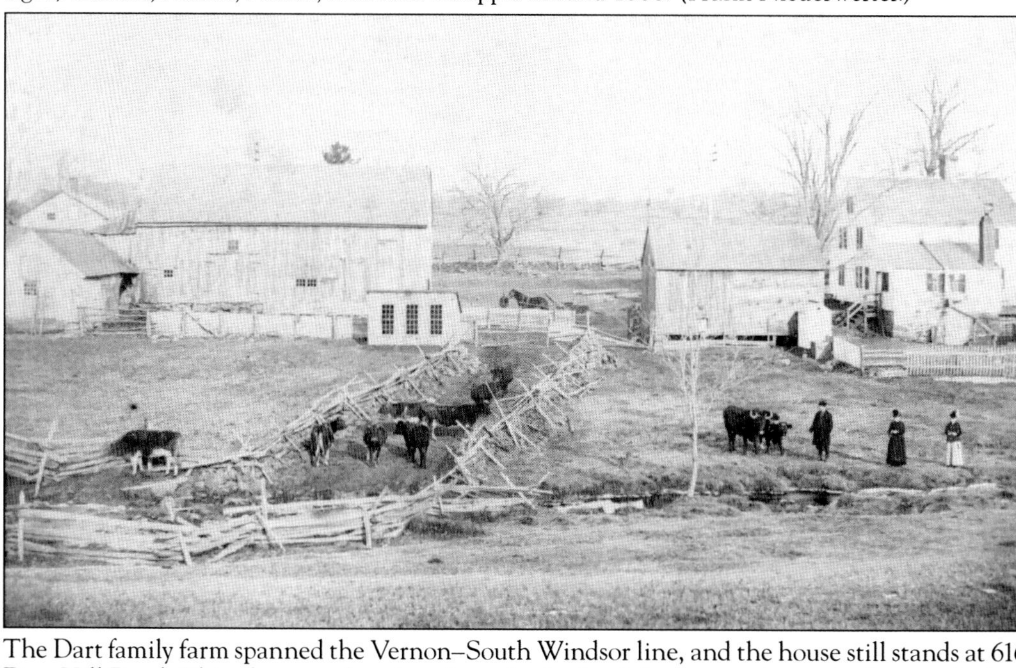

The Dart family farm spanned the Vernon–South Windsor line, and the house still stands at 616 Dart Hill Road. This photograph, taken from the back of the house, shows the barns, chicken coop, and cows, as well as the watercourse that crossed the property and gave the farm its name: Bonny Brook Farm. (Frank Niederwerfer.)

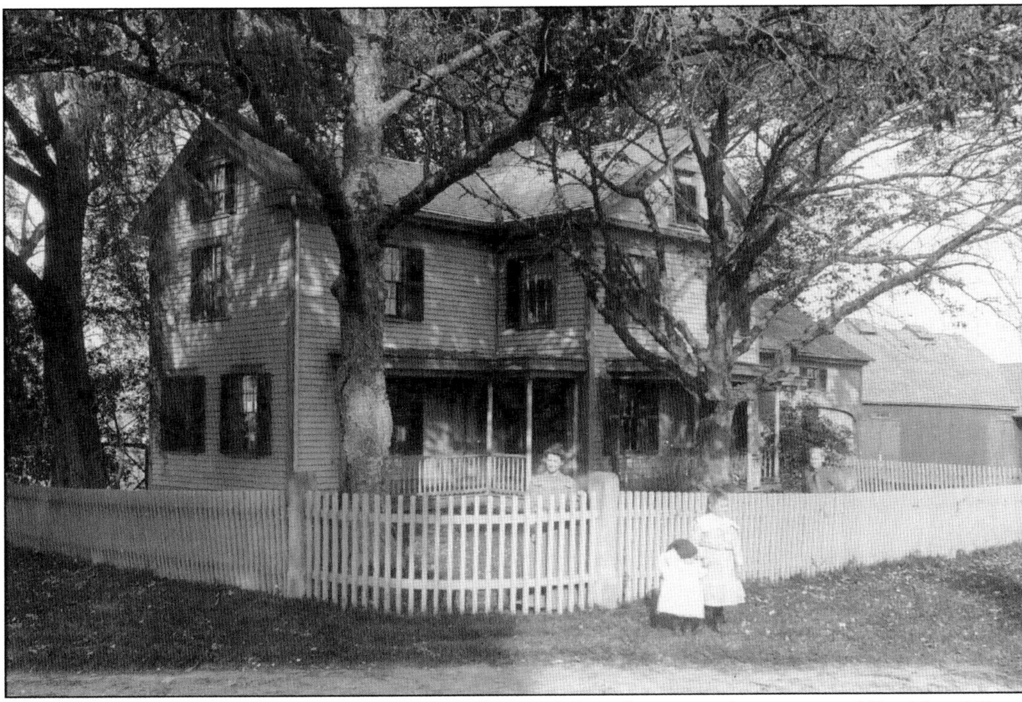

Above, Buckland family members stand in front of their home at the corner of Buckland Road and Deming Street in 1903. A 1982 newspaper article claimed that the house at 395 Buckland Road was haunted by the ghost of Clynton Buckland, the toddler in this photograph. Clynton grew up to be a farmer and practical joker, and the hauntings were said to be of a humorous sort. Below, Clynton Buckland (1900–1970), farmer and purported ghost, crouches in the field with his potato crop around 1940. In addition to farming, Buckland served in the Connecticut state legislature from 1951 to 1957. (Both, SWHS.)

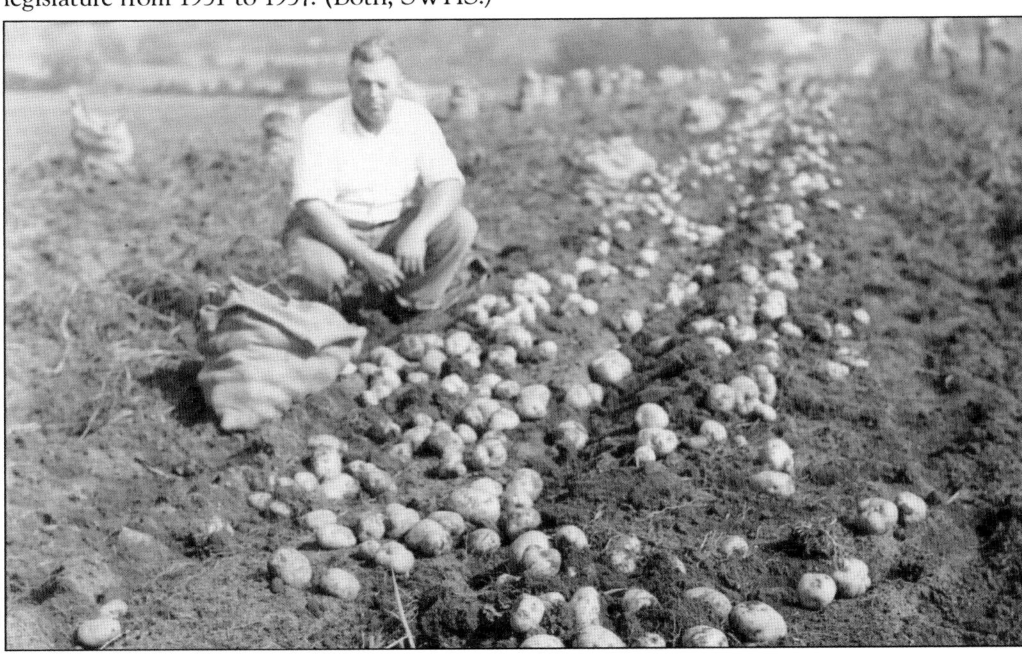

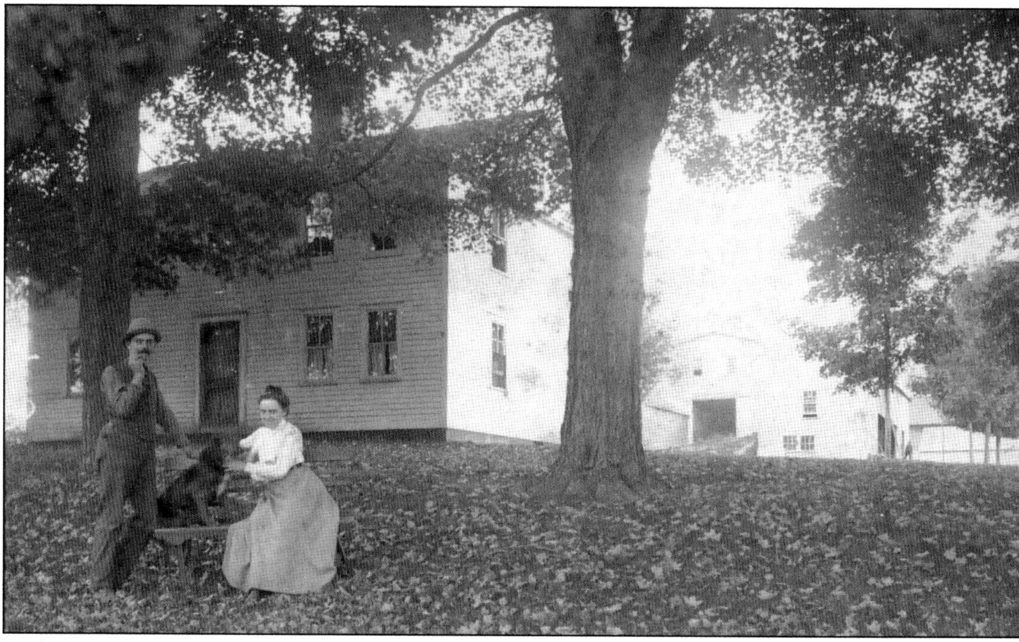

Walter N. Foster and his sister Naomi Foster and their dog sit in front of their home at 90 Foster Street in 1902. The Foster family has farmed the same land since 1790 and still farms it today. The house pictured here was built in 1822 and was added onto over the years. (Photograph by A.W. and G.E. Howes Photographers, Foster family.)

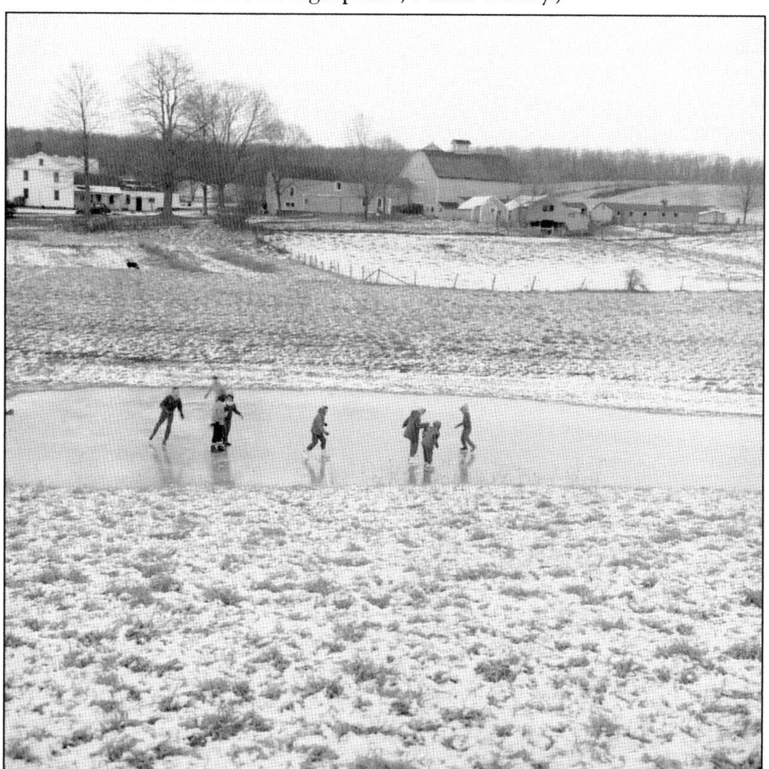

The house in the previous photograph is visible at far left in this image, taken on December 14, 1962, by a photographer for the *Manchester Herald News*. The small pond on Foster Farm has been a popular ice skating spot for generations of local children, and skaters still use it today when it ices over. (Barney Daley Collection, WMLM.)

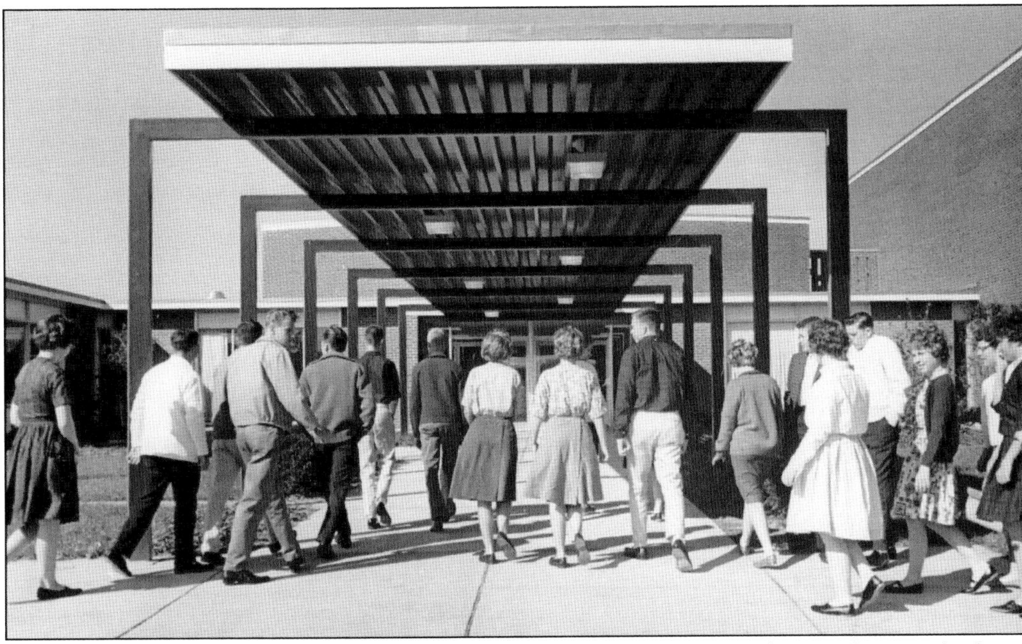

South Windsor saw rapid population growth in the mid-20th century. The population, which was under 3,000 in 1940, ballooned to over 9,000 by 1960, and Ellsworth Memorial High School on Main Street was straining at the seams. In 1963, a new South Windsor High School opened on Nevers Road in Wapping. (Photograph by Morton J. Boardman for the *Hartford Times*, Henry Adams Collection, WMLM.)

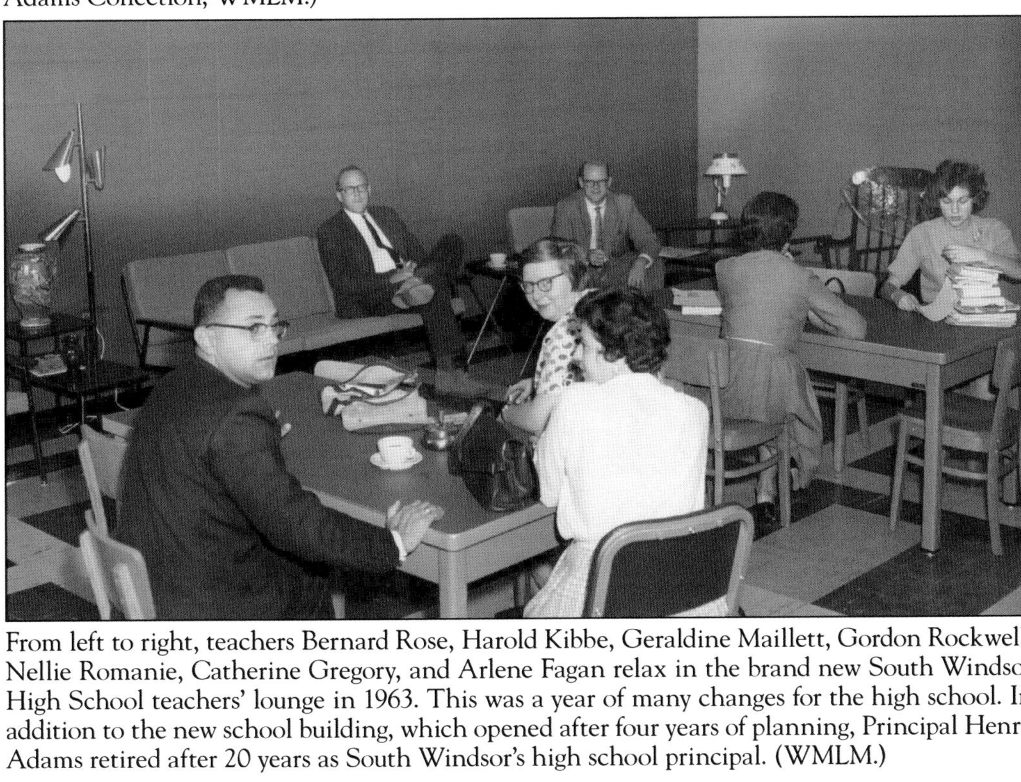

From left to right, teachers Bernard Rose, Harold Kibbe, Geraldine Maillett, Gordon Rockwell, Nellie Romanie, Catherine Gregory, and Arlene Fagan relax in the brand new South Windsor High School teachers' lounge in 1963. This was a year of many changes for the high school. In addition to the new school building, which opened after four years of planning, Principal Henry Adams retired after 20 years as South Windsor's high school principal. (WMLM.)

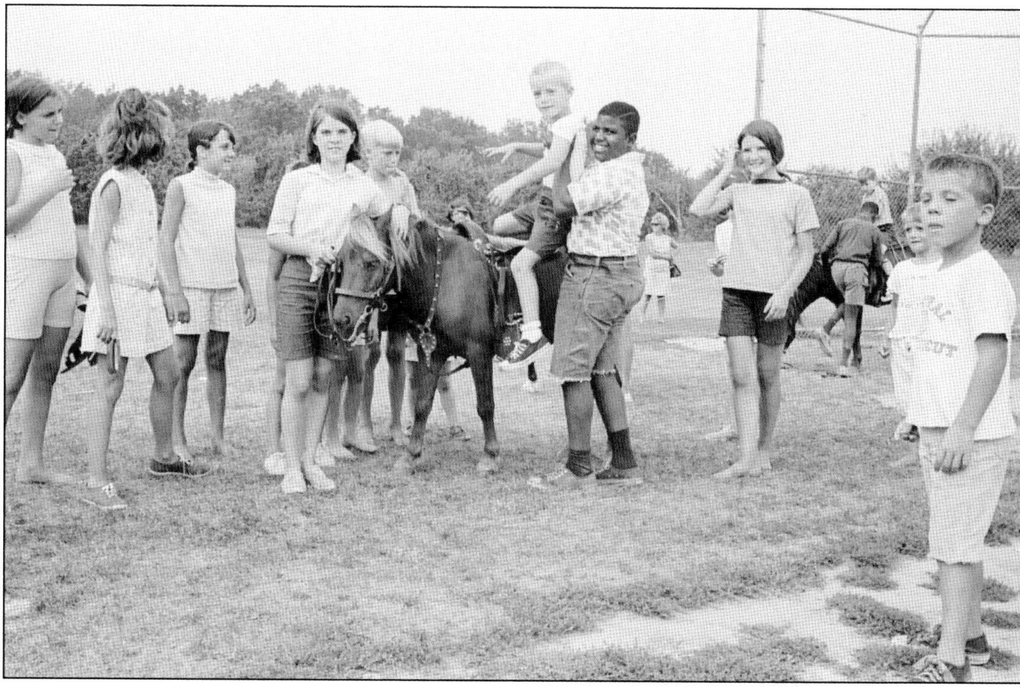

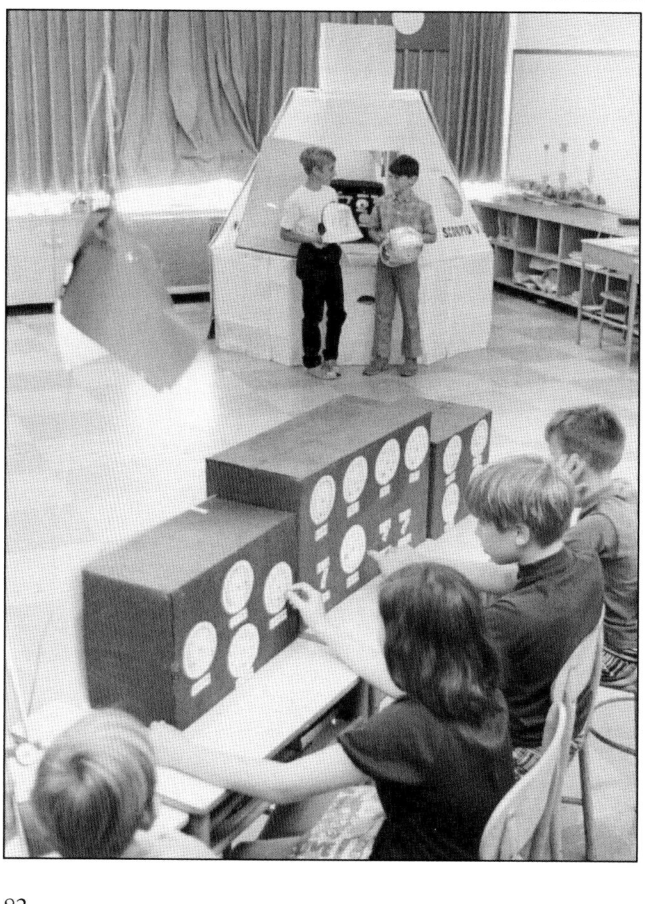

South Windsor's present elementary and middle schools were built in the 1950s and 1960s to accommodate the expanding population. Wapping Elementary School was built in 1953, Pleasant Valley School in 1958, Philip R. Smith (originally called Avery Street School) in 1959, Orchard Hill in 1964, Eli Terry in 1965, and Timothy Edwards Middle School in 1968. Here, children play at an Orchard Hill School carnival in August 1968. (Photograph by the *Manchester Herald*, Barney Daley Collection, WMLM.)

In 1971, Wapping Elementary students, perhaps inspired by South Windsor scientists' involvement with the Apollo moon missions (see page 96), simulated their own space mission with a lunar module and control room they constructed in their classroom. (Photograph by Albert E. Buceivicius for the *Manchester Herald*, Barney Daley Collection, WMLM.)

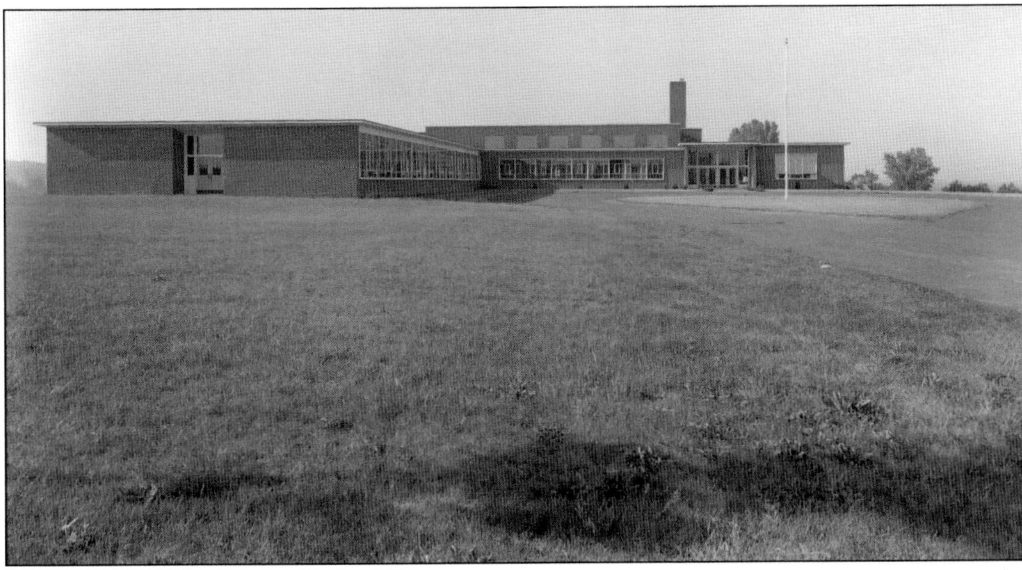

Wapping Elementary School on Ayers Road originally housed kindergarten through eighth grades. Aside from simply finding space for all South Windsor's new students, the town annual reports from the 1950s and 1960s include semi-panicked reports from the district superintendent about the difficulty of recruiting enough teachers each year to keep up with demand. (Photograph by Ellsworth Fairbanks, Barney Daley Collection, WMLM.)

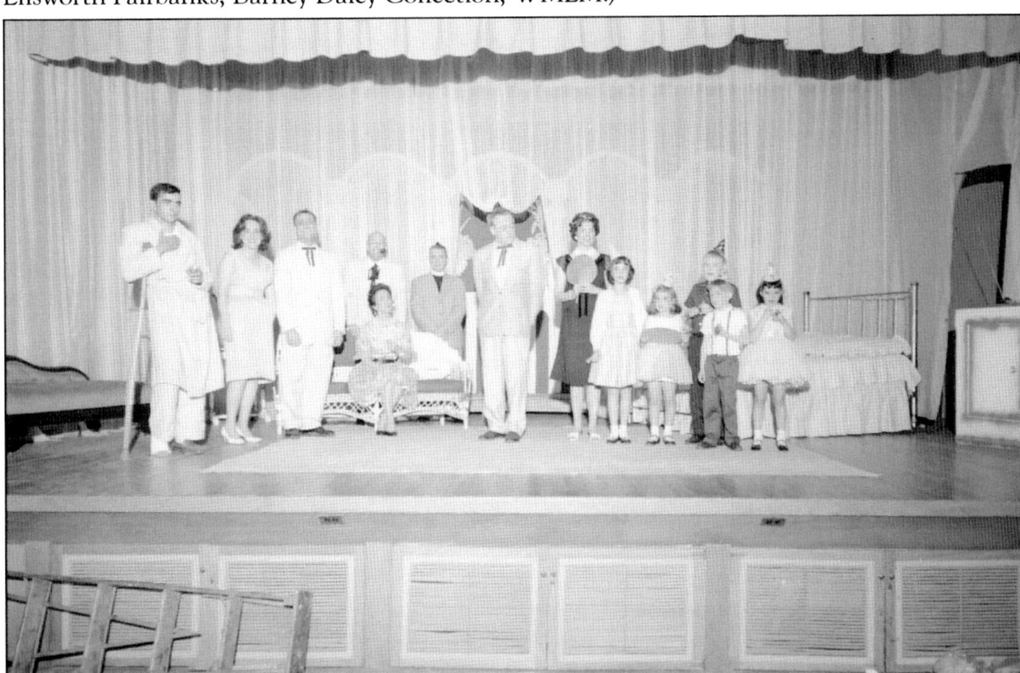

The South Windsor Country Players, a community theater troupe, held their first meeting in 1960 and staged their first play in 1961. This photograph from 1962 shows the cast of Tennessee Williams's play *Cat on a Hot Tin Roof*, which was performed at Wapping Elementary School. The troupe usually staged two plays a year until 1973, when it apparently disbanded. (Photograph by Ellsworth Fairbanks, WMLM.)

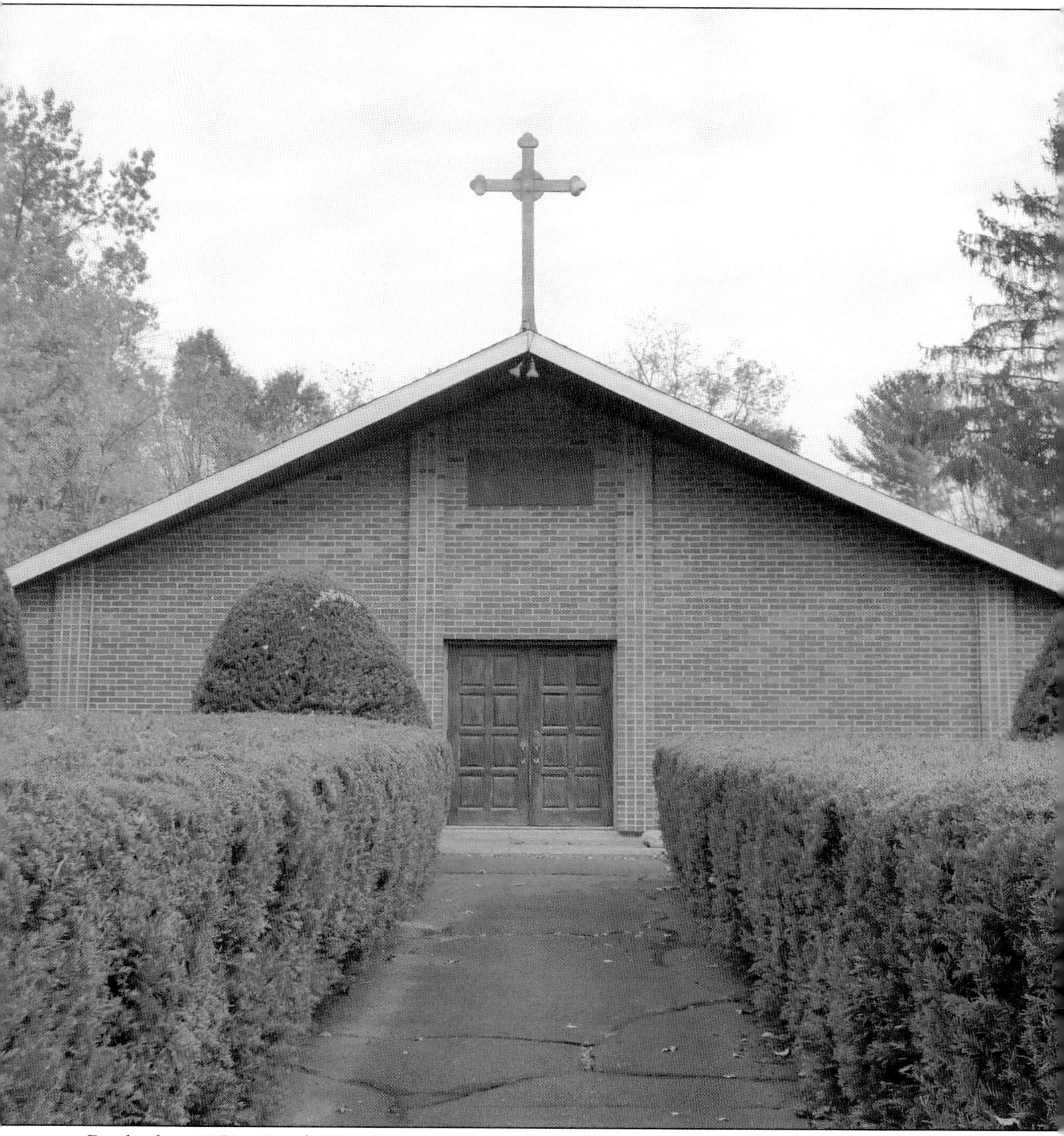

By the late 1950s, South Windsor's Jewish residents had gotten tired of traveling to surrounding communities to worship. They formed Congregation Beth Hillel in 1960 and held services for four years in the Wapping Community Church before building their first temple in 1964 at 1001 Foster Street Extension. By the 1990s, the congregation had outgrown the small brick building, and in 2000, the temple moved to a new, larger location on Governor's Highway. The old building now houses St. Lawrence Roman Catholic Church. (Photograph by Claire Lobdell.)

Four

Business and Industry

Some of South Windsor's most industrious days happened before the advent of photography. During the 18th century, Main Street was home to prominent clockmakers Daniel Burnap and Eli Terry, as well the talented yet morally suspect cabinetmaker Eliphalet Chapin, who fled town after being named in a lawsuit as the father of a child born out of wedlock. There were also shipyards along the banks of the Connecticut River building vessels that would sail between the United States and the Caribbean.

By the time photography took off in the mid-19th century, South Windsor's non-agricultural business was mostly limited to small manufacturing shops that employed a handful of workers, along with brick kilns and small grist, paper, cider, and sawmills. Unlike nearby towns that had button or silk factories, until the 20th century, it would have been hard to find a South Windsor manufacturing business with more than 20 employees.

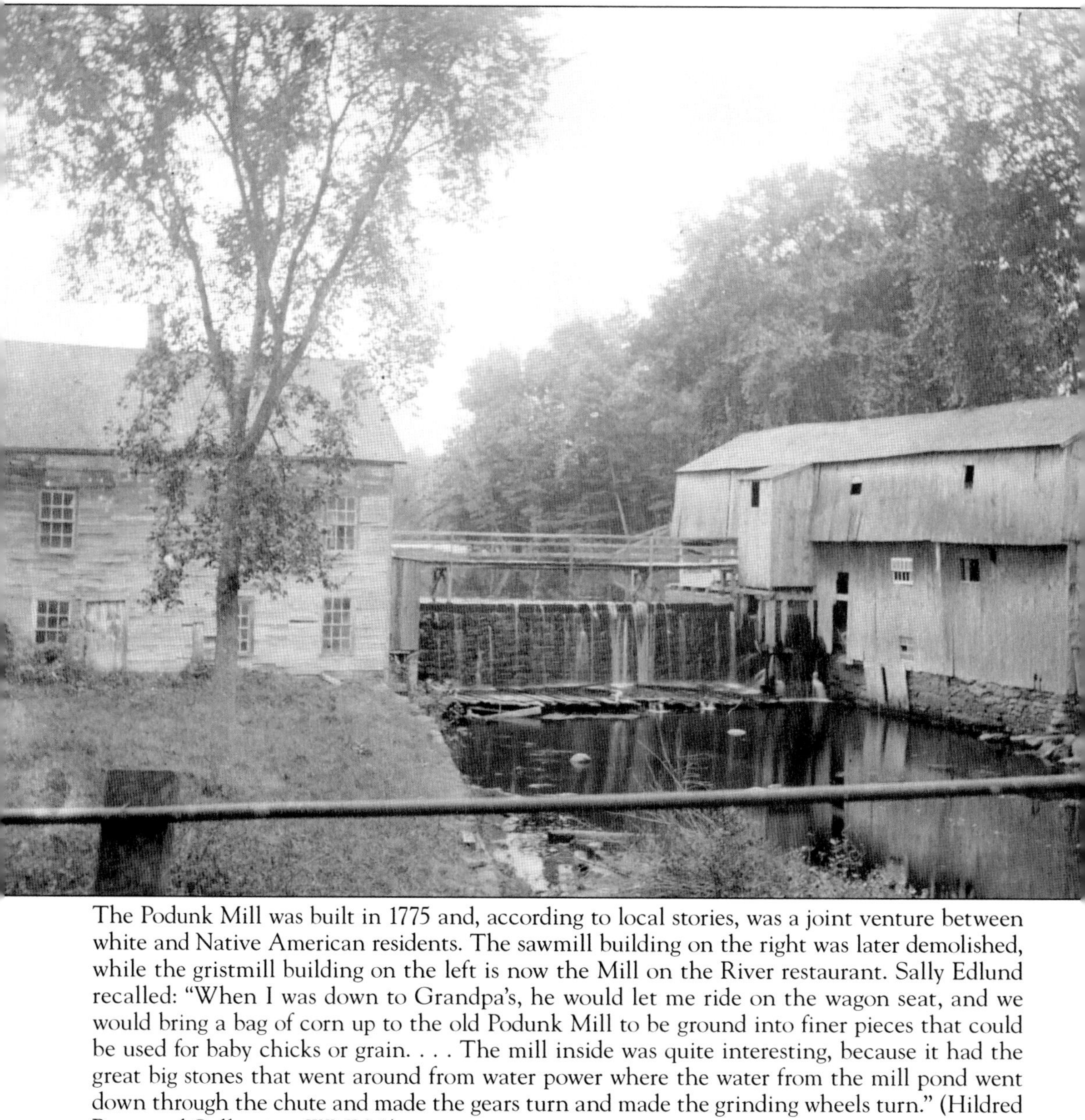

The Podunk Mill was built in 1775 and, according to local stories, was a joint venture between white and Native American residents. The sawmill building on the right was later demolished, while the gristmill building on the left is now the Mill on the River restaurant. Sally Edlund recalled: "When I was down to Grandpa's, he would let me ride on the wagon seat, and we would bring a bag of corn up to the old Podunk Mill to be ground into finer pieces that could be used for baby chicks or grain. . . . The mill inside was quite interesting, because it had the great big stones that went around from water power where the water from the mill pond went down through the chute and made the gears turn and made the grinding wheels turn." (Hildred Raymond Collection, WMLM.)

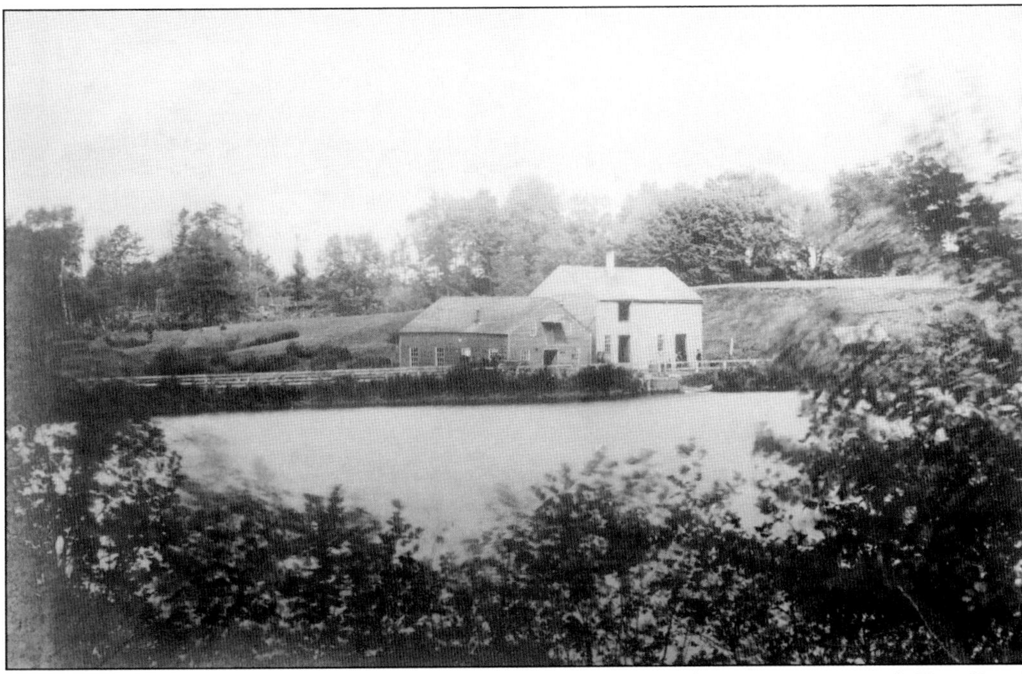

Rockwell's Mill, shown here in 1894, stood on Rye Street near the intersection with Troy Road. Dry Brook today is barely visible among all the surrounding vegetation, but in the 19th century, the brook was dammed to create a large mill pond that powered side-by-side grist and cider mills. Water from the pond would spill over waterwheels, which powered the machinery inside. While dams like this were a boon to mill owners, they were often built by the owners themselves or lay engineers without any formal training. Dam failures were common throughout the 19th century, including one in 1874 in Massachusetts on the Mill River, a tributary of the Connecticut River, that killed 139 people. (Both, Hildred Raymond Collection, WMLM.)

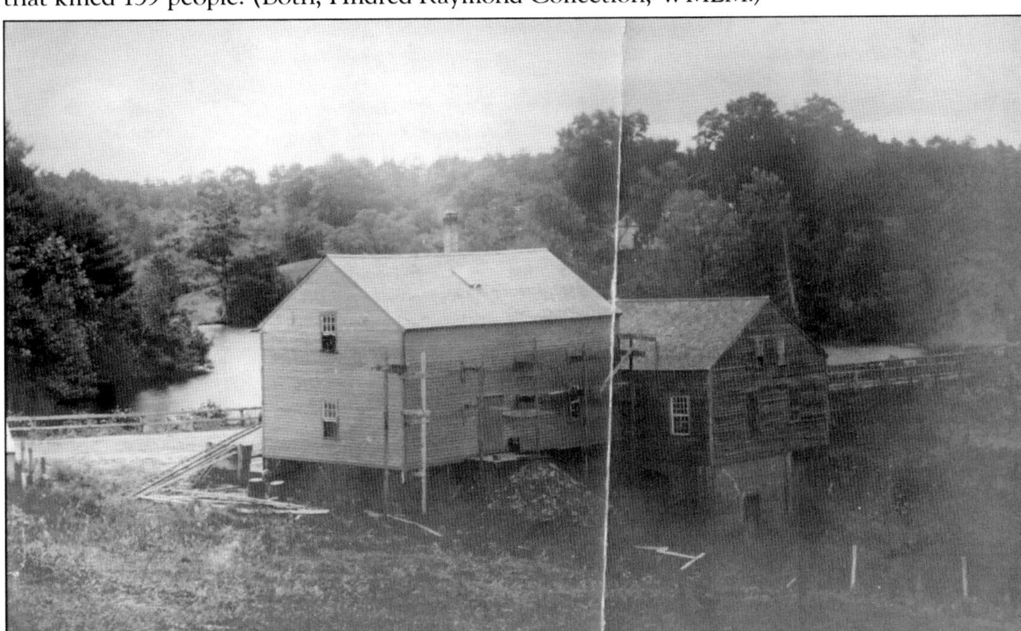

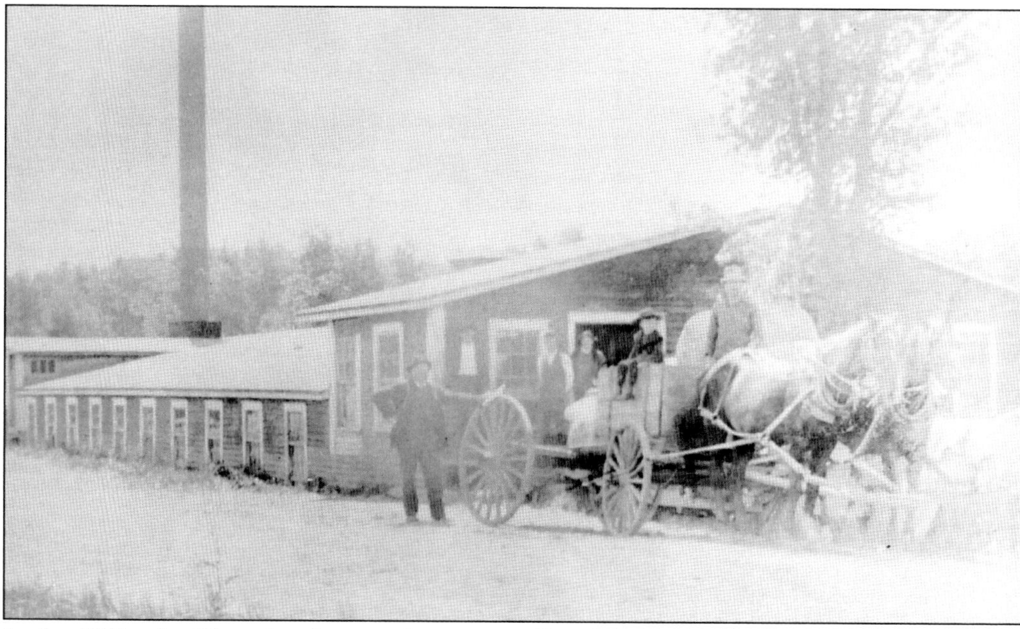

In the 1850s, the Clapp family started a paper mill on Pleasant Valley Road, then called Paper Mill Road. Powered by the dammed Podunk River, the mill made writing paper. The Clapps sold their mill in the 1870s to Conrad Wohlfart and James Gaskell, who made binder board there. After a fire, they sold the mill to Hollis G. Church in 1887. The mill suffered a second fire in 1895, and the dam burst the following night. The mill is pictured above in the 1880s, and below after the dam burst. (Both, WMLM.)

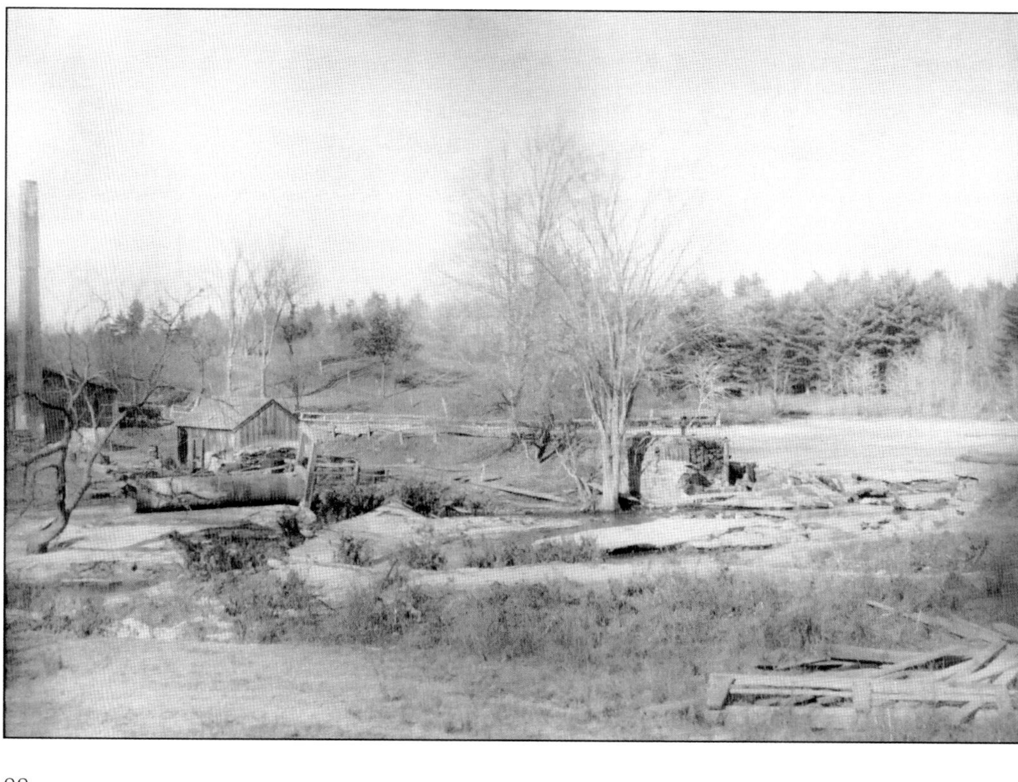

John A. Collins started the Collins Bus Service in 1912 with a horse-drawn sleigh that took children to school. In this photograph, taken between 1915 and 1919, his wife, Mabel Johnson Collins, stands in the front of the winter sleigh-bus with some of her passengers behind her. (Collins family.)

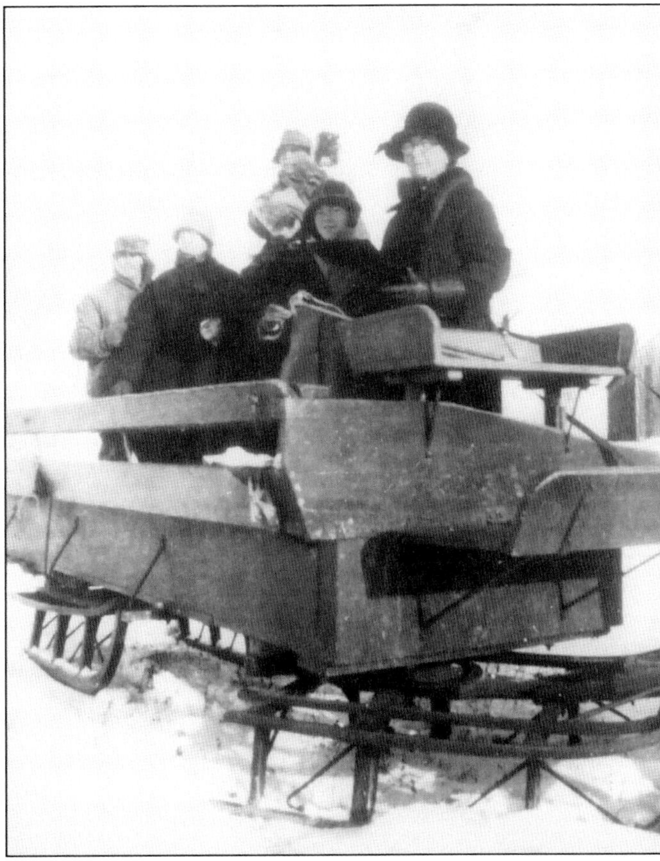

John A. Collins sits at the wheel of his bus around 1920. Generations of South Windsor children took Collins buses to school. During World War II, the company shuttled Pratt and Whitney Aircraft Company workers to the plant in East Hartford, and later transported tobacco workers to area farms. The company is still run today by Collins family members as Collins Bus Service/Post Road Stages. (Collins family.)

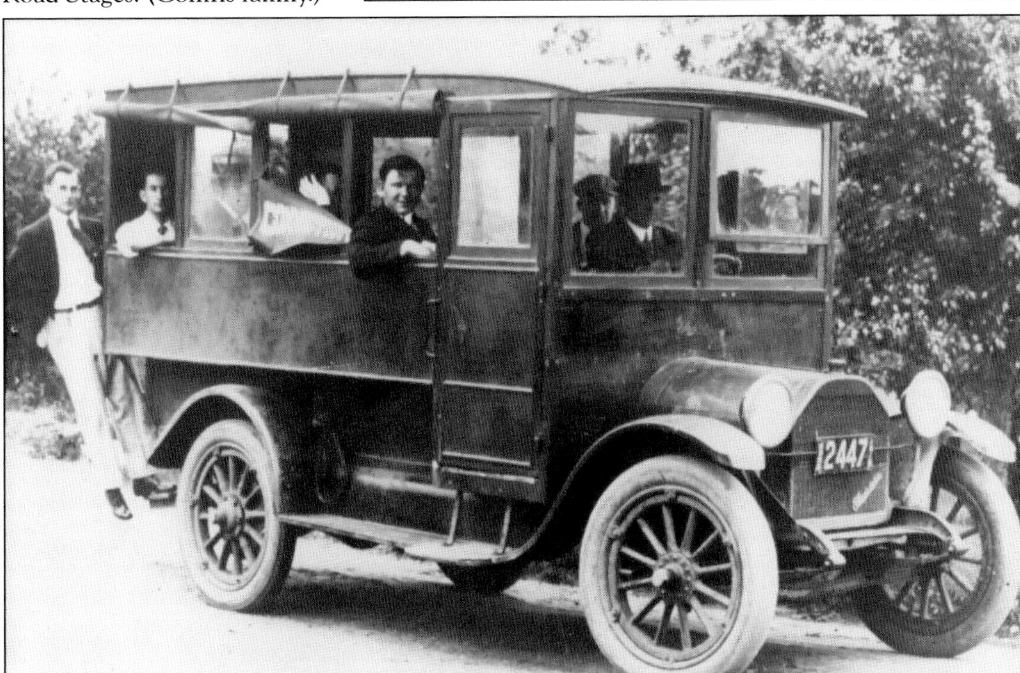

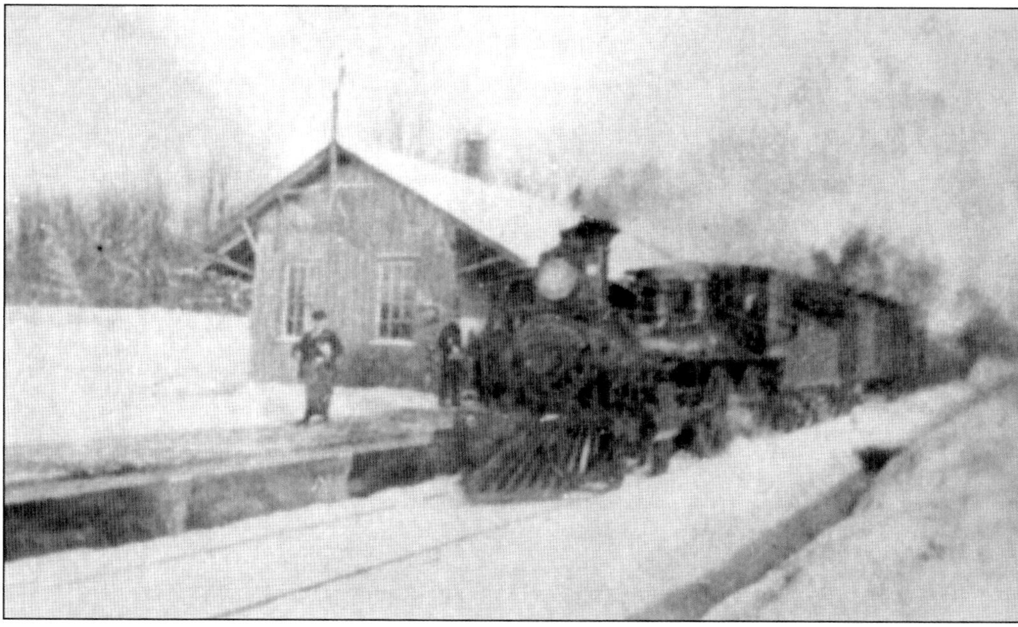

In 1876, a railroad line was built from Hartford to East Windsor and beyond, with two stations in South Windsor: one on East Windsor Hill near the intersection of what are now Sullivan Avenue and Route 5, and one near what is now the corner of Pleasant Valley Road and Route 5. This 1888 photograph shows stationmaster William B. Parmelee at the East Windsor Hill station. (Hildred Raymond Collection, WMLM.)

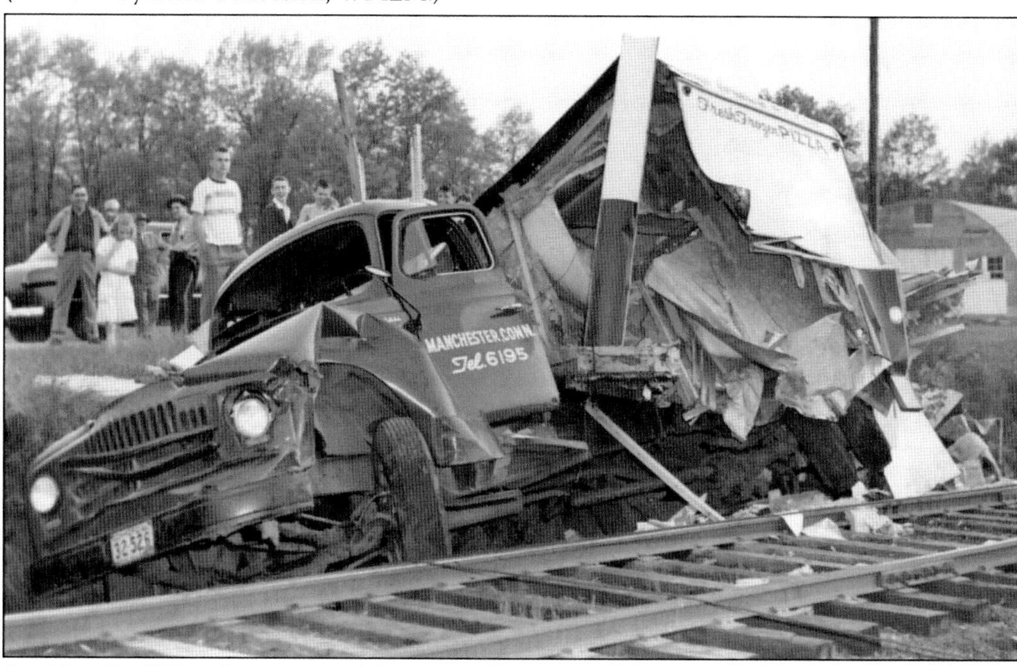

On May 11, 1953, a frozen-pizza delivery truck was struck by a train at the Troy Road railroad crossing near East Windsor Hill. The truck driver escaped with injuries to his shoulder, but his vehicle was totaled, and pizza pies were strewn around the tracks and nearby grass. (*Manchester Evening Herald* Clippings and Photograph Collection, WMLM.)

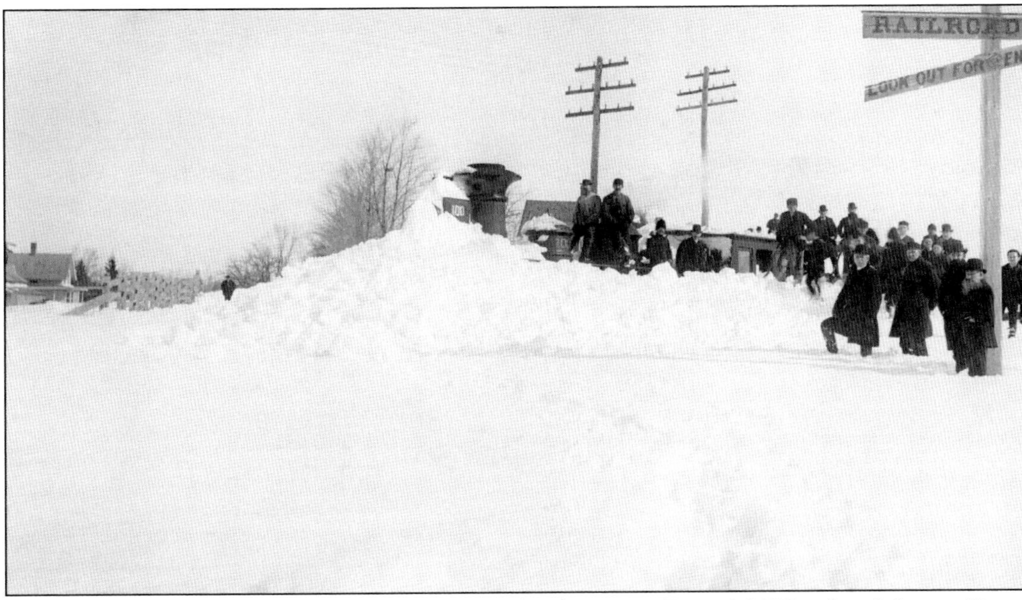

The railroad depot at Pleasant Valley Road—earlier known as Paper Mill Road and then as Depot Road—and what is now Route 5 is shown here in two different winters. Above, a group of men and boys stand by the snow-covered station and tracks around 1900. Below, the railroad depot, also a Western Union telegraph office, stands alone in the snow in 1938. (Above, Hildred Raymond Collection; below, photograph by Bernard McLaughlin, Barney Daley Collection, WMLM.)

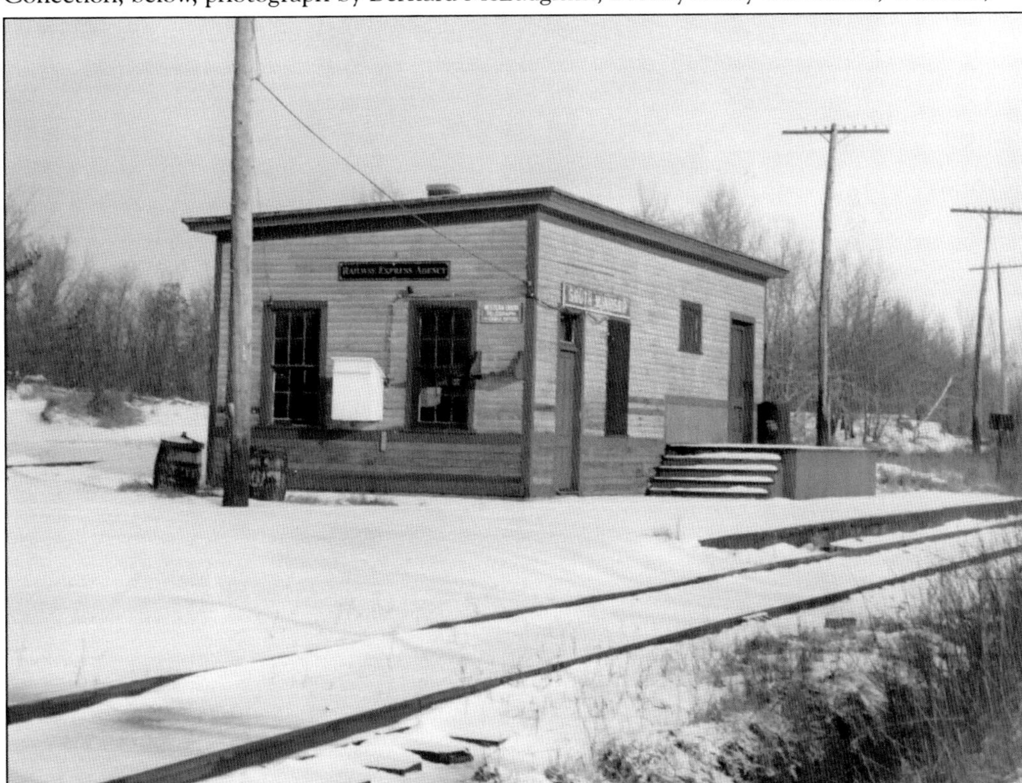

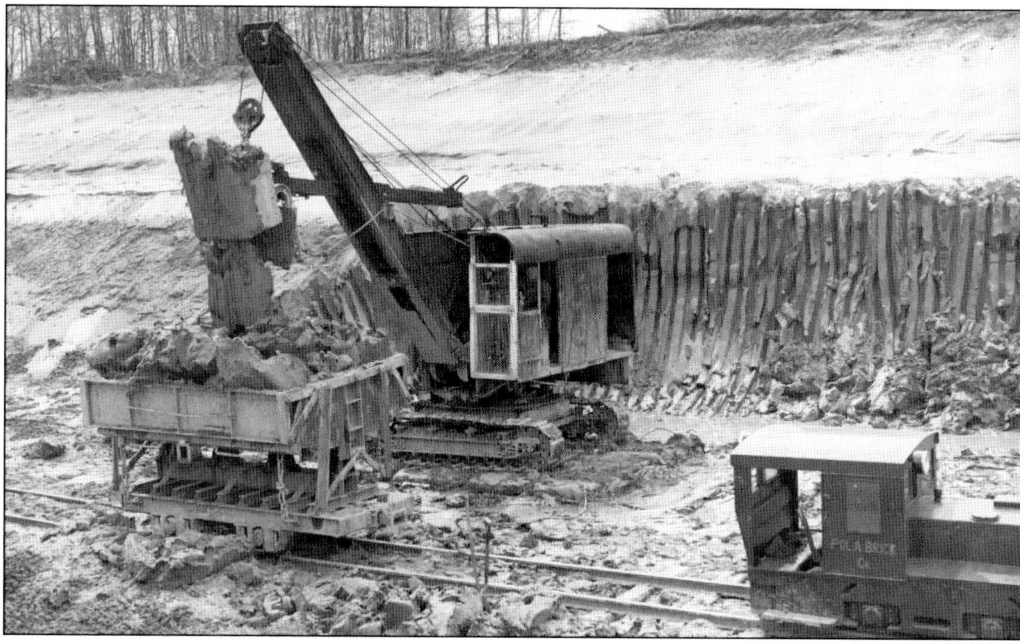

Brickmaking was one of the earliest industries here. Native Americans used local clay for pottery, shards of which are often found in farm fields. Some brick houses in town are made from clay dug on-site, and 19th-century maps of the town are dotted with the locations of commercial brick kilns. This photograph shows an excavator loading clay into a railcar at the Pola brickworks around 1940. (SWHS.)

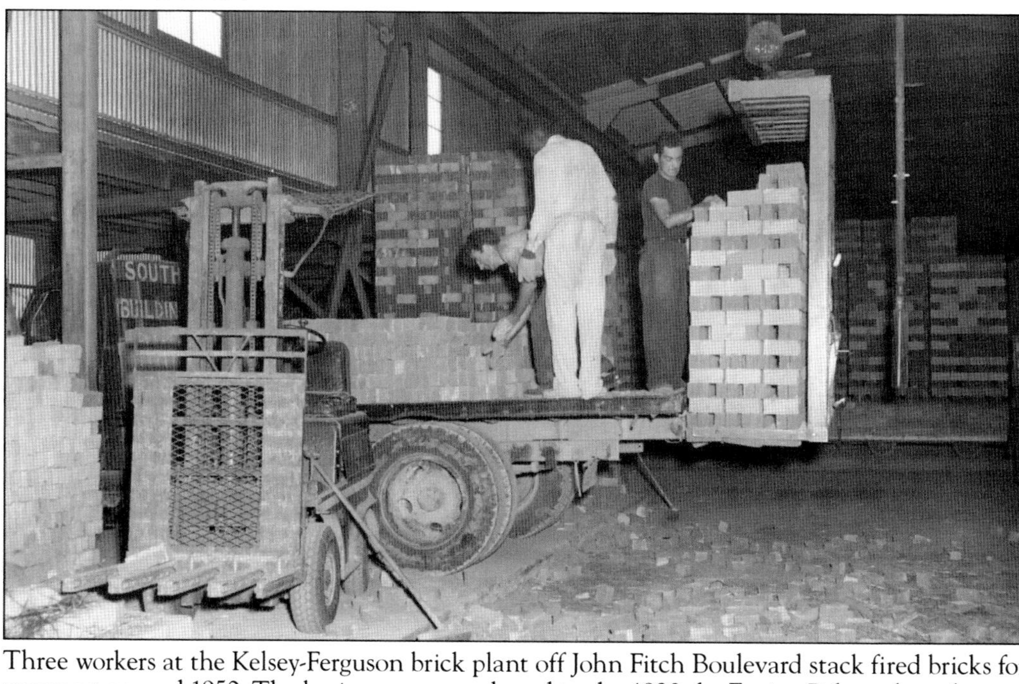

Three workers at the Kelsey-Ferguson brick plant off John Fitch Boulevard stack fired bricks for transport around 1950. The business was purchased in the 1920s by Enrico Pola and was known as the Pola brickworks. In the 1950s, it was sold to the Kelsey-Ferguson Company, which in turn was sold to Redland Brick in the 1990s. (SWHS.)

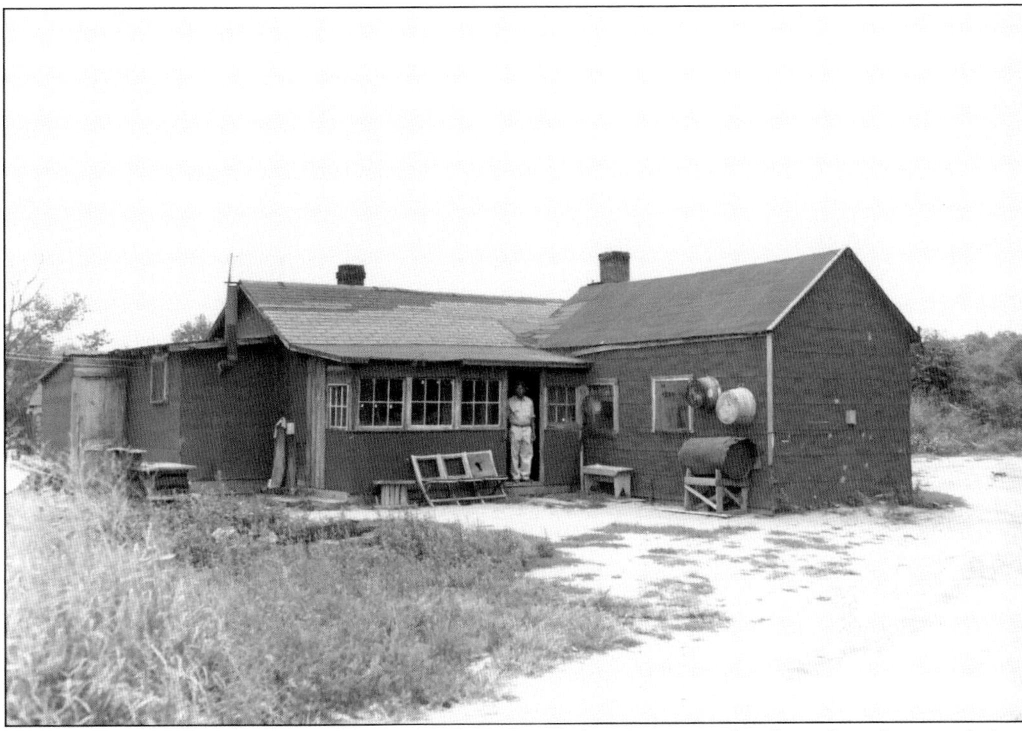

In the 1940s and 1950s, some African American Kelsey-Ferguson brickyard workers and their families lived on-site in company-owned homes that often lacked indoor plumbing and were poorly heated. Children who lived at the brickyards attended Union District School. The house above was the home of Raymond and Ann Baxter Newbold. There was also a small church on the site, the Church of God in Christ, which can be seen below with an outhouse next to it. (Both, SWHS.)

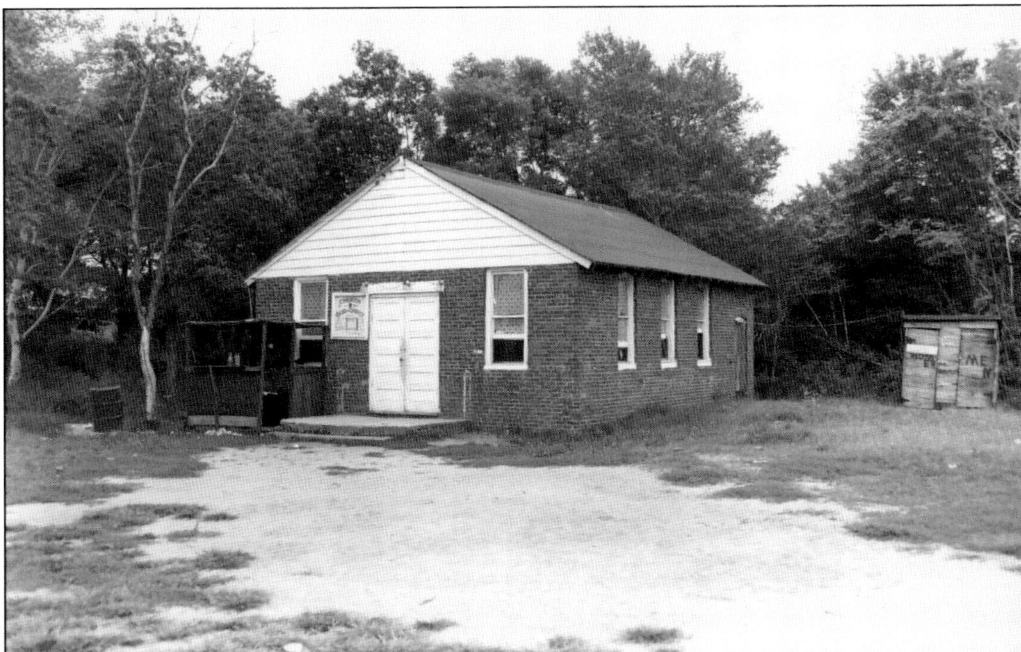

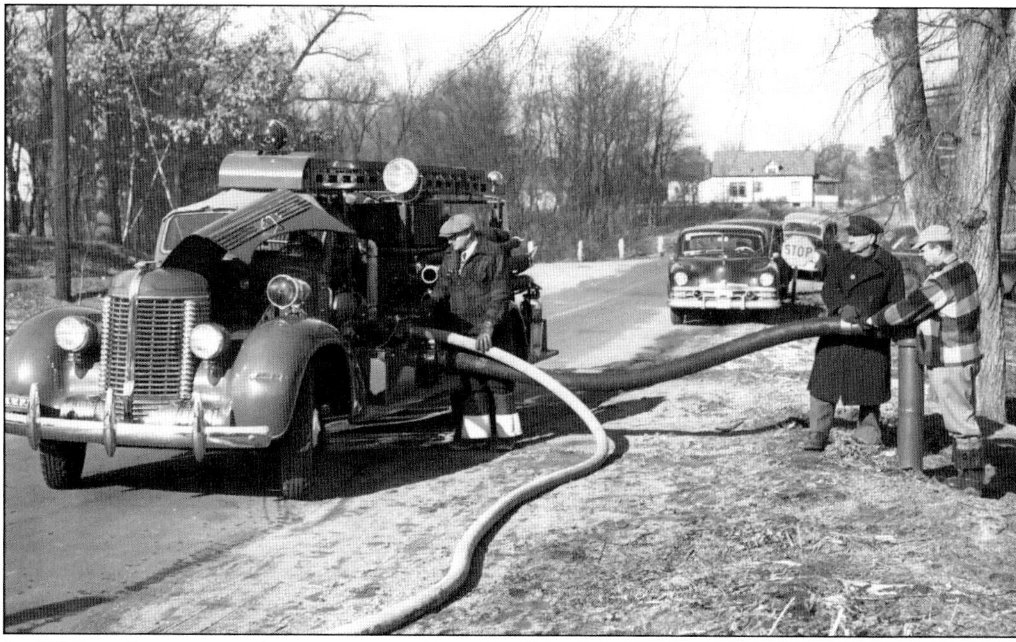

In 1938, with an expanding town population and citizens increasingly unhappy about the long wait times for fire engines to arrive from surrounding towns, the South Windsor Volunteer Fire Department was established. Above, around 1945, Chief George Enes stands next to the department's original fire engine no. 1, while Dick Jones (in plaid coat) and another firefighter stand by a hydrant. Below, members of the South Windsor Volunteer Fire Department pose around 1950 in front of the old Fire Station 3 on Sullivan Avenue (now an animal shelter). From left to right in the first row are Raymond Ellison, Raymond Hack, George Cox, Harold Dobb, Al Barbrick, and Chief Phil Crombie. (Both, Philip E. Crombie.)

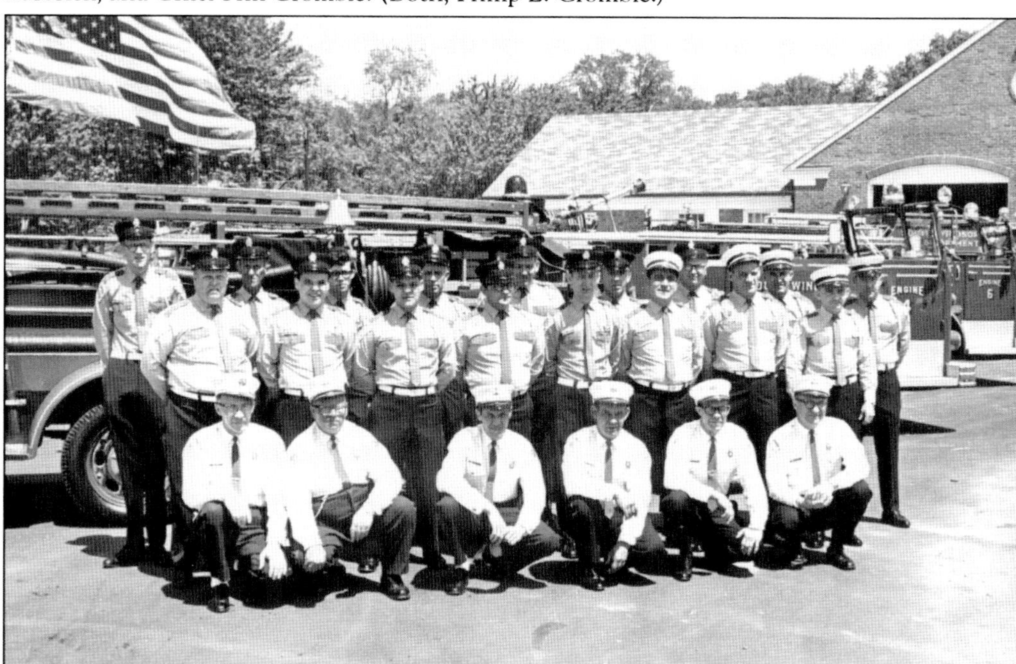

NuWay Tobacco Company was started by the Shepard family in 1955 to produce homogenized leaf cigar binder. Tim Shepard explained: "It's a process of taking tobacco by-products from the cigar manufacturers—all the tobaccos they use, so it's good tobacco. It's not taking the junk. . . . And you grind that into a talcum-powder consistency and mix it up with gums like guar gum, methyl cell gums, and make a slurry out of it, cast it on the belt, run it through dryers, and bring it off in a sheet form." In 1960, the company opened a plant on Sullivan Avenue that employed close to 100 workers at its height. At right, a NuWay employee watches a tobacco pulverizing and grinding machine. Below, Leo Chouinard (far right) and other employees watch a slitting machine. (Both, NuWay Tobacco Company.)

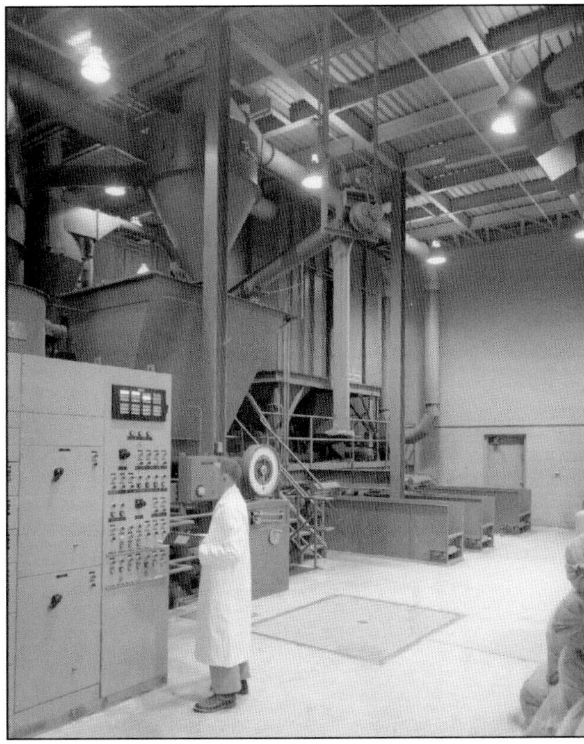

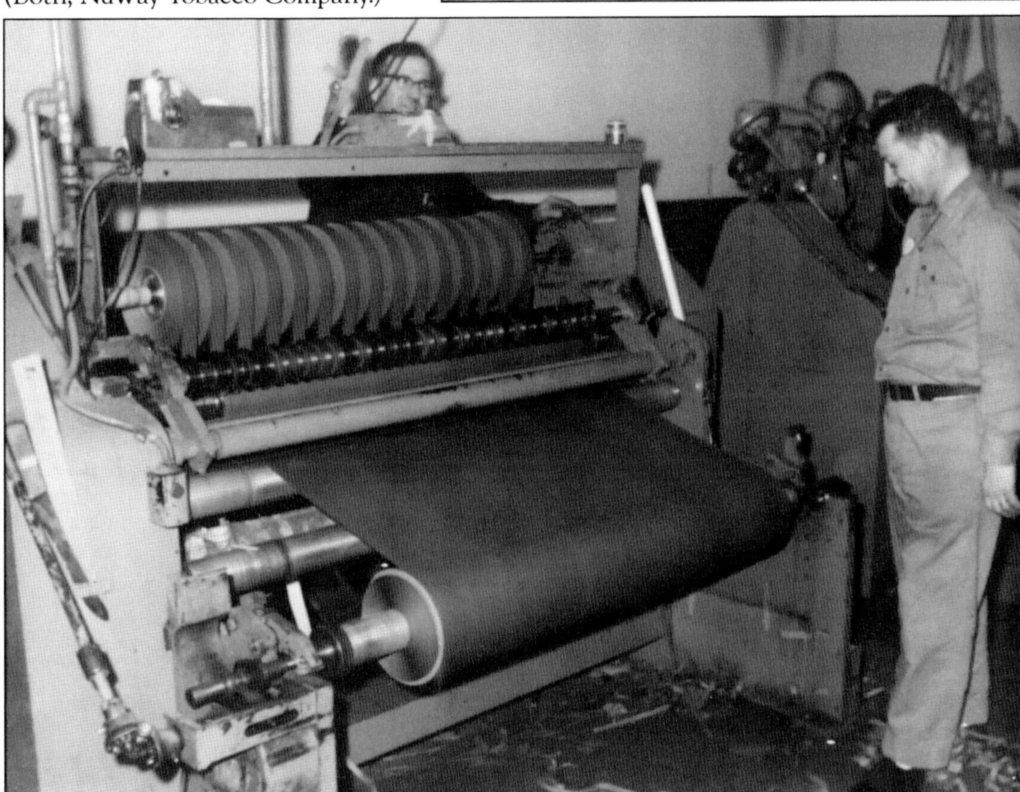

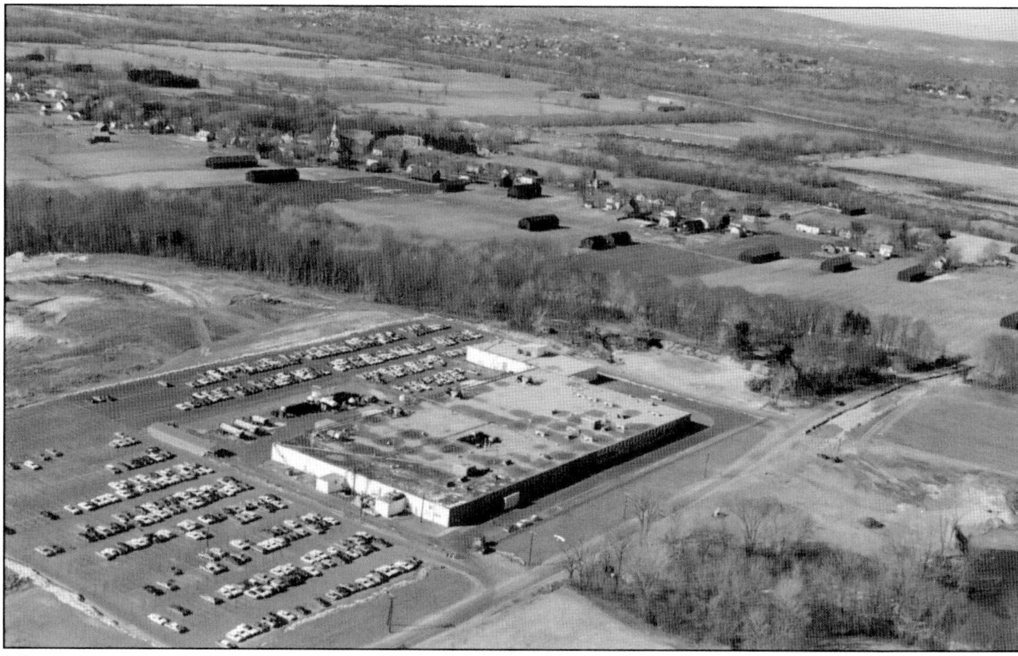

The Pratt and Whitney Aircraft Fuel Cell Operation (later renamed UTC Power) played a crucial role in manned space flight from 1966 to 2011. In a facility on Governor's Highway, employees designed the fuel cells that powered the Apollo missions starting in 1966 and all the space shuttle missions, starting in 1973. They also made fuel cells for commercial and public uses, including one installed at South Windsor High School in 2002. The company was sold in 2013. Above, high-tech and rural South Windsor are juxtaposed in this aerial view of the building taken around 1964. Below, engineers work on Apollo fuel cells in the late 1960s. (Both photographs by Pratt and Whitney staff photographers, Henry Cote.)

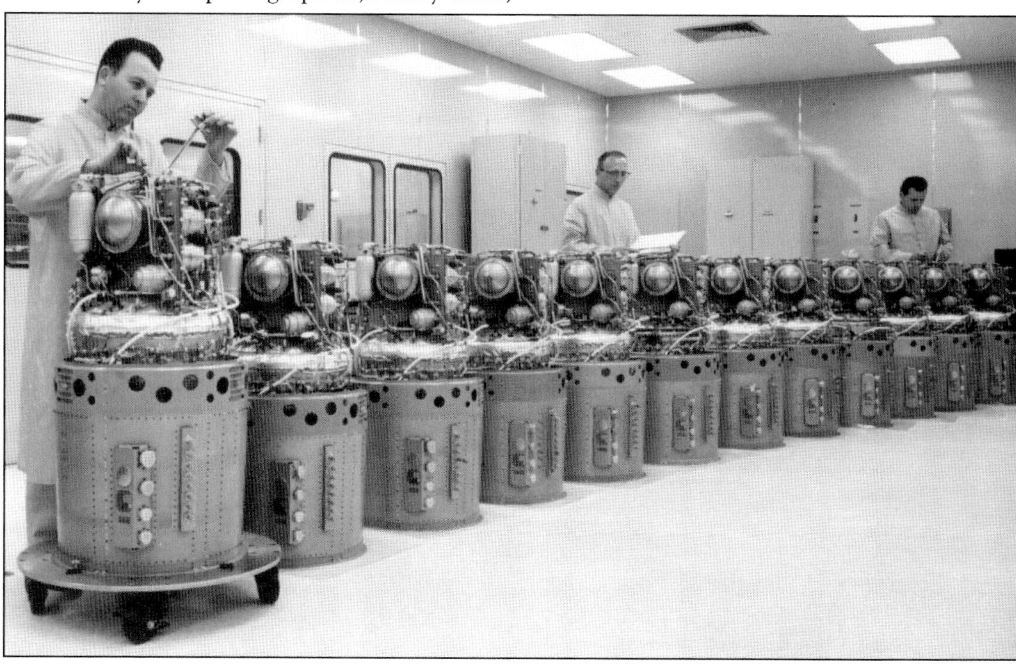

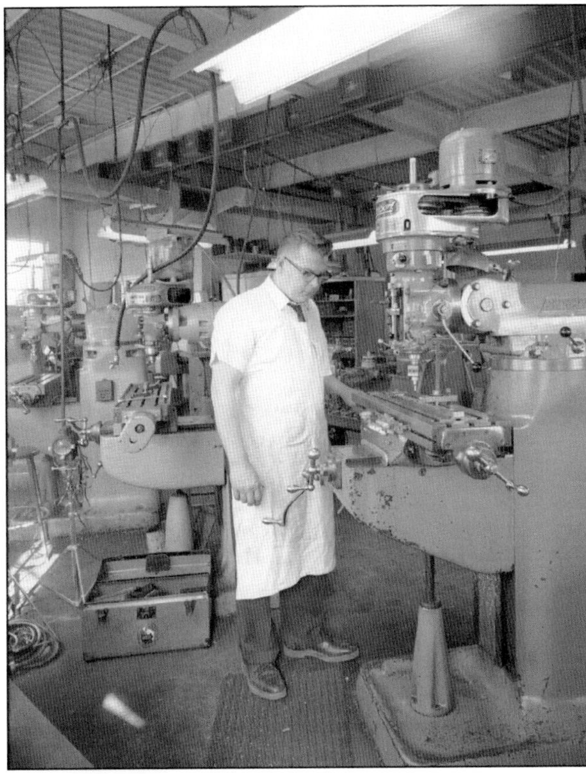

There were several machine shops throughout South Windsor from the mid-20th century on that made tools and parts for Pratt and Whitney, Sikorsky, United Technologies, and other Connecticut-based aerospace companies. Daniel Kobylanski's South Windsor Tool and Machine Shop on Pleasant Valley Road was one of these. Shown here around 1950, Kobylanski works on some of his precision machinery. (Both photographs by Ellsworth Fairbanks, Barney Daley Collection, WMLM.)

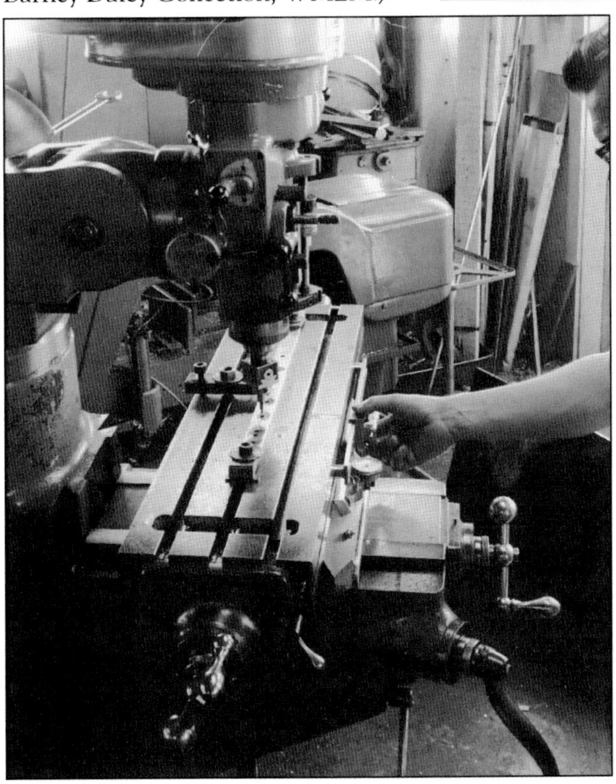

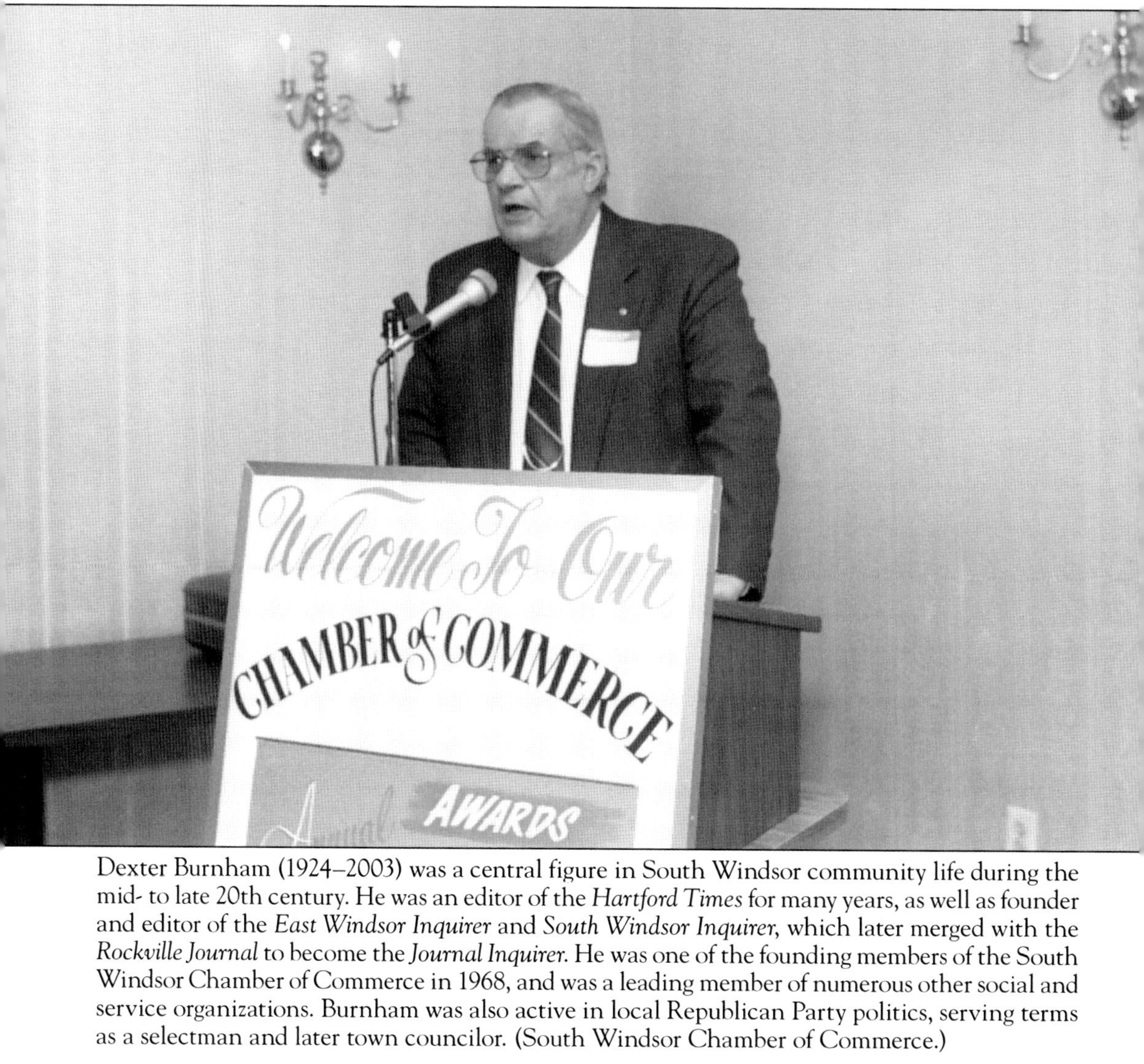

Dexter Burnham (1924–2003) was a central figure in South Windsor community life during the mid- to late 20th century. He was an editor of the *Hartford Times* for many years, as well as founder and editor of the *East Windsor Inquirer* and *South Windsor Inquirer*, which later merged with the *Rockville Journal* to become the *Journal Inquirer*. He was one of the founding members of the South Windsor Chamber of Commerce in 1968, and was a leading member of numerous other social and service organizations. Burnham was also active in local Republican Party politics, serving terms as a selectman and later town councilor. (South Windsor Chamber of Commerce.)

Five

FARMING

Generations of South Windsor families have grown tobacco on their lands, planting in the spring, harvesting in the fall, and hanging leaves in tobacco sheds with vented sides until the tobacco is fully cured. The varieties of tobacco grown here have changed through time. Native Americans smoked a type of wild tobacco native to this area, while white settlers brought up a variety from Virginia to use as pipe tobacco. As early as the beginning of the 19th century, farmers were planting a type of tobacco called shoestring that was used for cigar binders and wrappers—the outer two layers of a cigar. By the late 19th century, this had been mostly replaced by broadleaf, which local farmers still grow today. In the early 20th century, some farms also introduced Connecticut shade tobacco, which was modified from a Sumatran plant. Shade tobacco is grown under netting, which both shades the plant and creates a hotter, more humid microclimate.

Despite the prevalence of tobacco farming—and almost all South Windsor farms grew at least a few acres of tobacco at one time or another—the town has never been a monoculture. Orchards and dairy farms have rested cheek-by-jowl with poultry and sheep farms. Tobacco acreage has always been interspersed with corn, hay, potatoes, rye (for food and whiskey), and other crops to feed both people and livestock. It is only in the post–World War II era that South Windsor has shifted from a primarily agriculture-driven economy to more of a suburban bedroom community for nearby Hartford. Many farms still thrive around town, and the South Windsor Land Conservation Trust, incorporated in 1976, actively preserves undeveloped land so that generations to come can continue to enjoy open vistas along the Connecticut River and elsewhere in town.

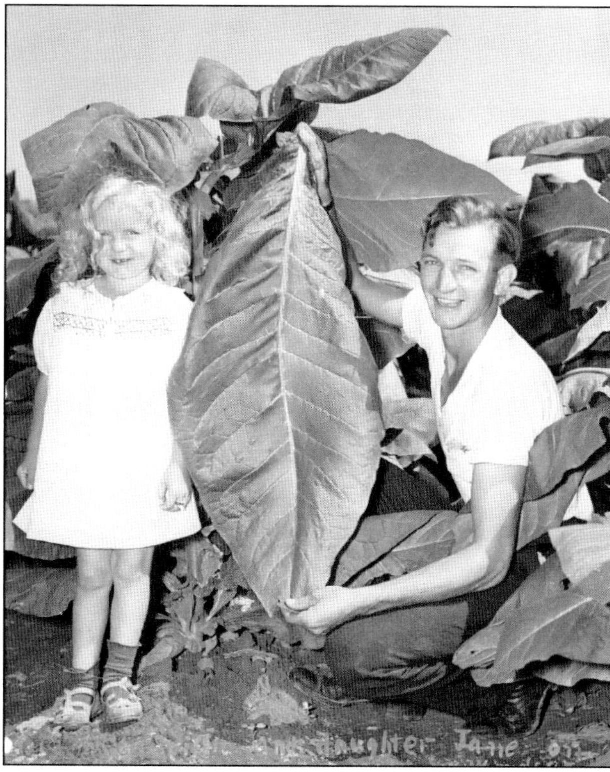

Charles G. Griffin (1906–1985) and his young daughter Jane pose in their tobacco field on Rye Street around 1940, showing just how large a leaf of broadleaf tobacco could be. Griffin was a part-owner of the Griffin-Fuller Tobacco Company, which owned shade tobacco fields in several towns, along with its own fertilizer plant. (Charles G. Griffin Collection, WMLM.)

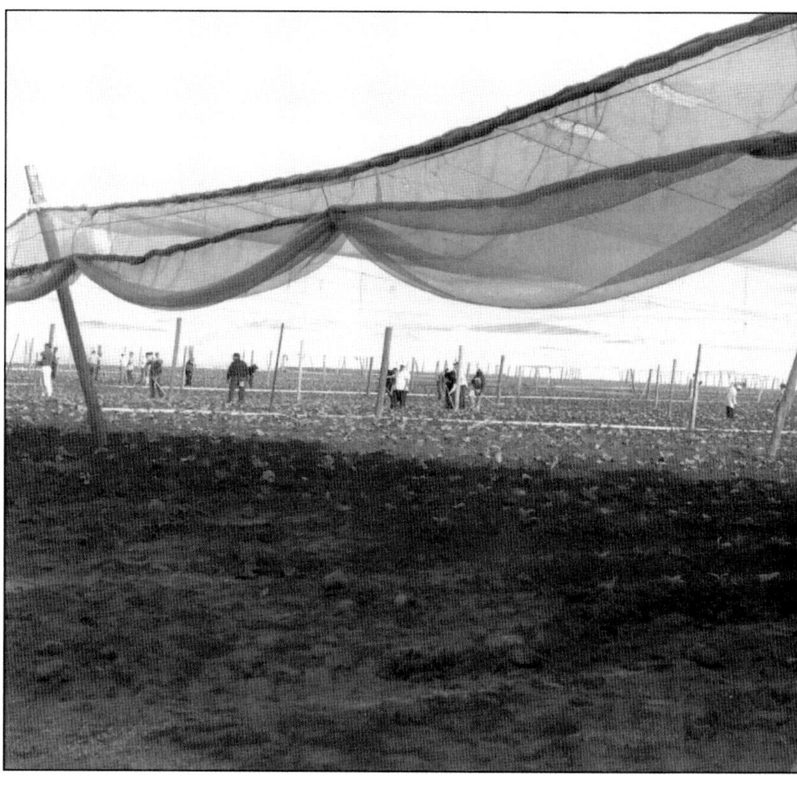

Waves of white translucent fabric ripple over fields of Connecticut shade tobacco grown by the Mulnite family. The thin cloth is held up by wooden stakes and covers the ends of the rows as well as the top to form a fully enclosed tent. (Photograph by Dexter Burnham, South Windsor Chamber of Commerce.)

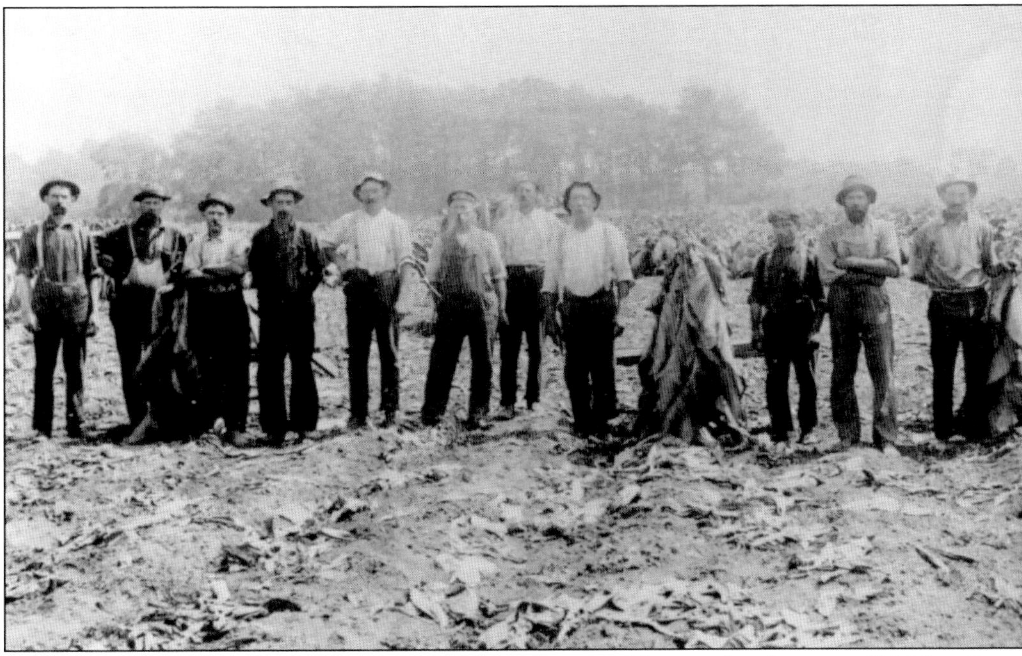

Farm workers stand in one of the Vibert family's tobacco fields near their house at 880 Main Street after harvesting tobacco in 1895. South Windsor's farmers often grew tobacco on any land they could. Joseph Vibert recalled: "We didn't have that much lawn to mow [at 880 Main Street] . . . the garden was right out the back door, but then the tobacco lot started right there." (WMLM.)

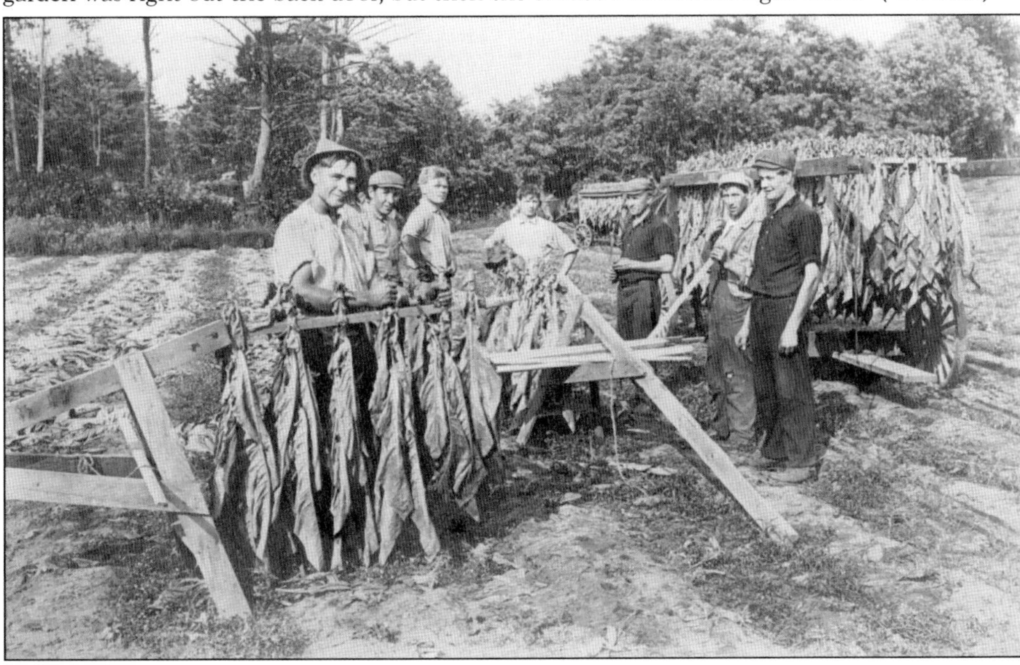

Workers at one of the Shepard family farms spear harvested tobacco plants onto wooden lath. The lath was then hung on horse-drawn carts, which carried the tobacco to barns called "sheds." Lath with hanging leaves were hung in two or three vertical levels in the tobacco shed to dry. (J.E. Shepard Collection, WMLM.)

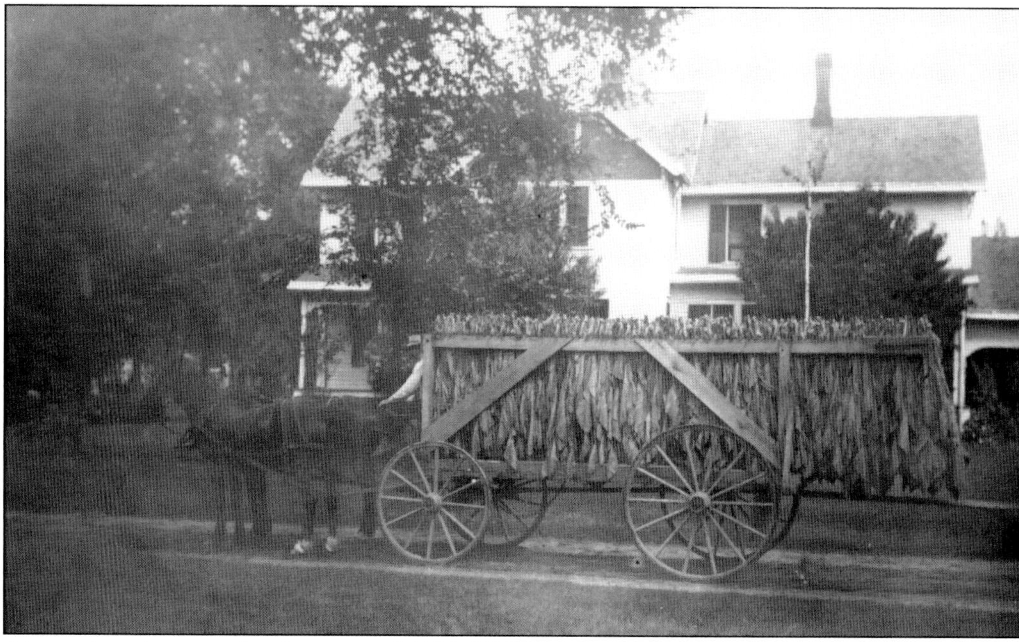

Above, in a photograph taken around 1900, Will Jennings drives a horse cart laden with speared tobacco past the house at 516 Main Street on the way to a tobacco shed. Below, a farmer stands outside of a tobacco shed on Rye Street with a trailer of hanging tobacco leaves pulled by a 1909 Nash Rambler. "I do remember horses in the field when they had riggings of tobacco, and people would just give them a slap on the tail and they'd just walk off and go to the barn—not the horse barn but the barn that you'd put tobacco in," remembered Tim Shepard. (Above, Hildred Raymond Collection; both, WMLM.)

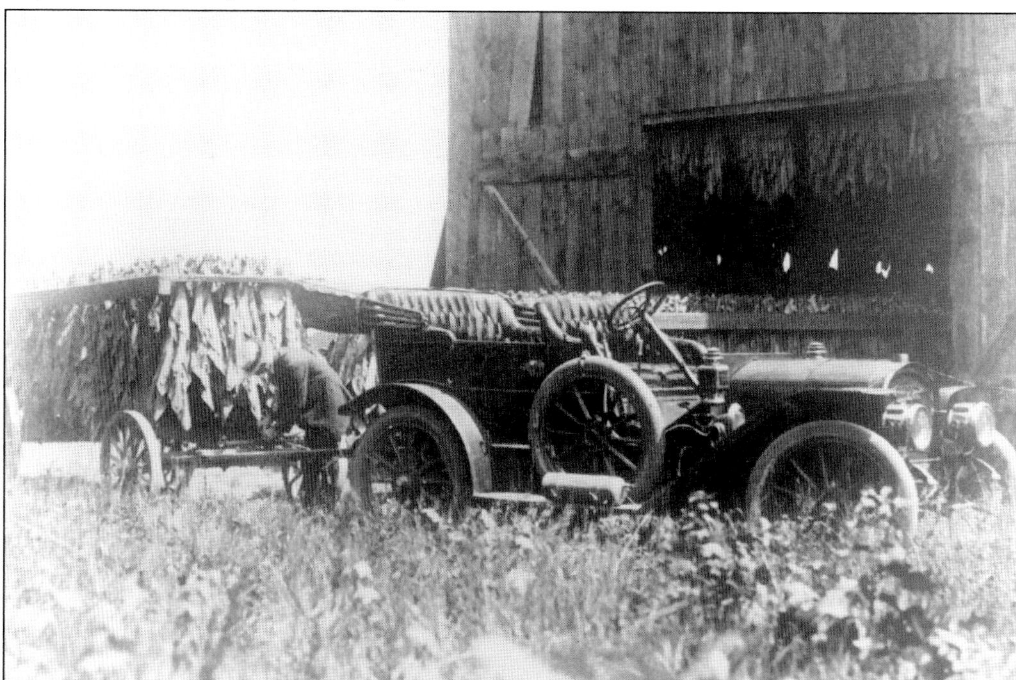

Olin Lane and another man hang tobacco leaves in a shed in 1946. Every step of the process, from chopping tobacco in the field, to spearing it on lath, to transporting it by cart, to hanging it in the shed, had to be done very carefully so as not to tear or break leaves. (Barney Daley Collection, WMLM.)

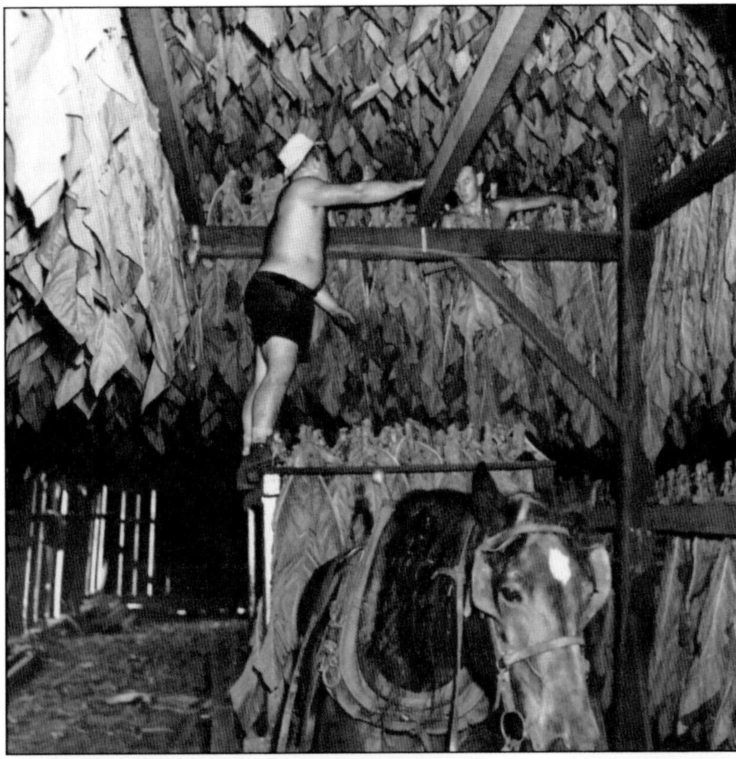

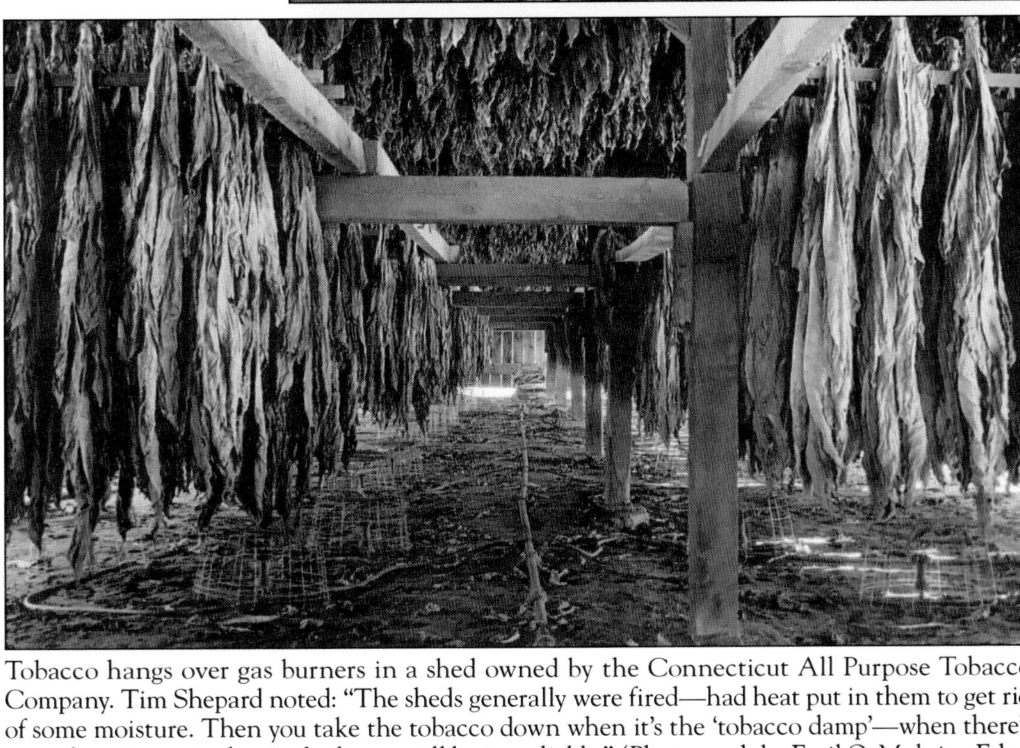

Tobacco hangs over gas burners in a shed owned by the Connecticut All Purpose Tobacco Company. Tim Shepard noted: "The sheds generally were fired—had heat put in them to get rid of some moisture. Then you take the tobacco down when it's the 'tobacco damp'—when there's enough moisture in the air the leaves will be just pliable." (Photograph by Emil O. Mulnite, Edna and Norman Priest Collection, WMLM.)

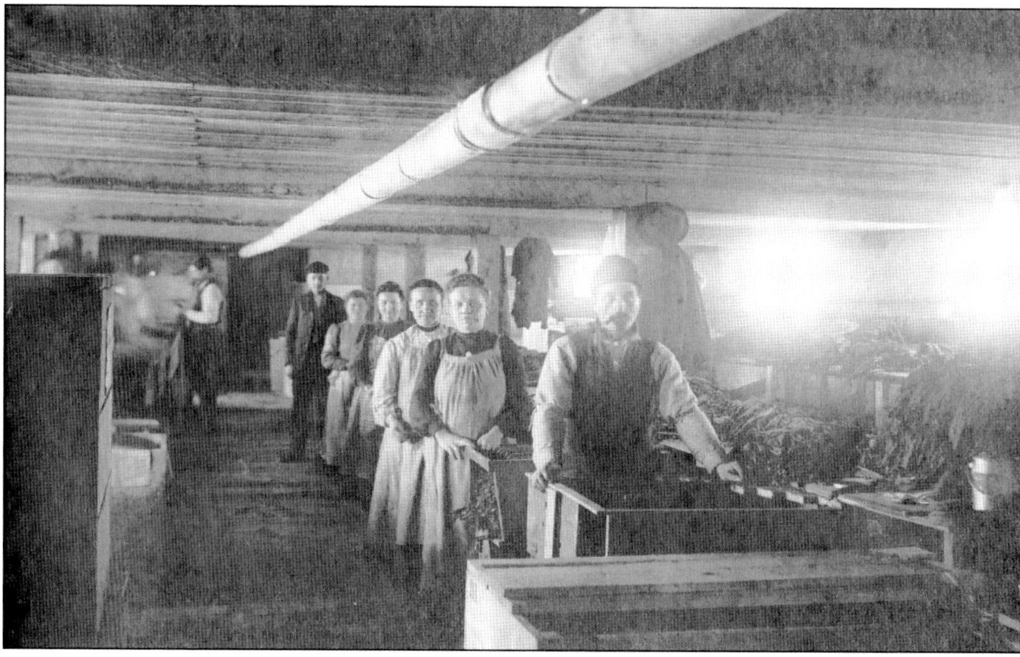

These two images from the 1870s or 1880s show men and women in a dimly lit, low-ceilinged room, sorting dried and cured broadleaf tobacco leaves by soundness, texture, color, and size. The leaves were then packed into large cases or crates and placed in a "sweat room," in which the leaves fermented and were stored for future use in cigar manufacturing. These workers may have been early employees of the J.E. Shepard Company. (Both, J.E. Shepard Collection, WMLM.)

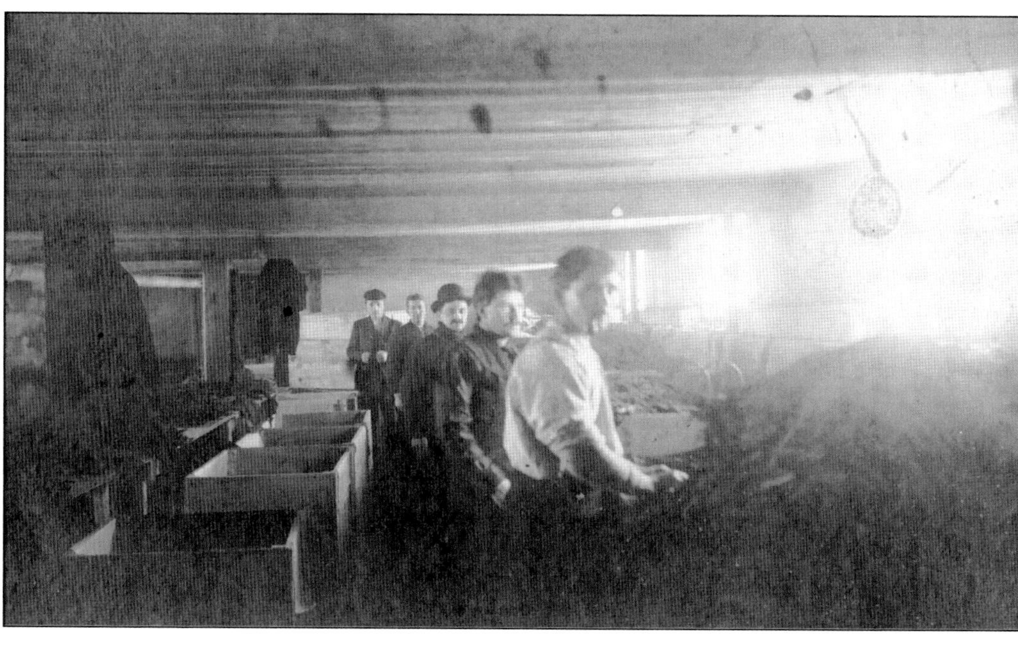

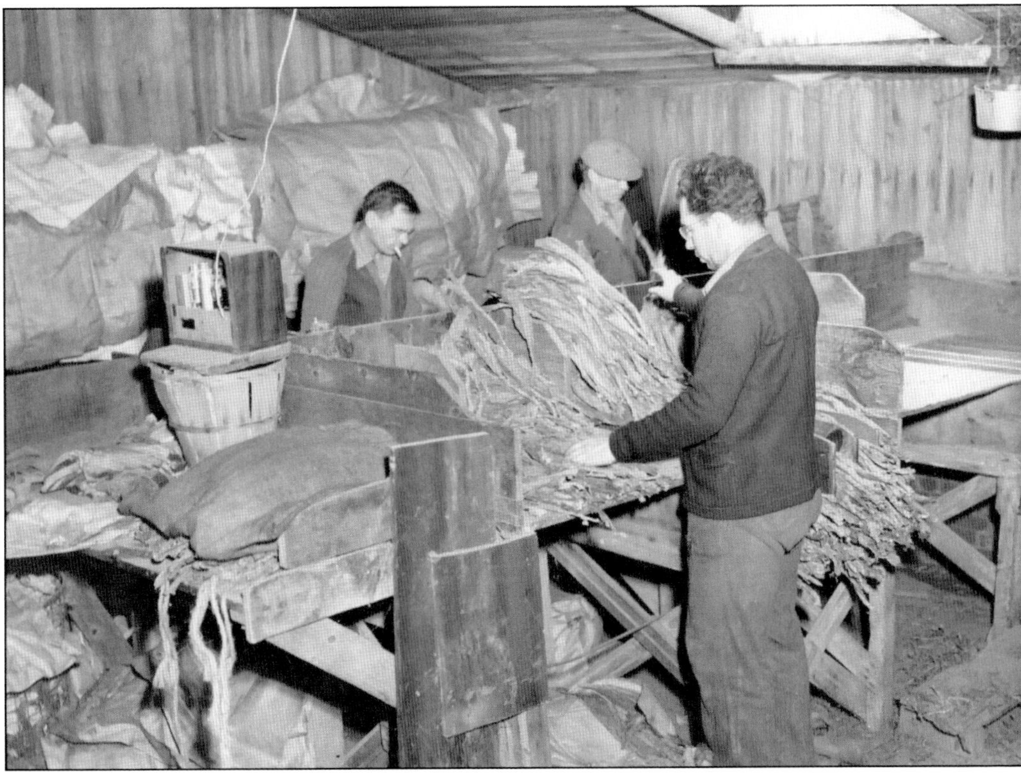

From left to right, Barney Daley, Edwin Reardon, and Andrew Reardon sort tobacco at 465 Main Street in 1946. Tim Shepard recalled: "When somebody sorted here they would sort into various grades, and within those grades there were a lot of different qualities of tobacco versus sizes and colors and so forth." (Barney Daley Collection, WMLM.)

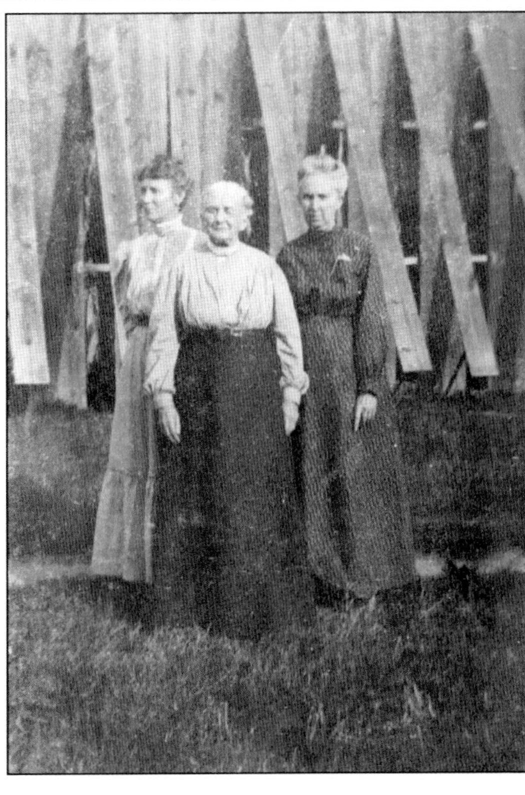

From left to right, Lena Burnham, Roxy Eveline Gillette Burnham, and Sarah Burnham pose outside their family's tobacco shed in 1885. The slats on the side are propped open to allow the leaves to dry. Because the crop was the main source of family wealth, many South Windsor families in the 19th century took formal portraits by their tobacco fields or sheds. (Gillette Family Collection, WMLM.)

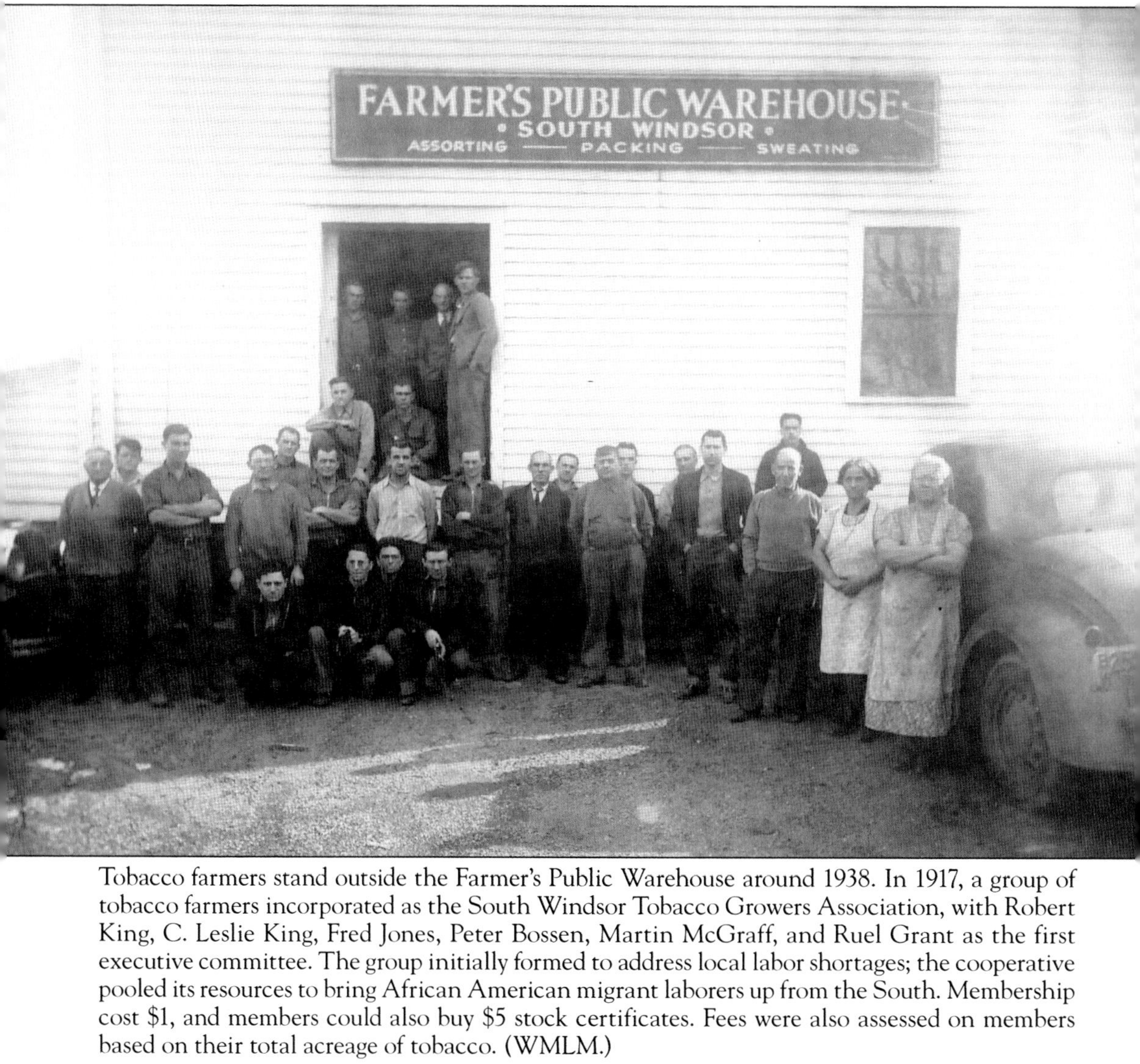

Tobacco farmers stand outside the Farmer's Public Warehouse around 1938. In 1917, a group of tobacco farmers incorporated as the South Windsor Tobacco Growers Association, with Robert King, C. Leslie King, Fred Jones, Peter Bossen, Martin McGraff, and Ruel Grant as the first executive committee. The group initially formed to address local labor shortages; the cooperative pooled its resources to bring African American migrant laborers up from the South. Membership cost $1, and members could also buy $5 stock certificates. Fees were also assessed on members based on their total acreage of tobacco. (WMLM.)

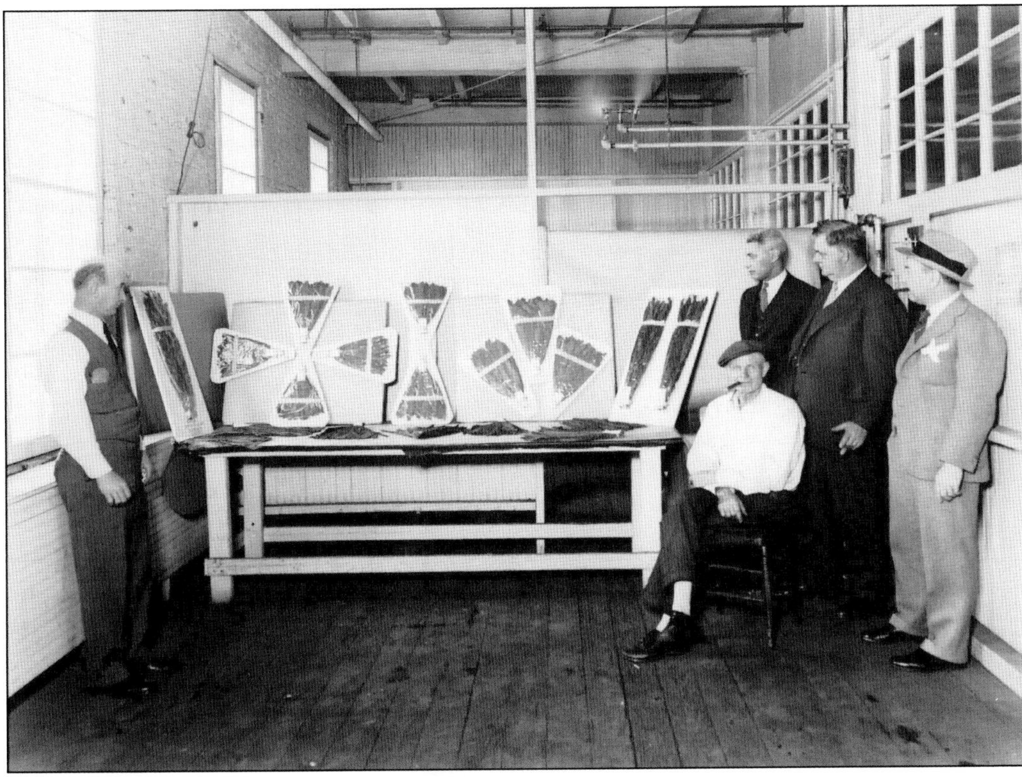

A group of men, possibly tobacco growers or buyers, look at tobacco leaf samples. One of the samples is labeled "Connecticut Broadleaf Binder Grade," and another is labeled "Connecticut Shade." Much of the tobacco produced here was purchased by buyers for large cigar manufacturers and sent to the Caribbean for cigar production. (Photograph by Wyckoff Mills, Charles G. Griffin Collection, WMLM.)

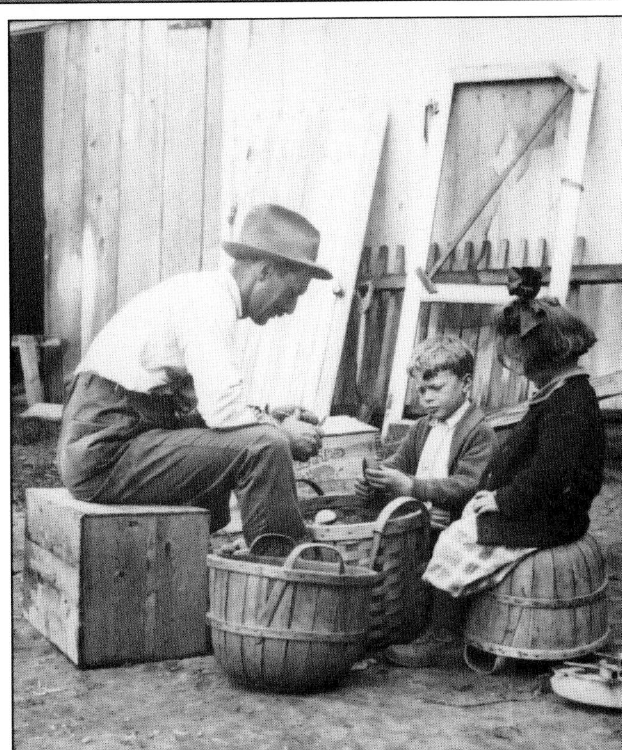

John Selden Clapp Sr., with his children John Jr. and Olive, cuts seed potatoes around 1917 in the yard at their farmhouse at 59 Sullivan Avenue, known as the Increase Clapp house. Later in life, John Jr. remembered how difficult it was for a young child to cut the potatoes so that each piece had an eye that could germinate. (Photograph by Edith S. Watson, Hildred Raymond Collection, WMLM.)

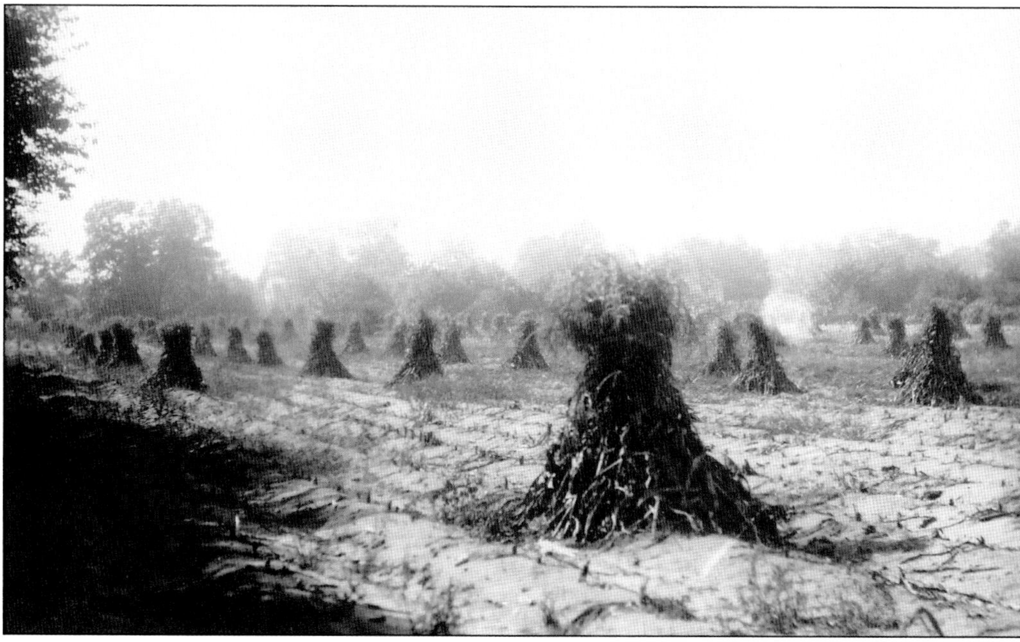

Corn shocks stand drying in a field near Sullivan Avenue in this photograph from the late 19th or early 20th century. Professional photographer Edith S. Watson was particularly known for her images of rural life. Starting in the 1890s, she made numerous long trips through rural Canada, photographing families at work in First Nations villages and religious minority communities. (Photograph by Edith S. Watson, Watson Family Collection, WMLM.)

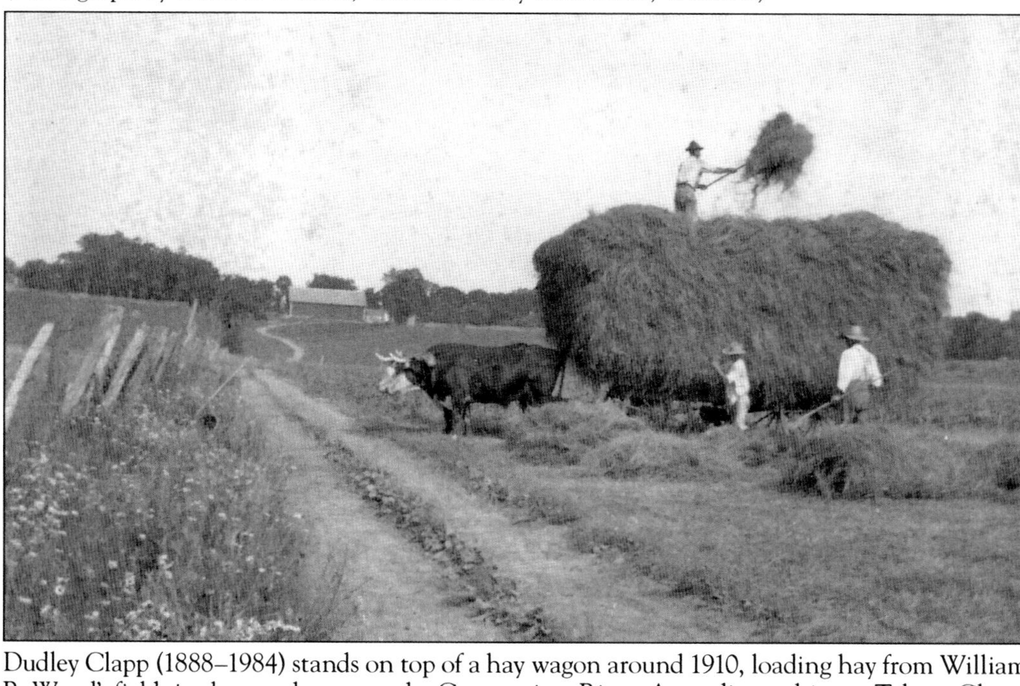

Dudley Clapp (1888–1984) stands on top of a hay wagon around 1910, loading hay from William R. Wood's fields in the meadows near the Connecticut River. According to his son Talcott Clapp, Dudley prided himself on his square-cornered haystacks. The hay was then used to feed Will Wood's large herd of cattle. (Hildred Raymond Collection, WMLM.)

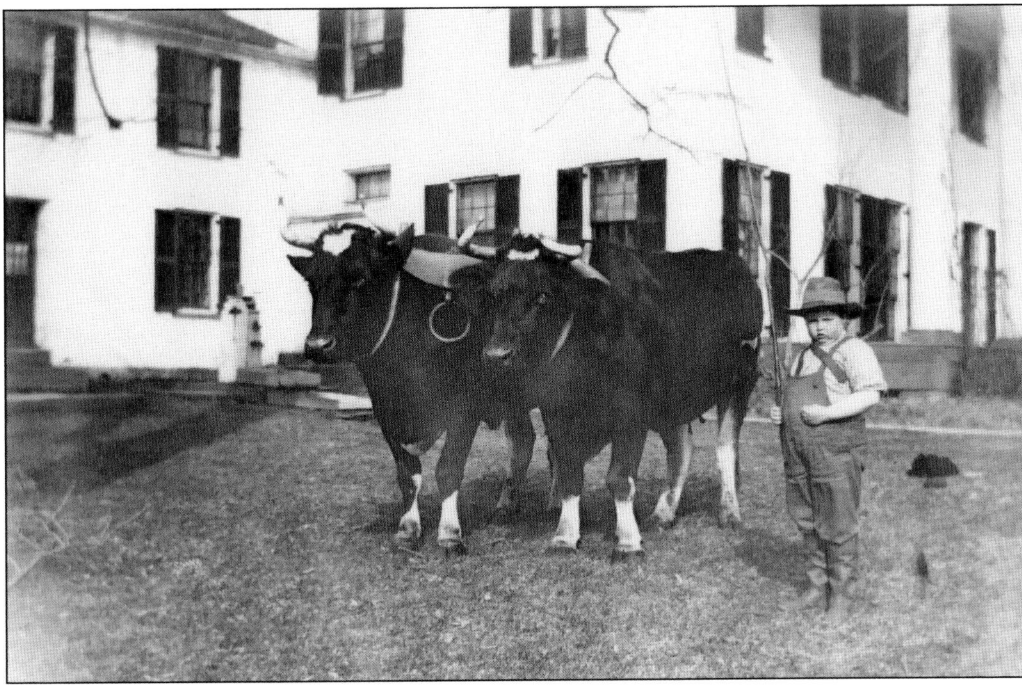

Billy Bowler, the son of one of William Wood's employees, stands with an ox team in the yard of Wood's house at 1837 Main Street. One of Wood's primary businesses was cattle dealing. He was probably aided in this business by the close proximity of the Pelton Slaughterhouse, which was adjacent to the railroad tracks by what is now Route 5. (Hildred Raymond Collection, WMLM.)

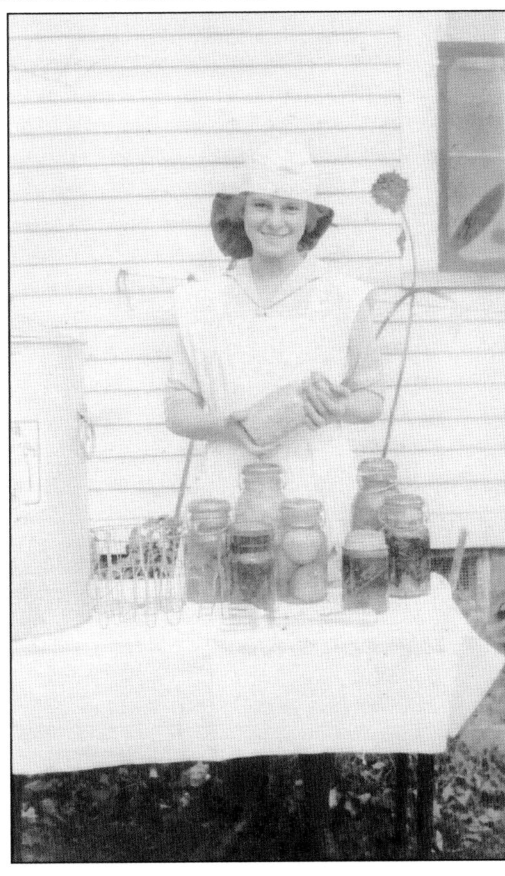

In the days before commercial refrigeration, home canning was much more widespread and necessary than it is today. Here, Miriam Baker, one of the daughters of the family that operated Town Farm, poses with canning supplies and some of her prize-winning jarred and canned food around 1917. (Hildred Raymond Collection, WMLM.)

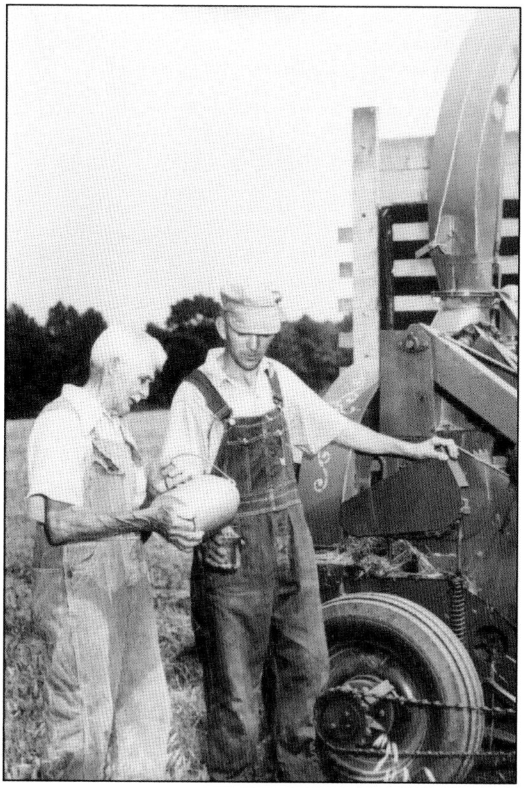

Richard Niederwerfer brings his son Frank Niederwerfer Sr. a drink of water on the family farm on Niederwerfer Road around 1953. They are standing next to their new corn cutter-harvester. The elder Niederwerfer immigrated to the United States from Germany as a toddler in 1871. He passed away less than a year after this photograph was taken. (Frank Niederwerfer.)

Men and a barefoot boy stand in Elisha Morton's peach orchard on Rye Street at the South Windsor–East Windsor line at harvest time in 1891. Because of their soft skin and tendency to bruise easily, peaches are some of the most delicate fruit to harvest and have to be handled carefully during picking and transportation. This orchard is now gone, replaced with houses. (SWHS.)

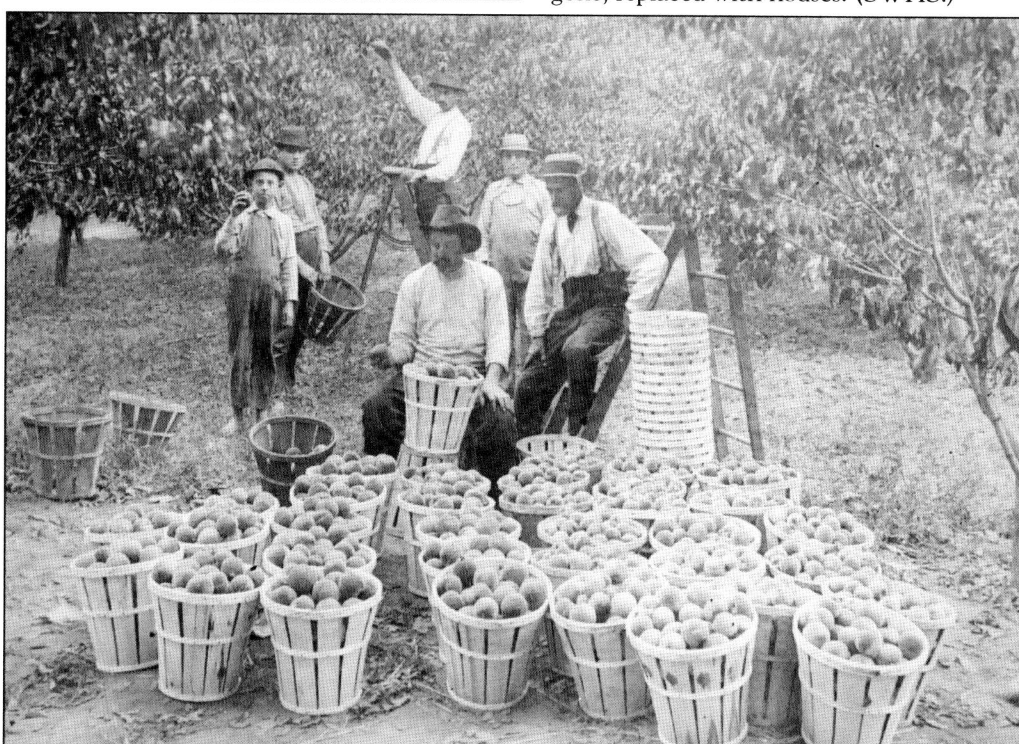

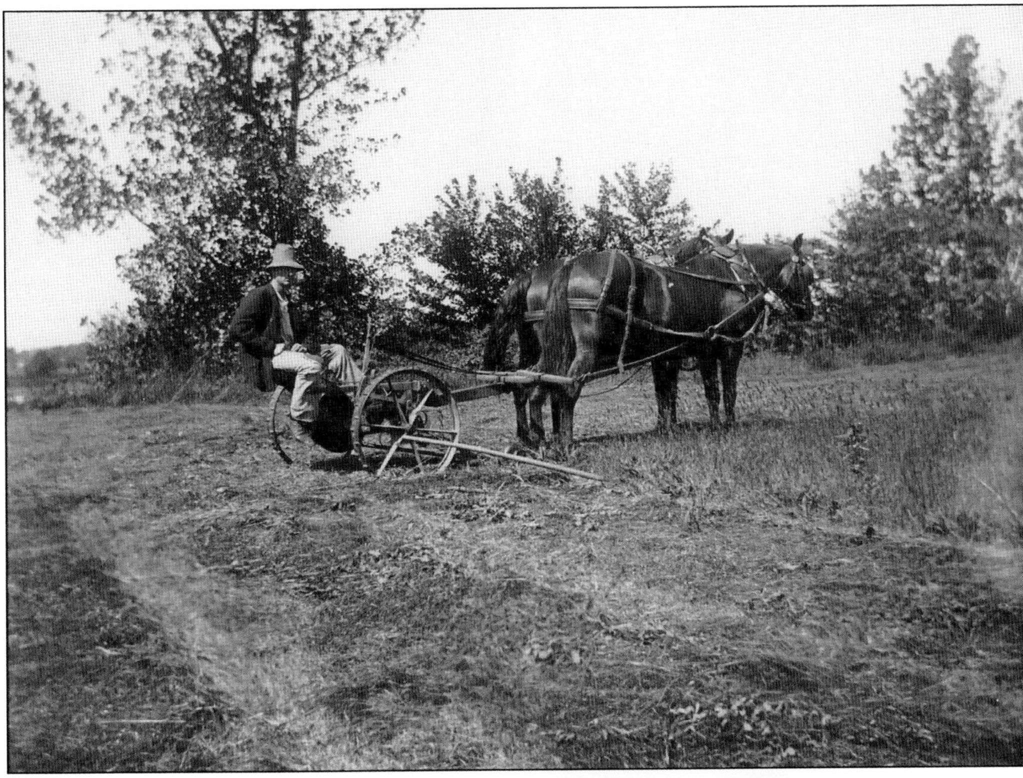

Ed Bancroft sits on a horse-drawn grass cutter, mowing Meadow Hill in the late 1890s. In colonial days, the meadows were a common grazing field during parts of the year. "Depending on what your acreage was, you were assessed so many feet along the meadow hill, and you were responsible for a fence," said Joseph Vibert. After the harvest, livestock grazed in the common field. (Hildred Raymond Collection, WMLM.)

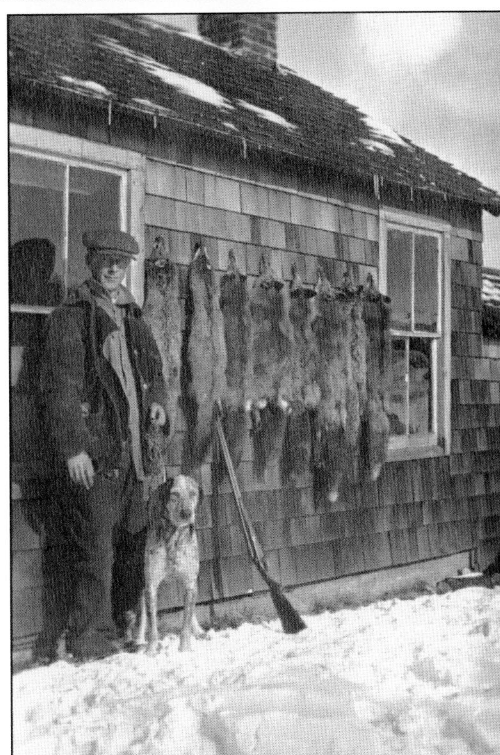

Fred Chapman and his hunting dog Lion stand by fox pelts hanging on the outside of a building around 1920. Chapman was a farmer, and like many farmers, he needed seasonal work to supplement his income in the winter. In addition to fur trapping, Chapman also owned a portable sawing rig that people would hire to cut lumber for building and firewood. (SWHS.)

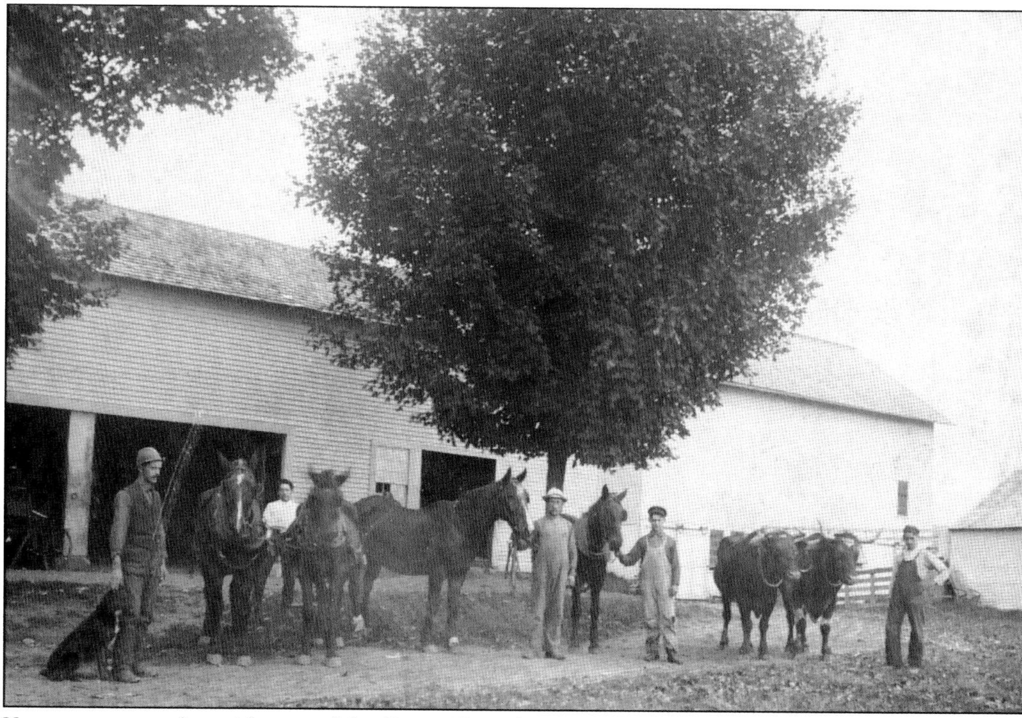

Young men stand outside one of the Foster Farm barns in 1902 with horses and cows. Foster Farm grew tobacco and other crops and ran a commercial dairy, delivering bottled milk to customers in South Windsor and surrounding towns. Below, one of the Foster Farm milk delivery wagons is shown in the early 1900s. The farm has been in the same family since 1790 and today is best known for its corn maze. (Above, photograph by A.W. and G.E. Howes; both, Foster family.)

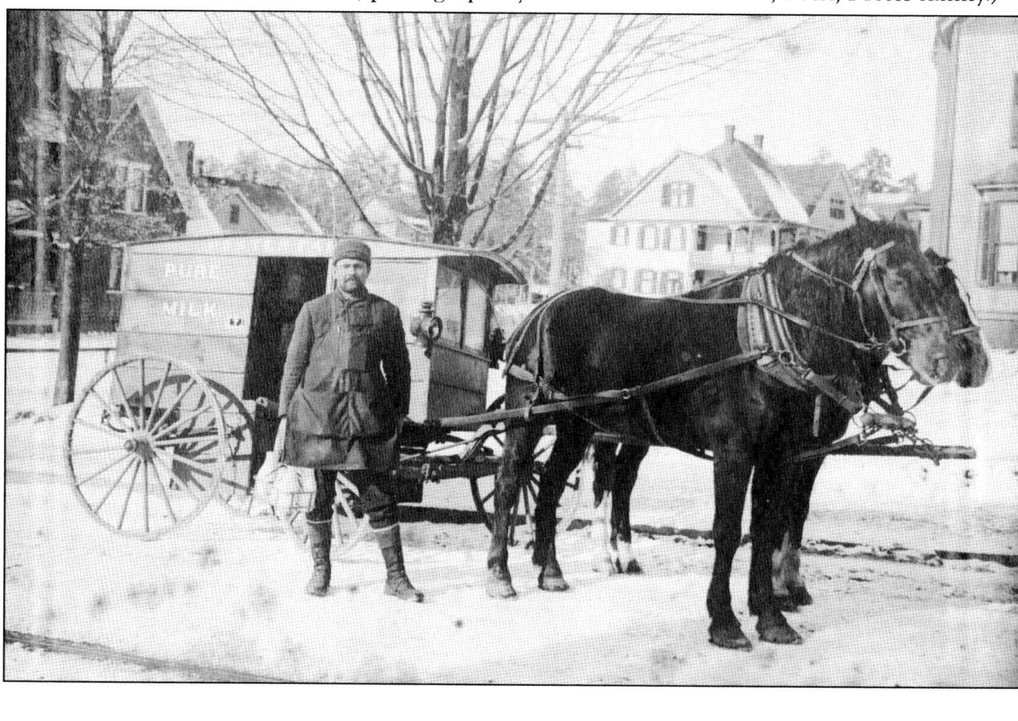

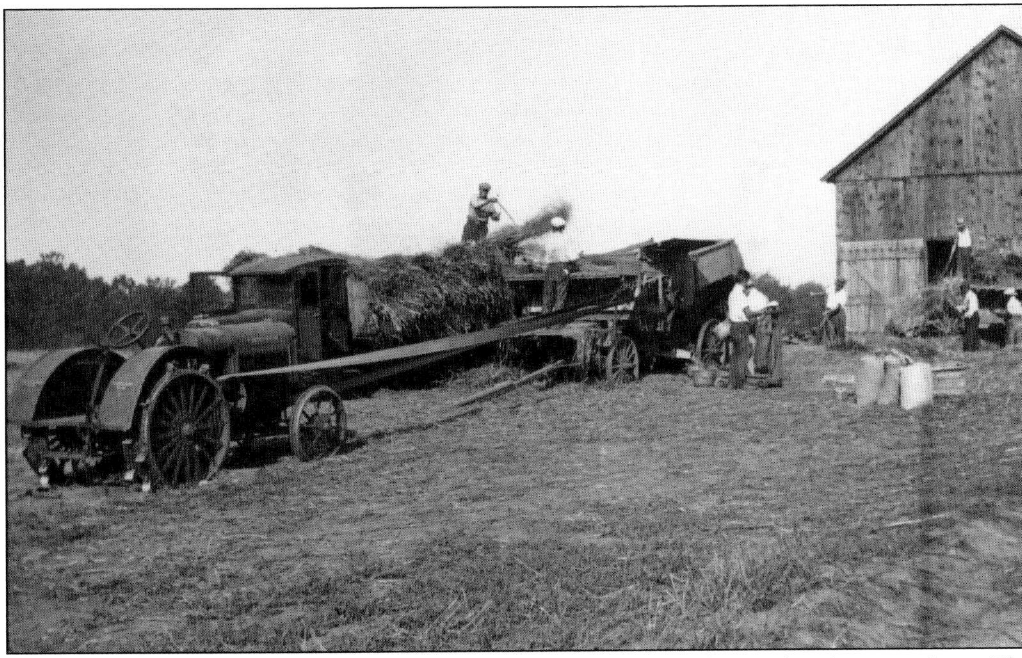

Workers on Upper Strong Road in 1935 feed straw into a tractor-driven threshing machine. The straw would have then been used for animal fodder. Jane Wadach Gutt estimated that in the 1930s, "let's say 90 or more percent of the people at least had chickens, and another 50 percent or more had a cow or two. And then there were horses for the crops and things like that." (Ted Bancroft Collection, WMLM.)

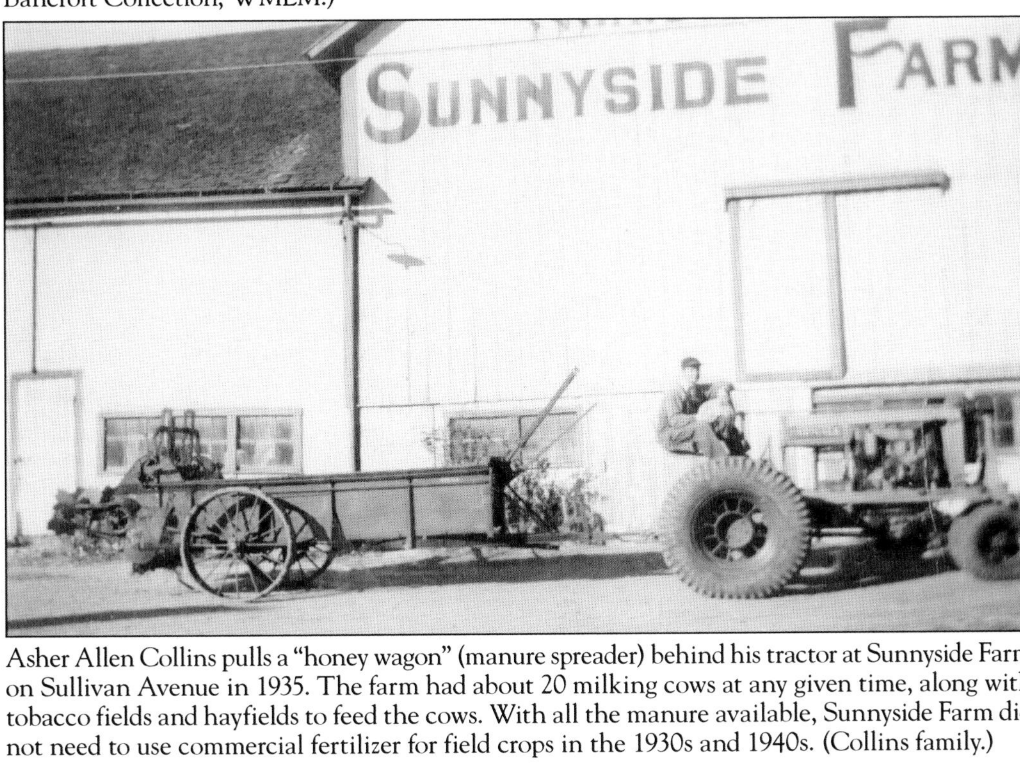

Asher Allen Collins pulls a "honey wagon" (manure spreader) behind his tractor at Sunnyside Farm on Sullivan Avenue in 1935. The farm had about 20 milking cows at any given time, along with tobacco fields and hayfields to feed the cows. With all the manure available, Sunnyside Farm did not need to use commercial fertilizer for field crops in the 1930s and 1940s. (Collins family.)

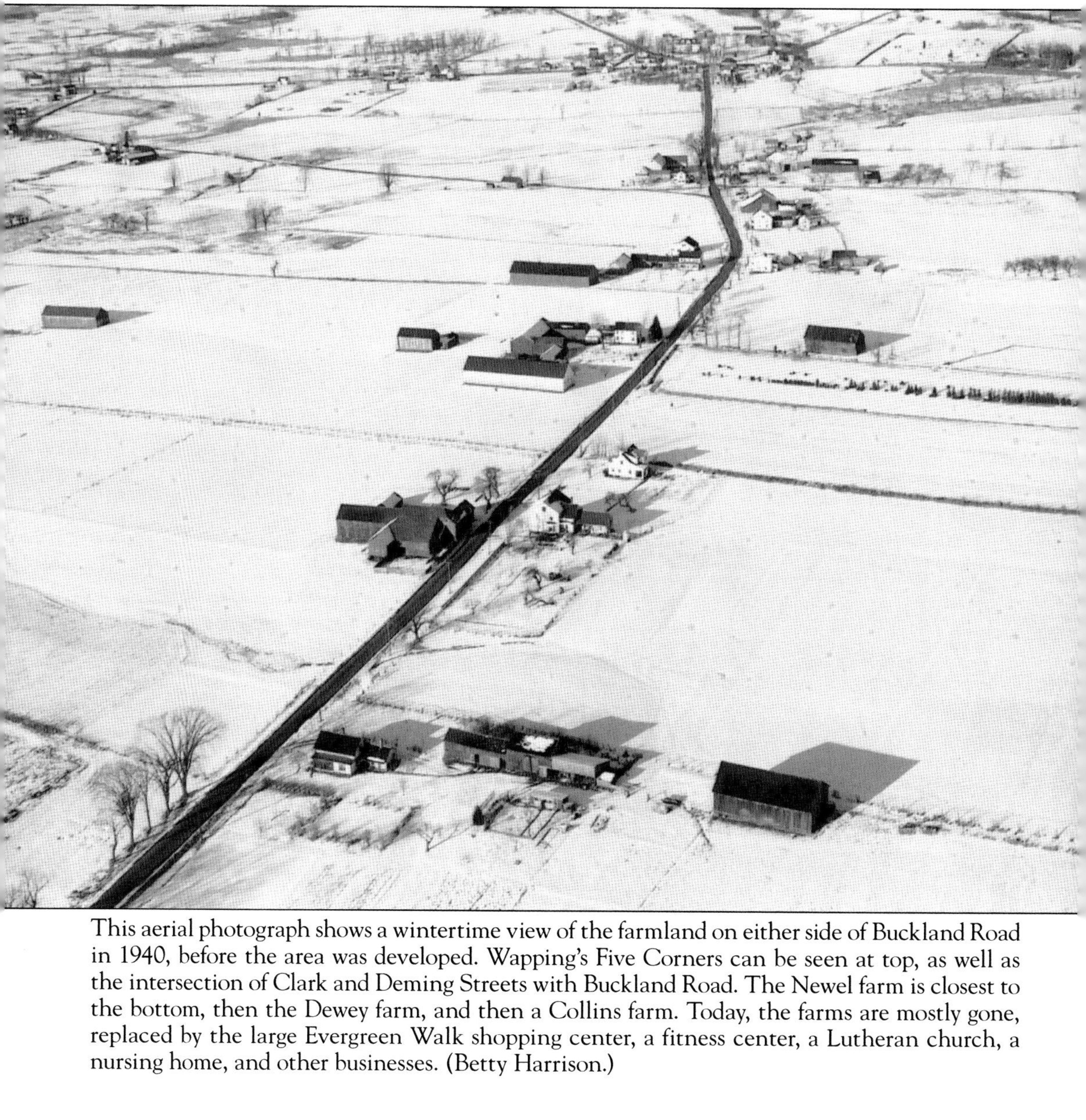

This aerial photograph shows a wintertime view of the farmland on either side of Buckland Road in 1940, before the area was developed. Wapping's Five Corners can be seen at top, as well as the intersection of Clark and Deming Streets with Buckland Road. The Newel farm is closest to the bottom, then the Dewey farm, and then a Collins farm. Today, the farms are mostly gone, replaced by the large Evergreen Walk shopping center, a fitness center, a Lutheran church, a nursing home, and other businesses. (Betty Harrison.)

Six

Pleasant Valley, Long Hill, and the South Side of Town

If South Windsor was largely a rural town until the Cold War era, the south side of town around Pleasant Valley Road and the East Hartford town line was especially sparsely populated, with some residents even calling the area a wilderness. In fact, it was so sparsely populated that students in the area attended a one-room schoolhouse until 1952. Two mills in the area, the paper mill and the Podunk Mill, owed their existence to the Podunk River, and some of the homes on Pleasant Valley Road were built as housing for millworkers. In later years, the Podunk River was used for recreational purposes, feeding the Spring Pond swimming area.

The busiest part of this section of town was the intersection of Pleasant Valley and Ellington Roads, with Long Hill Road intersecting Pleasant Valley nearby. Before Route 84 was built, Ellington Road was one of the main routes between New York City and Boston. Drivers would stop for lunch or an overnight stay at Burnham Station, which sat at the intersection with Pleasant Valley Road. The highway system dramatically changed the area, diverting traffic from Ellington Road and carving out a section of Long Hill Road to become Route 291.

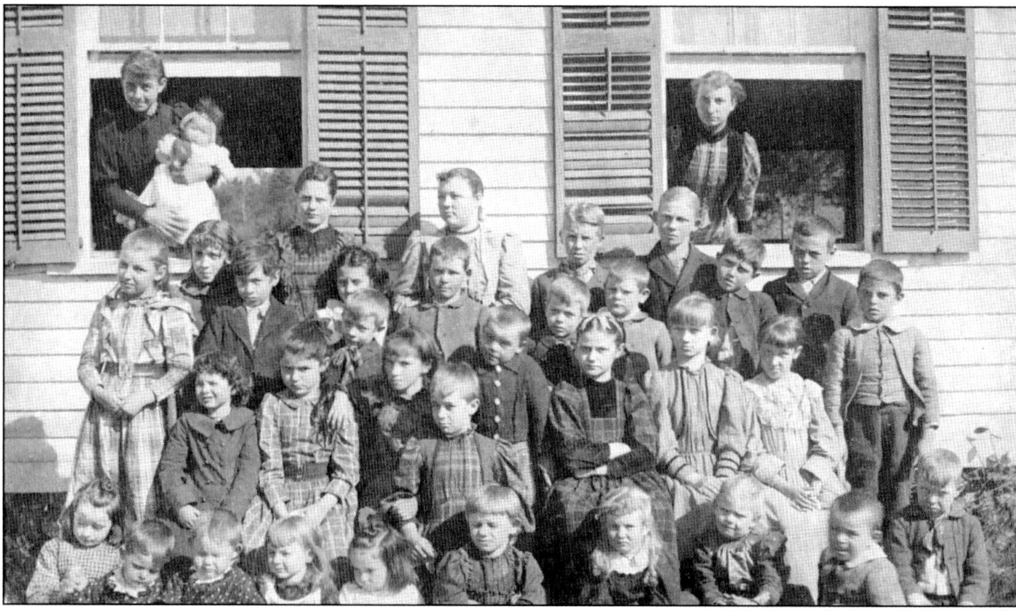

The Pleasant Valley Schoolhouse, also known as the District 5 school, served as a public school from 1862 to 1952. It now houses the South Windsor Historical Society. Sally Edlund recalled: "Well, the schoolhouse was just the one room, and it had a double door in the front, but one door was never used when I was there. We went in the north door, and they had a little coat room there, and then it had one main room. . . . When they moved the school back to a place with a foundation underneath it, they had put in indoor plumbing [in the basement] which was a boy's and a girl's toilet and a sink in the middle." The 1892 students (along with an infant) are pictured above, and the 1936 students are below. (Both, SWHS.)

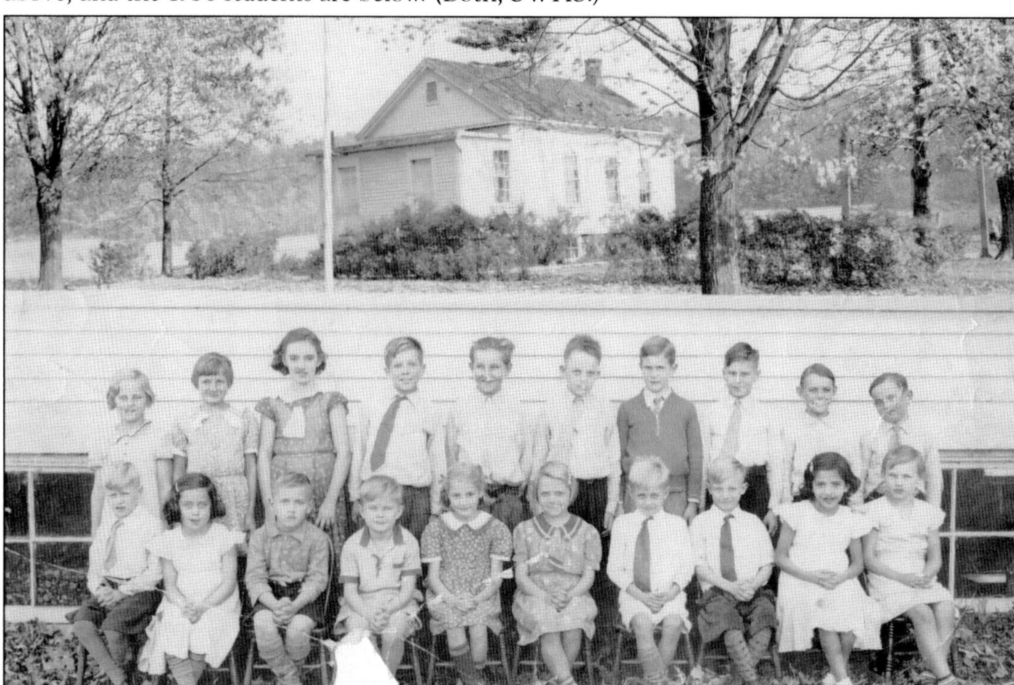

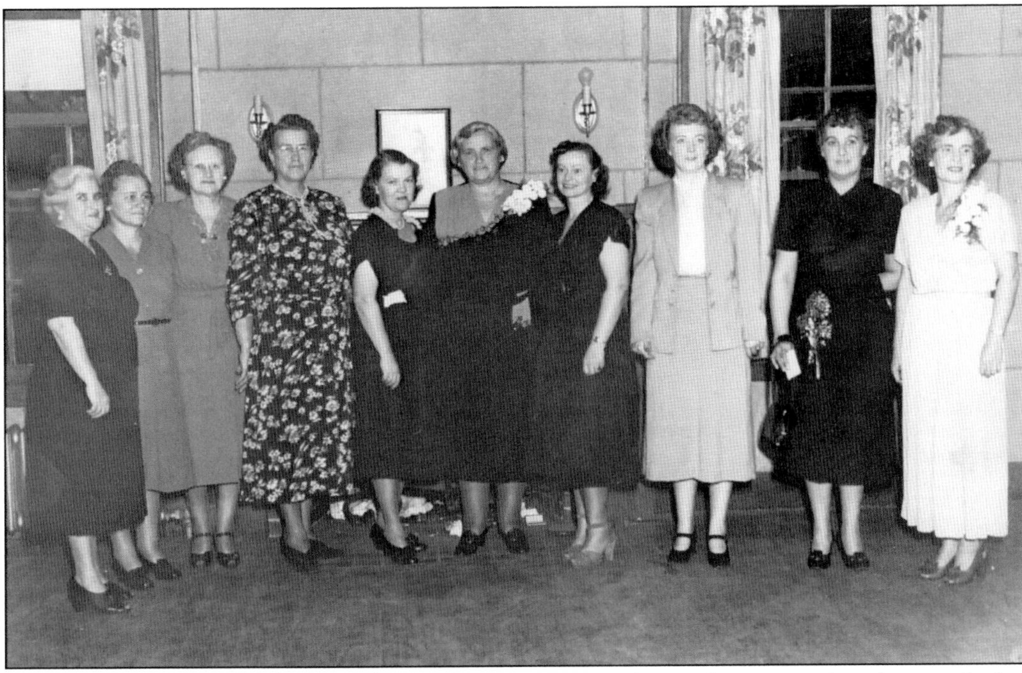

The Pleasant Valley Club, started in 1924, was a women's social organization that worked to improve the school and community. After the Pleasant Valley schoolhouse closed in 1952, the Pleasant Valley Club used it as a clubhouse until 1970, when it disbanded and turned the building over to the town. Above, from left to right, are members Margaret Turner, Helen Fairbanks, Lena Elmore, Louise Johnson, Betty Burnham, Ellen Thresher, Lillian Hack Anderson, Pearl Burnham, Lillian Skinner, and Blanche Page. Below, the club hosts a banquet. (Both, Pleasant Valley Club Collection, WMLM.)

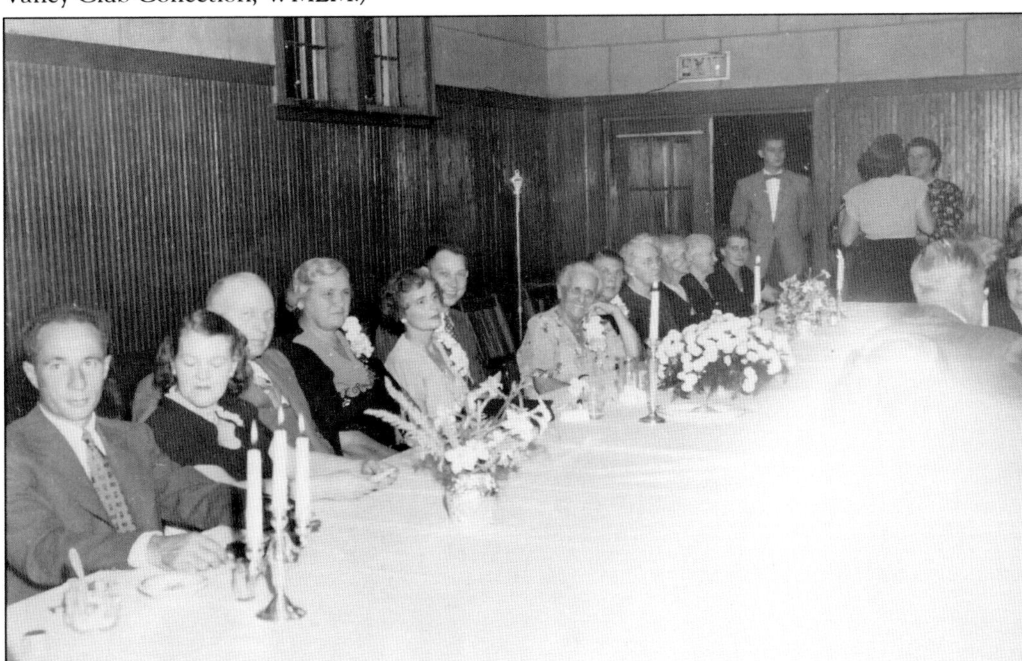

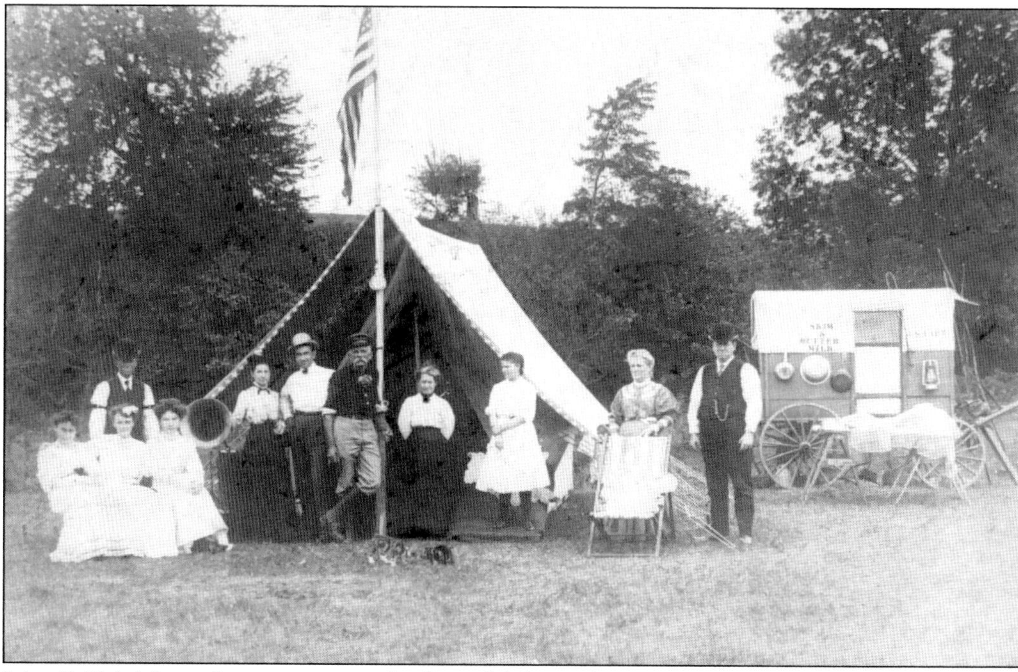

John S. Taft (above, leaning against the flagpole), his wife Mary, and their children Joseph, Mabel, and Clara, lived at 240 Pleasant Valley Road in the house pictured below. The house, now demolished, was near the present site of Veteran's Memorial Park. John was a farmer and Civil War veteran. The camp site in the photograph above was near their home, and this picture may have been taken at an Independence Day celebration. Taft's son, Joseph, was a milk peddler and probably sold his wares out of the cart at right above, which is stenciled with the words "Skim & Butter Milk." (Above, Hildred Raymond Collection; below, Doris Burgdorf Collection; both, WMLM.)

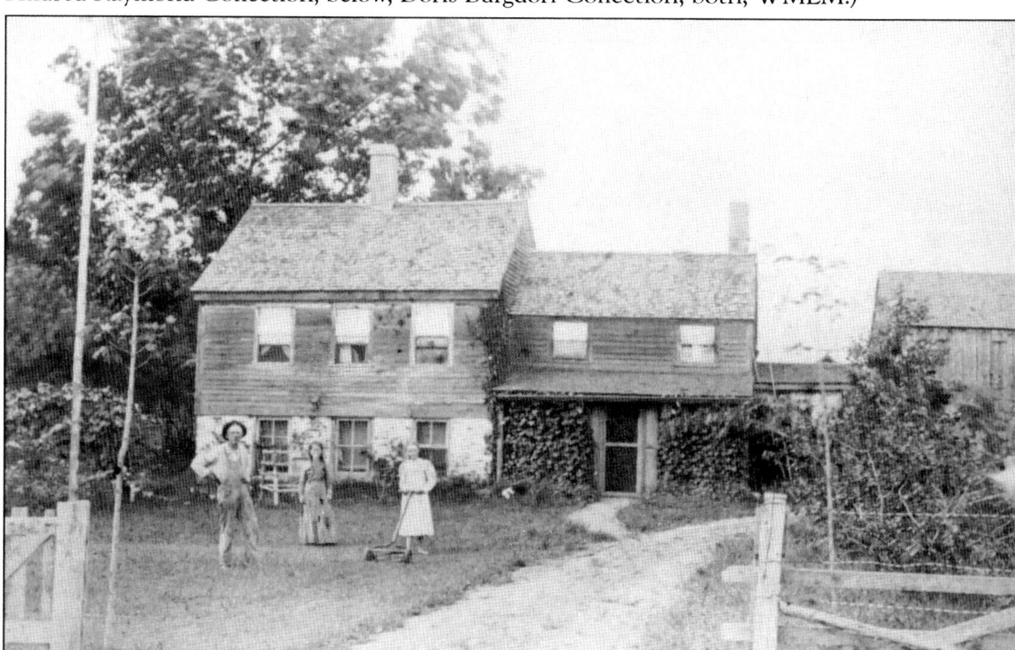

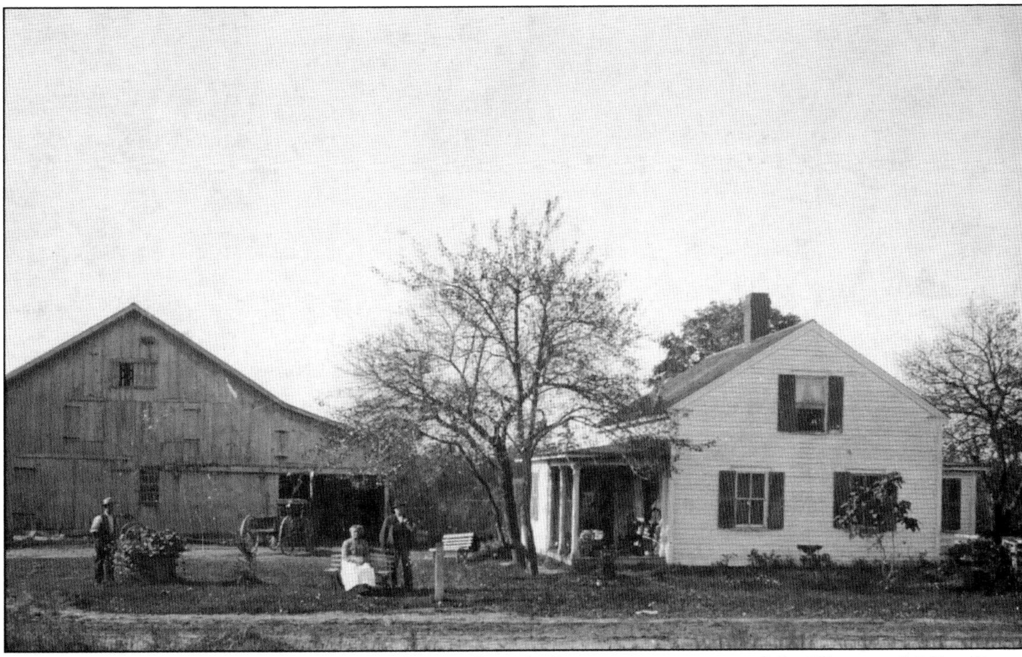

Mary Webber Church and Hollis Gardiner Church, former proprietors of the Pleasant Valley Paper Mill, pose in front of their home at 479 Pleasant Valley Road in 1902. The house still stands, but the barn has been torn down. After the fire and dam failure that destroyed their factory in the 1890s, the Churches switched to farming. (Photograph by A.W. and G.E. Howes, Ordway Family Photograph Collection, WMLM.)

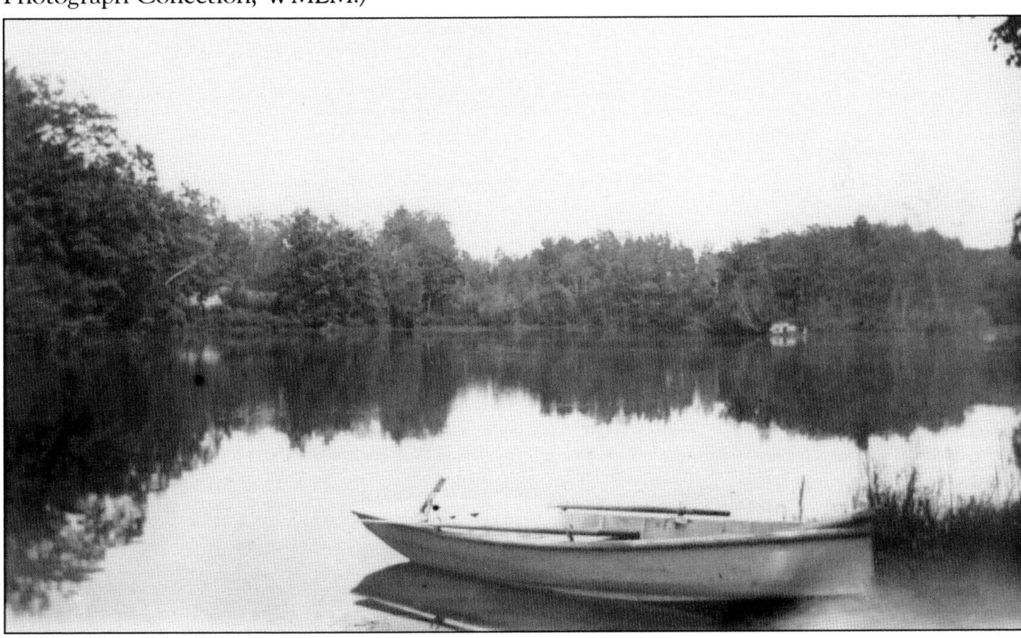

Mill Pond, behind the Podunk Mill (see page 86), served as more than simply the power source for the mill. Jane Wadach Gutt remembered: "The owner of the gristmill had rowboats that could be rented out for fishing mostly. . . . There was ice cutting, and the ice was then put up into a building at the top of the hill next to the grist mill." (Hildred Raymond Collection, WMLM.)

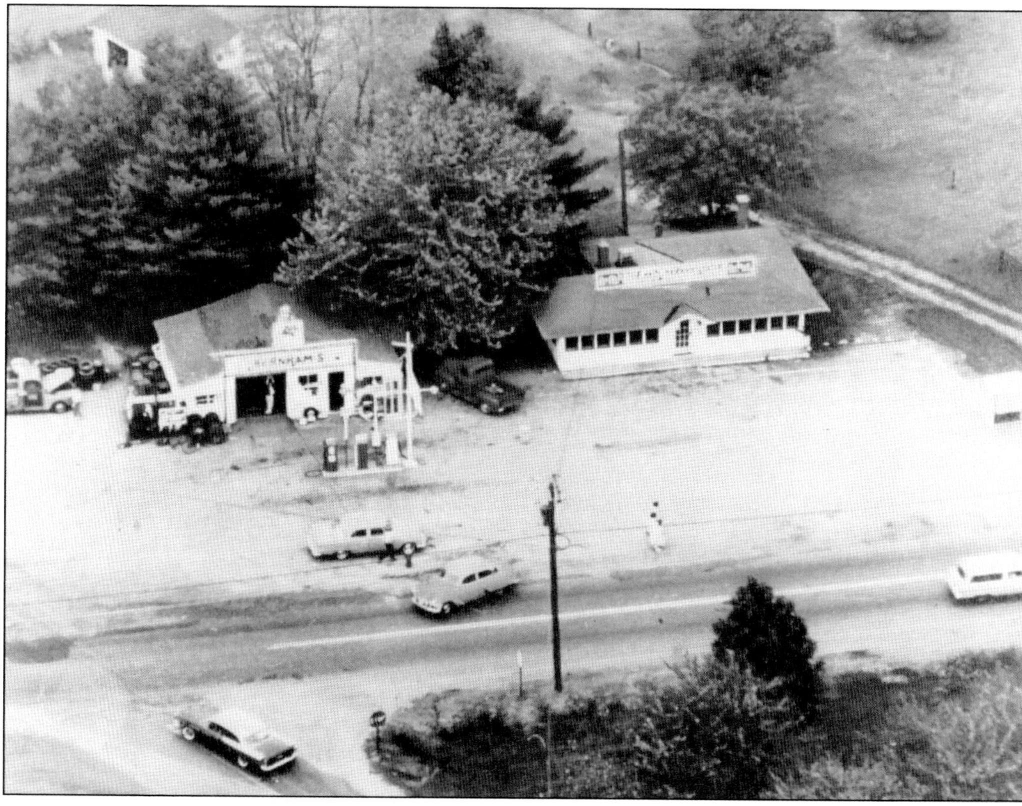

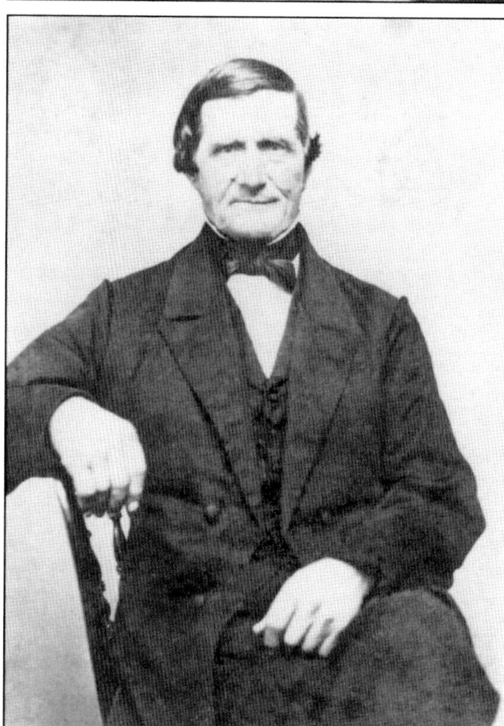

Burnham Station, at the corner of Pleasant Valley and Ellington Roads, was a gas station and store that sold penny candy in the early to mid-20th century. Sally Edlund added, "Burnham's also ran quite a famous lunchroom which was right north of the gas station and they were well known as the stop to take between Boston and New York, because Ruth Burnham made wonderful chicken pies and desserts, and they also had three cabins in the woods where you could stay overnight if you wanted to." (WMLM.)

Harvey Elmore (1799–1873) was elected to the Connecticut state legislature in 1842 and 1844. In 1845, he led a successful effort to separate South Windsor from East Windsor. Elmore was born with the last name Elmer but changed it in adulthood. He lived at 87 Long Hill Road, which he remodeled in 1843. The back section of the house dates from the late 18th century, while the Greek Revival front of the house is from the 1843 construction. (Gary S. Pitcock.)

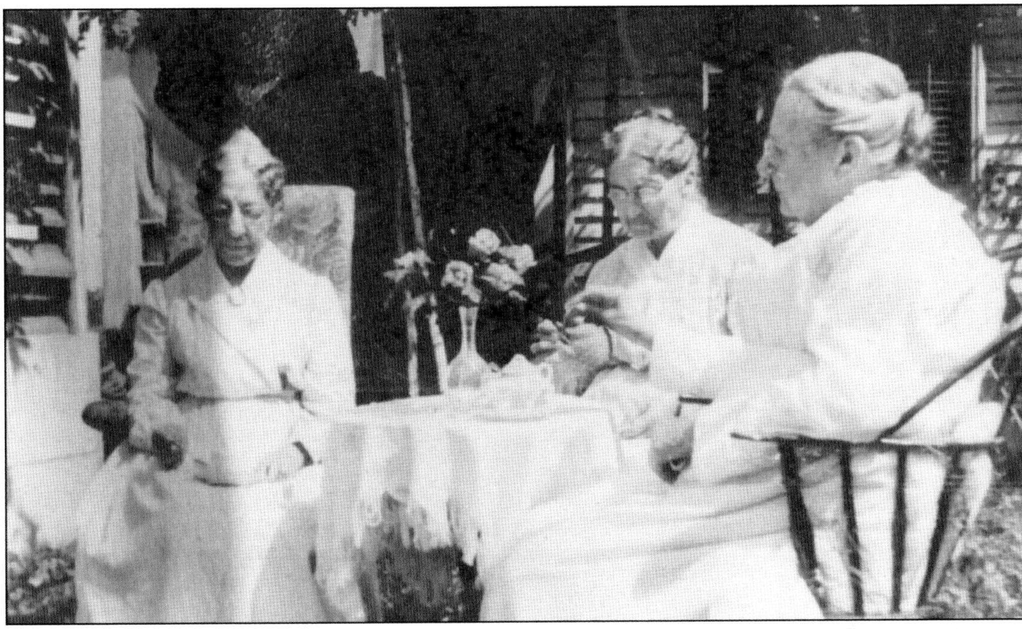

Mary Janette Elmore (right), the only daughter of Harvey Elmore, holds a high tea in the yard of her house at 87 Long Hill Road with two of her neighbors, the Williams sisters, sometime around 1900. In 1911, Mary Janette Elmore (1832–1922) wrote and illustrated her memoirs. In 1976, the manuscript was rediscovered and published by the South Windsor Historical Society. (Gary S. Pitcock.)

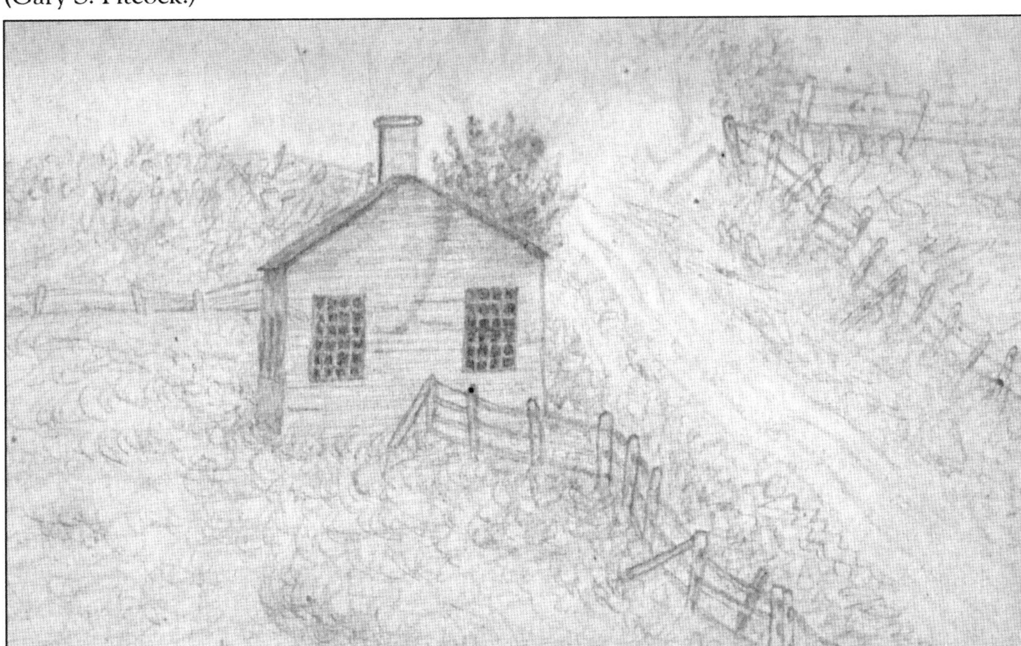

A one-room schoolhouse on Long Hill Road once stood approximately where Route 291 now passes under the road. Mary Janette Elmore included this small pencil sketch of the schoolhouse as it appeared in 1842 in her book *Long Hill*. (Gary S. Pitcock.)

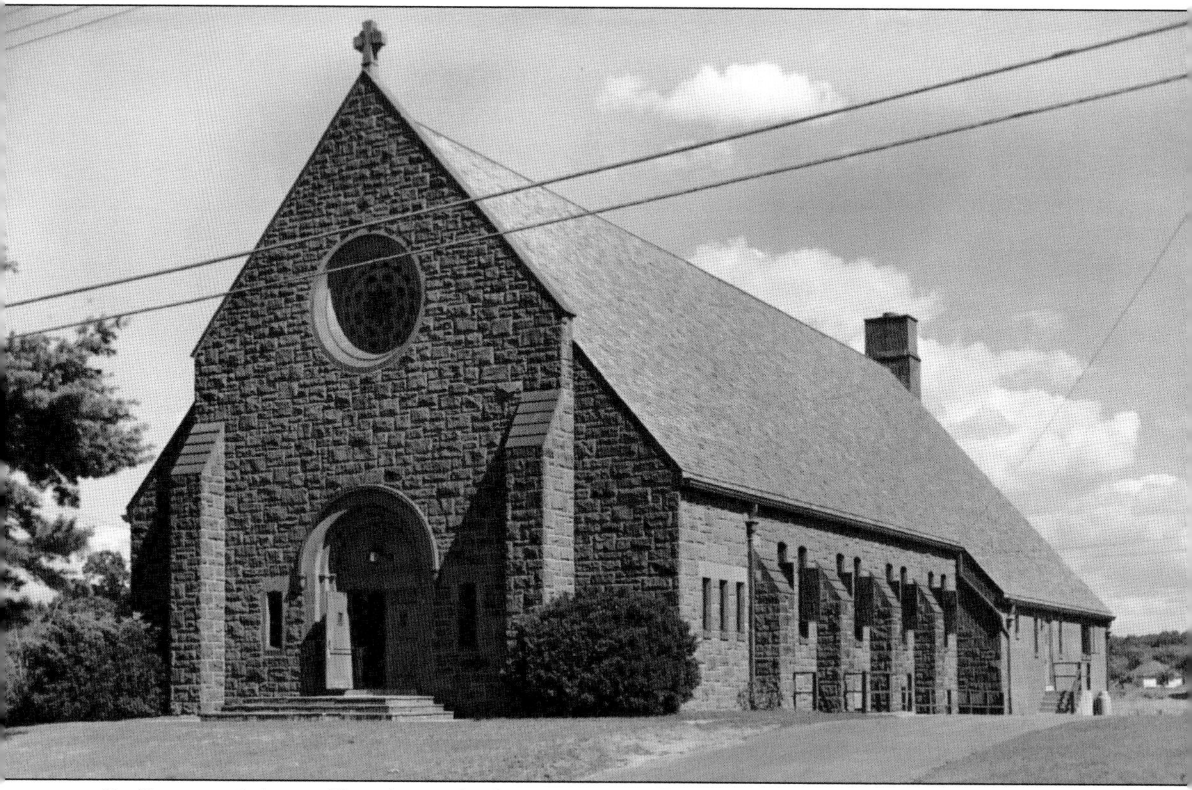

St. Francis of Assisi Church was built in 1942 on Ellington Road, but its Norman style makes it look much older. Although it is faced with brownstone, much of the church is made of brick from the Pola brickyards in town. The Pola family even donated some of the materials to finish the church when building materials and funds grew scarce during World War II. (Photograph by Ellsworth Fairbanks, Barney Daley Collection, WMLM.)

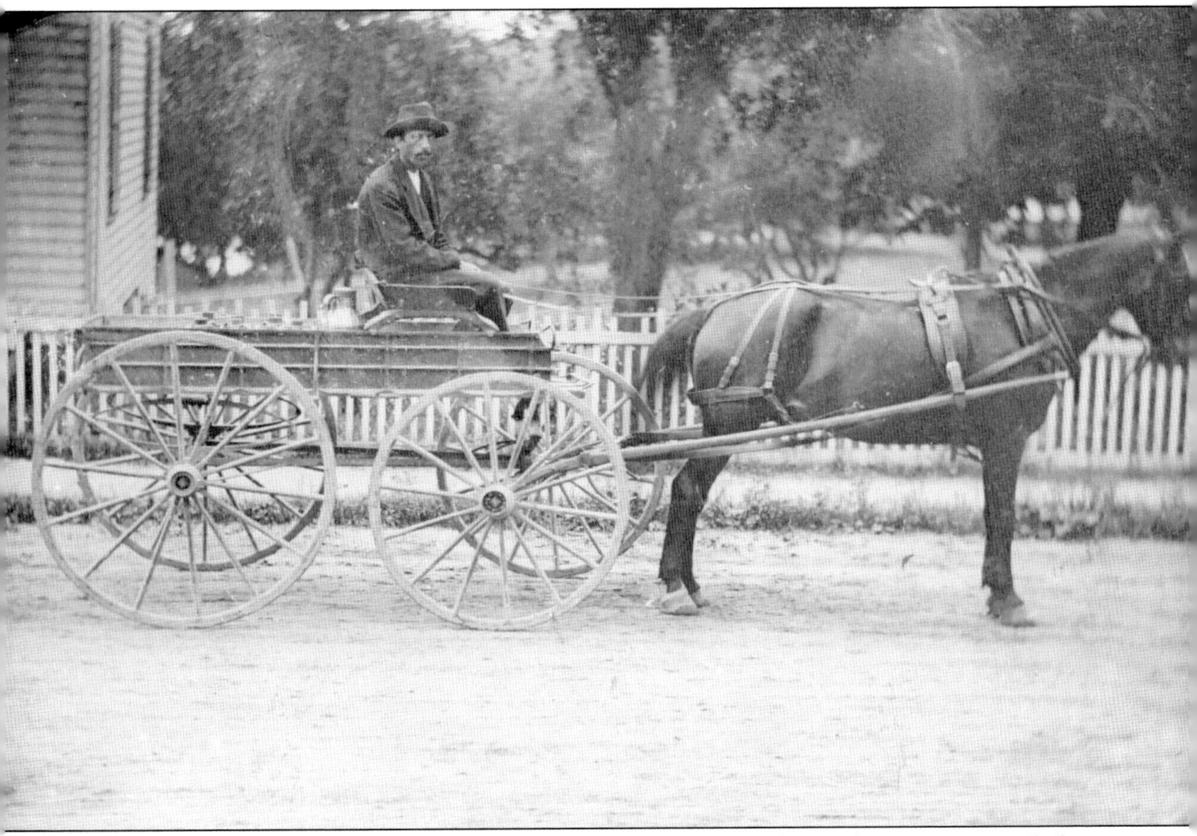

This small tintype shows tobacco farmer Henry C. Hayes, who lived near the intersection of what are now Smith and Wheeler Streets. Hayes was related to many other local families by blood and marriage. In 1864 and 1865, he helped his sister-in-law Mary Burnham while her husband was off fighting in the Civil War. In one heartbreaking letter to her husband, she wrote of his help after their infant son's death, "Henry took charge of things. He went down after the coffin and got the grave dug that contains our little treasure." Hayes was no stranger to small graves, as three of his own five children died in childhood. (Gary S. Pitcock.)

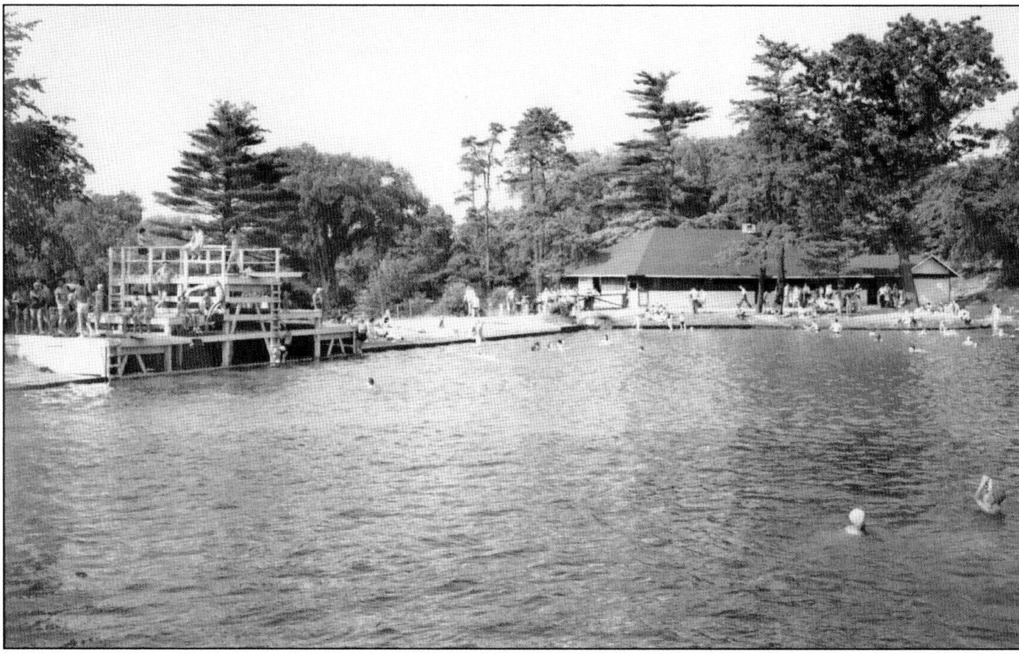

Before it was transformed into Veteran's Memorial Park and converted into a pool, Spring Pond really was a pond. Bob Raymond reminisced: "Well, it was a private enterprise then, run by the Cowles. . . . The local kids would go out there. We all learned to swim. In those days it looked like a big pond. The older you got the smaller it got." (Lorraine Jones Collection, WMLM.)

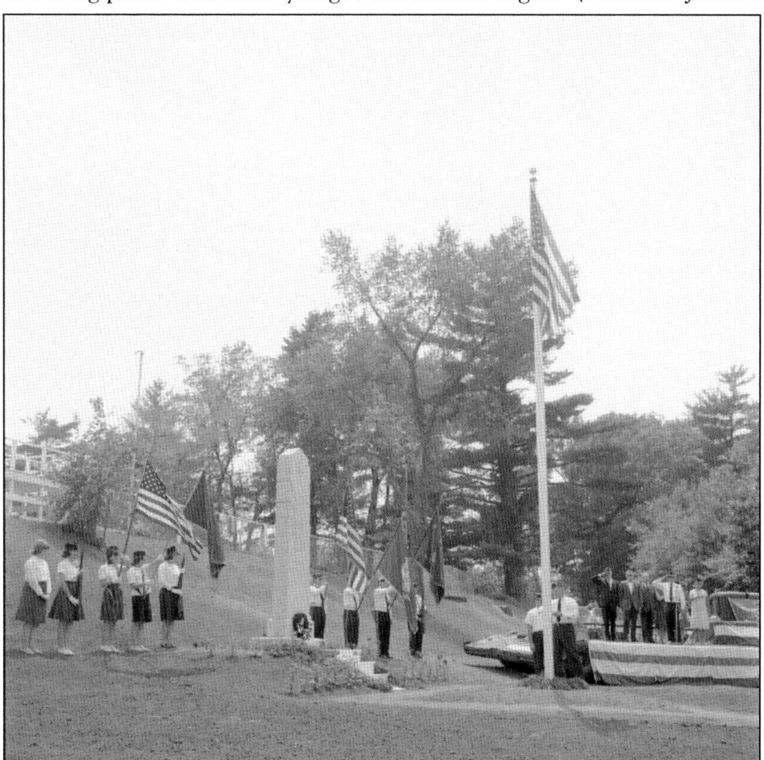

When it opened as a public swimming hole in 1940, Spring Pond was privately owned. Later, it was sold to the town. On July 6, 1965, Spring Pond was rechristened Veteran's Memorial Park, with a large monument honoring all veterans. Later, smaller granite monuments were added that honor South Windsor soldiers who died in different wars. (Photograph from the *Manchester Herald Newspaper*, Barney Daley Collection, WMLM.)

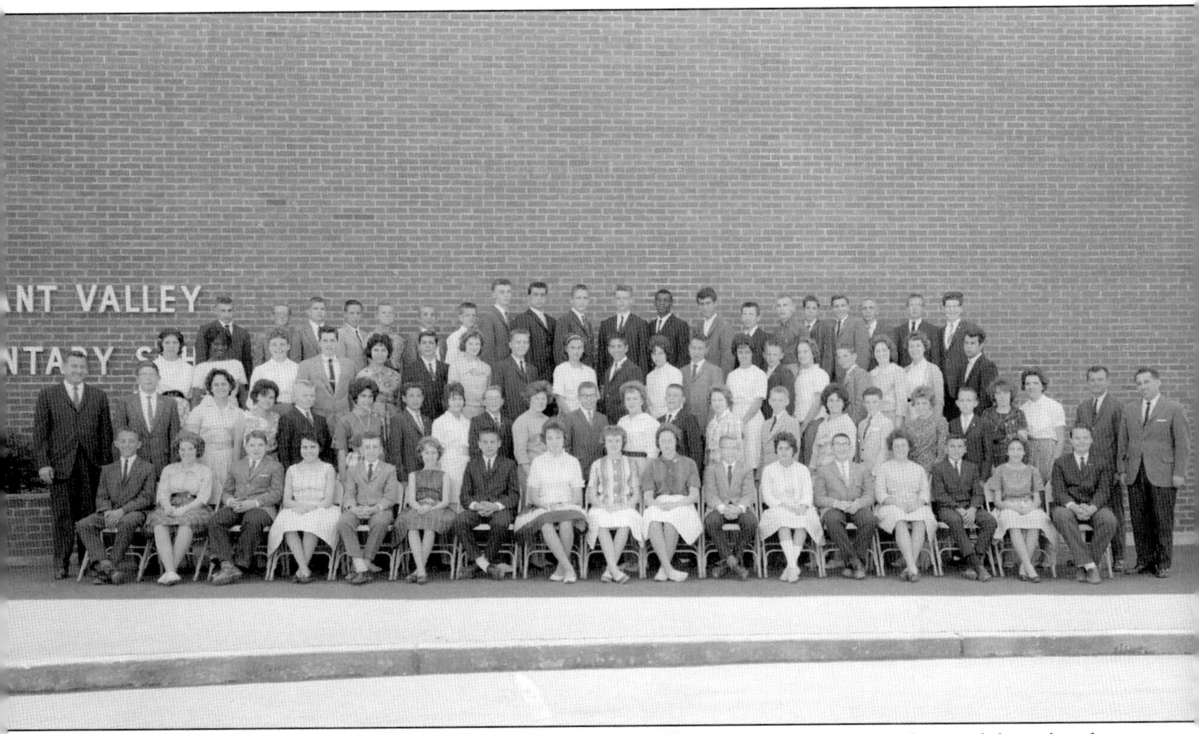

The 1962 eighth-grade graduating class from Pleasant Valley Elementary sits in front of the school with its teachers and administrators. The school on Ellington Road opened in 1958 and originally housed kindergarten through eighth grade. Today, the school houses kindergarten through fifth grade, while middle schoolers go to Eli Terry Middle School. (Photograph by Ellsworth Fairbanks, Barney Daley Collection, WMLM.)

Bibliography

Bortolan, Ruth. Recorded interview by Louise Evans, July 18, 2011. Wood Memorial Library Oral History Program.

Burgdorf, Doris. *A Country Mile: A Guided Tour through South Windsor's Designated Historic District*. South Windsor, CT: South Windsor Historical Society, 1995.

———. Recorded interview no. 3 by Maureen Bourn, July 31, 2007. Wood Memorial Library Oral History Program.

Carney, Francis Peter "Butch." Recorded interview by Davida Foy Crabtree, January 7, 2012. Wood Memorial Library Oral History Program.

Collins, Sherman, and Charlotte Andross Collins. Recorded interview by Jan Kennedy, April 27, 2007. Wood Memorial Library Oral History Program.

Crombie, Philip Sr. Recorded interview by Sherman Tarr, May 25, 2016. Wood Memorial Library Oral History Program.

Daley, Barney E. *Five Thousand Years at Podunk*. South Windsor, CT: B.E. Daley, 1984.

———. *God's Acre*. South Windsor, CT: B.E. Daley, 1984.

———. Recorded interview no. 1 by Jim Daly, May 8, 2013. Wood Memorial Library Oral History Program.

———. *Tobacco Parish: A Collection of South Windsor's Memories*. South Windsor, CT: B.E. Daley, 1998.

Edlund, Fred. Recorded interview by Jan Kennedy, March 16, 2007. Wood Memorial Library Oral History Program.

Edlund, Sally M. Recorded interview by Linda Sunderland, April 18, 2011. Wood Memorial Library Oral History Program.

Elmore, Mary Janette, Doris Burgdorf, Jack Burgdorf, and Jean Klein. *Long Hill, South Windsor, Connecticut "Reminiscences:" A Family Record of Early American Life*. South Windsor, CT: South Windsor Historical Society, 1976.

Files, Terry. Recorded interview by Anthony Macro, April 7, 2015. Wood Memorial Library Oral History Program.

Gutt, Jane Wadach. Recorded interview by Jean Klein, July 19, 2007. Wood Memorial Library Oral History Program.

Nicholson, Richard. Recorded interview no. 2 by Anthony Macro, May 3, 2012. Wood Memorial Library Oral History Program.

Nielsen, Charles Robert. Recorded interview no. 1 by Jean Klein, April 30, 2009. Wood Memorial Library Oral History Program.

———. Recorded interview no. 2 by Jean Klein, date unknown, Wood Memorial Library Oral History Program.

Prior, Janet. Recorded interview by Linda Sunderland, September 15, 2015. Wood Memorial Library Oral History Program.

Raymond, Robert E. Recorded interview no. 1 by Anthony Macro, May 28, 2008. Wood Memorial Library Oral History Program.

———. Recorded interview no. 2 by Anthony Macro, June 10, 2011. Wood Memorial Library Oral History Program.

Risley, Ruth Baker. Recorded interview no. 2 by June Cooke, December 1994. Wood Memorial Library Oral History Program.

Rooney, Frances. *Working Light: The Wandering Life of Photographer Edith S. Watson*. Ottawa, ON: Carleton University Press, 1996.

Shepard, Charles Beach "Tim." Recorded interview by Kathy Kerrigan, January 16, 2015. Wood Memorial Library Oral History Program.

Starr, Robert S. III. Recorded interview by Louise Evans, October 25, 2007. Wood Memorial Library Oral History Program.
Stiles, Henry Reed. *The History and Genealogies of Ancient Windsor, Connecticut; Including East Windsor, South Windsor, Bloomfield, Windsor Locks, and Ellington, 1635–1891.* Hartford, CT: Press of the Case, Lockwood & Brainard, 1891.
Stiles, Jane M. *History of the Changes in the Main Street of South Windsor, Connecticut, 1800–1874.* Unpublished manuscript, 1874.
Vibert, Edith Miller. Recorded interview by John Koenig, May 28, 1976. Wood Memorial Library Oral History Program.
Vibert, Joseph Watson Jr. Recorded interview no. 1 by Jean Klein et al., September 22, 2003. Wood Memorial Library Oral History Program.
———. Recorded interview no. 2 by Jean Klein, October 2, 2003. Wood Memorial Library Oral History Program.
———. Recorded interview no. 3 by Jean Klein, November 23, 2003. Wood Memorial Library Oral History Program.
Waldron, Cynthia Collins, and Pamela Bowen. Recorded interview by Jan Kennedy, November 7, 2014. Wood Memorial Library Oral History Program.
Watson, Lois Foster. *Wapping Five Corners: A History of Wapping Community Church.* Self-published, 1992.
Wolcott, Samuel. *Memorial of Henry Wolcott: One of the First Settlers of Windsor, Connecticut, and of Some of His Descendants.* New York, NY: A.D.F. Randolph, 1881.

About the Organization

Wood Memorial Library was built in 1927 by William R. Wood, a farmer, cattle dealer, and lifelong bachelor. He built the library in memory of his parents, Dr. William Wood and Mary Ellsworth Wood, and their portraits hang on opposite sides of the main first-floor room of the library. Although the Colonial Revival building resembles a house, it was always used as a library, with book collections on the first floor and performance space on the second floor. After building it, William R. Wood presented the building to the town of South Windsor, along with an endowment to fund the library's operations. He provided the building fully furnished, down to complete sets of china and silverware.

In 1964, a collection of Native American artifacts was put on permanent display on the second floor, and the building was renamed Wood Memorial Library and Museum. The Wood also has a permanent display of mounted birds in the first-floor Albert Morgan room, paintings and furniture on the first and second floors, and exhibit space in the basement gallery and second floor.

Wood Library operated as a town library until 1970, when the town closed it. Faced with losing their beloved library, a group of Main Street residents incorporated as Friends of Wood Memorial Library and re-opened the building in 1971 as a privately funded organization. The Friends operate the organization to this day, with a lending library, programs and performances for all ages, a field trip series for third graders, art exhibits, and archives. The building is open to the public on Mondays and Thursdays from 10:00 a.m. to 8:00 p.m.